"Philosophy is the punk rock of subjects? The party to whi̲c̲.̲.̲.̲ ̲e̲v̲e̲r̲y̲o̲n̲e̲ ̲i̲s̲ ̲i̲n̲v̲i̲t̲e̲d̲.̲ ̲I̲f̲ ̲t̲h̲a̲t̲ ̲i̲s̲ ̲w̲h̲a̲t̲ philosophy is, as Moreland and Groza ably argue, then I'm in! *Unraveling Philosophy* is philosophy at its best: comprehensive in scope, written with swagger, theologically grounded, and inspiring. This book serves as one-stop introduction to Christian philosophy. Pick up this book and join the party."

—**Paul M. Gould**, associate professor of philosophy of religion and director of the Master of Arts in Philosophy of Religion Program, Palm Beach Atlantic University

"The risen Christ taught us that the greatest commandment includes loving the Lord with all our minds. These scholars demonstrate both a love for the mind of Christ and a love for the history of philosophical thought. They skillfully engage and explain philosophy in a way that is accessible for the everyday reader. I believe this resource can be a great encouragement for anyone intimidated by philosophy to think deeply for the love of the Lord."

—**Ronjour Locke**, instructor of preaching and urban ministry and director of the Center for Preaching and Pastoral Leadership, Southeastern Baptist Theological Seminary

"Moreland and Groza's *Unraveling Philosophy* does for the new student of philosophy what Alexander the Great's sword did when he faced the Gordian Knot—it slices open a complex tangle of rope that seemed impossible to unravel, thereby opening the world for intrepid minds to explore and master."

—**Ben Phillips**, dean, College of Christian Studies, Charleston Southern University

"Groza and Moreland have written an accessible, sound, mind-engaging and heartwarming book that helps the reader figure out things that make life worth living: goodness, truth, and beauty. I wish I had read this book when I was 20 years old. I plan to give out a copy to many Finnish students."

—**Mikko Sivonen**, academic dean, Agricola Theological Seminary, Finland

"For some time, I've been searching for an introductory text in philosophy that was highly readable, unashamedly Christian, and highlighted the rarely recognized fact that philosophy is all about achieving the good life. Thanks to Moreland and Groza my quest has ended. I will certainly use this book in my courses and suggest that you also consider it."

—**Robert Stewart**, professor of philosophy and theology and Greer-Heard Chair of Faith and Culture, New Orleans Baptist Theological Seminary

UNRAVELING

PHILOSOPHY

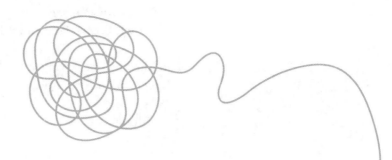

UNRAVELING

AN INTERACTIVE GUIDE

PHILOSOPHY

ADAM GROZA & J.P. MORELAND

B&H
ACADEMIC
BRENTWOOD, TENNESSEE

To Dr. Benjamin Arbour (1981–2020),
beloved colleague and friend

CONTENTS

1

Philosophy Is Not Boring

What interests you? There is probably something that keeps your attention and captivates your imagination. People talk about "finding your passion." One way to find your passion is to think about your interests. What are some things that hold your attention? What started your interest in those things, and why do they interest you? Be brutally honest with yourself about this. Nothing is more important than knowing yourself in this way. Deep in your core, what attracts, engrosses, captivates you?

Boring is the opposite of interesting. If something is boring, you probably will not pay attention to it. You will consider it dull, uninteresting, and tiresome. You might have enrolled in a philosophy class thinking that it would be boring, but philosophy is not boring. The goal of this book is to help you understand philosophy in a way that connects with your interests (and passions), helps you discover and cultivate new ones, and minimizes boredom.

Do not mistake deep for boring. Something is deep if it requires thought, earnest reflection, and analysis. A movie that is deep can be watched multiple times without being boring. A song that is deep makes you think. Just because something is deep does not mean it is boring.

Philosophy is deep but not boring. You may have to read something twice to get the meaning, just as you may have to watch a movie twice to understand it or listen to a song twice to appreciate

1

the sound. That you do not get something the first time does not make it boring. Some of the best things in life require a second read, watch, or listen.

Philosophy is like jazz music. Jazz music challenges the listener and is for many an acquired taste. Once you learn to hear what jazz musicians call "the head" (i.e., the main melody in a song) and the clever ways that musicians bend notes and shape melody against uneven percussion, you come to understand and enjoy the art and science of jazz. Philosophy, like jazz, is an acquired taste.

What is philosophy? There are different ways to answer that question. Philosophy is a subject you study in college, a section in the local bookstore, and a term used to describe questions we ask about meaning and purpose. If someone wants a deeper understanding of definitions and concepts in any subject, we say that they are "philosophical."

Philosophy deals with life's most important questions related to goodness, truth, and beauty. Everyone thinks about these things in relationships, politics, music, and elsewhere. What does it mean to be a good friend? Which political party (if either) is telling the truth? What makes something beautiful? Philosophy is life. As philosopher Martin Heidegger said, "you cannot be outside philosophy looking in; human beings always stand within philosophy."[1]

Philosophy is not a spectator sport. In order to study philosophy, you must understand the questions and follow the arguments. Doing so will naturally draw you into the conversation. Your own perspective and beliefs will be engaged and challenged. In the study of philosophy, everyone is on the field; no one is in the stands. Philosophy will help you, a participant in life, make the most of the time you have been given (Eph 5:16).

Philosophy as Exploration

Think of philosophy as a type of human exploration or adventure. Television shows or documentary movies about explorers feature people who go places that are new to them in the world, or perhaps where no human has ever been. These explorers use rockets to blast into space, canoes and ships to cross water, horses and wagons to cross forests and deserts, and submarines to explore the depths of the ocean; these are the tools of physical exploration.

The primary tool of philosophical exploration is reason; using the power of the mind and the rules of logic to think about questions that matter and to make sense of human experience.

---

[1] Martin Heidegger, *Introduction to Philosophy—Thinking and Poetizing*, trans. Philip Braunstein (Bloomington: Indiana University Press, 1990), 1.

Philosophy is mental exploration. By asking questions and using imagination, we can explore unseen worlds and better understand the world in which we live and the lives we are living.

When you think about philosophy, do not think primarily about a classroom or a bookstore; think instead about the things that matter most to you, about what they mean and why they matter. If explored well, philosophy can help you better understand and appreciate the good things in life, and to enjoy life to the fullest.

Martin Luther King Jr. was a key leader in the American civil rights movement. He believed in nonviolent protest as a means of bringing about change. Few people realize that his commitment to nonviolence was philosophical in nature. King reasoned that you cannot defeat hate and violence with more hate and violence; the way to defeat hatred is with love.[2] His philosophical commitment to nonviolence led to the greatest social advancements of the twentieth century.

Another person who knew the value of philosophy was Socrates, who lived in Greece at the same time that the biblical characters of Esther, Ezra, and Nehemiah were exiled in Babylon. Socrates never wrote anything down, so we only know about him through his student Plato.

Plato shared an important story about Socrates in *The Apology* that shows how philosophy can be interesting, impactful, and life changing. Socrates was arrested and put on trial for corrupting the youth. He wanted people to really know and understand things rather than mindlessly accepting what they were taught. As in our own day, many people used words like *justice*, *love*, and *courage* without really knowing what they meant. By encouraging people to ask questions, Socrates was seen as a threat. There is an important lesson to be learned: those who seek to control others will always be threatened by those who see truth as a means to freedom.

Socrates was given a choice to either stop asking questions and live or to keep asking questions and die. Which would you choose? Socrates chose to die, saying "the unexamined life is not worth living." Better to die loving what is true than to live without freedom of thought. Philosophical exploration is a high-stakes journey.

Philosophy and Freedom

Philosophy is also an exercise in human freedom. Even a person who is physically constrained (like Socrates) can use his or her mind to explore the universe of ideas. Socrates chose to die by drinking hemlock (a type of poison). He was unwilling to allow his freedom of thought to be taken away. He saw that as the worst kind of slavery: if your body is free but your mind is

---

[2] See Martin Luther King Jr., *Strength to Love*, Gift ed. (Minneapolis: Fortress, 2010), 47.

enslaved, you are not truly free. Sadly, many people who possess freedom of thought fail to use it and are unknowingly enslaved to false ideas.

Humans are meant to be free. Physical freedom refers to freedom of movement. Intellectual freedom refers to freedom of thought. Without either freedom, something meaningful and joyful in life is missing. Parents oftentimes ground their children, taking away some kind of freedom as a punishment. The loss of freedom probably has a negative impact on the child's happiness.

Freedom and happiness go together. We know this is true in regard to physical freedom, but it is also true in regard to freedom of thought. The importance of human freedom stems from how God created humans in his image (Gen 1:27). God is free, and humans are created to be free as well.

In the New Testament, Paul warned the believers in Colossae against being taken captive by false ideas: "Be careful that no one takes you captive through philosophy and empty deceit based on human tradition, based on the elements of the world, rather than Christ" (Col 2:8).

It may seem as though Paul was warning his readers against all philosophy, but a careful reading of the passage reveals that Paul was warning against philosophy based on human tradition and not on Christ. There is a way to do philosophy that is faithful to Christ, and a way to do philosophy that is unfaithful to Christ. The goal of this book is to help you understand philosophy, and to do philosophy in a way that is faithful to Christ.

Someone who says "Be careful" is alerting you of danger. Paul said it is dangerous to be taken captive (literally, to be carried away) by philosophy described as "empty deceit based on human tradition." Christians should beware of ideas and belief systems that go against what the Bible teaches about Jesus Christ.

Some have mistakenly thought that Christianity and philosophy have nothing in common. The African church father Tertullian famously asked, "What has Jerusalem to do with Athens, the Church with the Academy, the Christian with the heretic?" He was right to recognize the divide between man's thoughts and God's Word. The Old Testament prophet Isaiah said of this divide:

> "For my thoughts are not your thoughts,
>   and your ways are not my ways."
> This is the LORD's declaration.
>
> "For as heaven is higher than earth,
>   so my ways are higher than your ways,
> and my thoughts than your thoughts." (Isa 55:8–9)

Yet, most Christians recognize that general revelation provides a common ground for Christians and non-Christians to use observation, reason, and logic to begin a discussion of truth. General revelation refers to the world itself and the truths that can be known apart from salvation. Examples of truths that can be known from general revelation include God's existence (Ps 19:1; Rom 1:19), mathematical facts (2+2=4), and basic moral principles ("murder is wrong").

Philosophy done in faithfulness to Christ functions as a bridge in at least three ways. First, it bridges the gap between believer and nonbeliever through conversation about agreed-upon facts. Philosophy helps both dialogue partners find common ground. Second, it bridges the gap between the human mind and God, who intends to point humans back to himself using things like nature, reason, and morality. Even the idea of God itself is part of general revelation; as Aquinas said, "knowledge of God's existing is naturally implanted in everybody. Therefore, that God exists is self-evident."[3] Third, philosophy can bridge what is visible and invisible or what is physical and immaterial. Many philosophical conversations explore the relationship between the visible and invisible and between the material (physical) and the immaterial (spiritual) world.

When Paul warned against empty philosophy, he was reminding us that Jesus is "the way, the truth, and the life" (John 14:6). False ideas that are contrary to Christ and his Word turn people into mental captives. People are literally enslaved to systems of thought (i.e., philosophy), and Jesus came to set us free (Gal 5:1). Living free is first and foremost about thinking rightly about God, yourself, others, and the world: good actions usually follow true thoughts and beliefs (Prov 23:7).

Dutch theologian and statesman Abraham Kuyper famously said, "There is not a square inch in the whole domain of our human existence over which Christ, who is Sovereign over all, does not cry: 'Mine!'"[4] Jesus is Lord over everything, and that includes our minds and thoughts, our hearts and our beliefs.

Question 1.1

Philosophy, like jazz, is an _____ taste.

---

[3] Thomas Aquinas, *Summa Theologiae*, translated by Gerald Massey (Part one, question 2, article 1).

[4] Abraham Kuyper, "Sphere Sovereignty" in *Abraham Kuyper: A Centennial Reader*, ed. James D. Bratt (Grand Rapids: Eerdmans, 1998), 488.

Question 1.2

True or false: Deep subjects that require thought are generally boring.

Question 1.3

The primary tool of philosophy is _____.

Question 1.4

Which two historical figures does the author use to demonstrate how one's philosophy affects one's actions?
- a) Martin Luther King Jr. and Socrates
- b) Ezra and Nehemiah
- c) Socrates and Plato
- d) Jesus and the apostle Paul

Question 1.5

What do you think of Socrates's claim that "the unexamined life is not worth living"?

_____

_____

Question 1.6

True or false: The apostle Paul warned against being taken captive by *all* philosophy.

Question 1.7

Philosophy functions as a bridge between:
- a) _____ and _____
- b) _____ and _____
- c) _____ and _____

Loving God with All Your Mind

Part of what it means to reflect God's image is to love God with your whole being. Jesus told his disciples to "Love the Lord your God with all your heart, with all your soul, and with all your mind" (Matt 22:37).

Philosophy invites us to take our thoughts and beliefs seriously, to define our terms, and to make sure our beliefs are consistent. When our beliefs are true and consistent, and when our actions reflect our beliefs, we exhibit what the Bible calls *integrity*.

Loving God with all your mind requires that you take control of your thoughts. The apostle Paul said, "We take every thought captive to obey Christ" (2 Cor 10:5). It is bad to be taken captive by philosophy but good to take your thoughts captive. What does that mean? It means to control your thoughts, to think what is true, to consider an idea before you believe it, and to consider how your beliefs should affect your actions. The freedom to think and reason is the opposite of being brainwashed, which means to have your thinking controlled by outside sources (media, advertisement, education, etc.) rather than to be in control of your own thoughts and to be accountable for your actions based upon your beliefs.[5]

The Bible talks often about the importance of self-control. The idea of self-control applies both to your physical life (i.e., your body) and to your mental life (i.e., your thoughts). Philosophy helps you "take thoughts captive" and develop self-control in regard to your thoughts and ideas.

Jesus fulfilled God's law perfectly (Heb 4:15); he loved God with all his mind and was in total control of his thoughts, his ideas, and his beliefs. He was not taken captive by any false ideas popular in his culture that were untrue, and he challenged others to do the same. Jesus is the perfect example of faith and reason working in harmony. To follow Jesus is not just about what you do with your body; it is about your mind: God cares about your intellectual life, the thoughts you entertain, and the beliefs you cultivate.

In his sermon "The Battle for the Mind," Welsh physician and preacher Martyn Lloyd-Jones said that from beginning to end the Bible is a book that urges people to think.[6] In fact, he says, our problem is that we do not think enough. God invites us to reason and think (Isa 1:18) and to ready our minds for action (1 Pet 1:13). To love God, and to follow Jesus, we must learn to think well.

---

[5] See Kathleen Taylor, *Brainwashing: The Science of Thought Control*, 2nd ed. (Oxford: Oxford University Press, 2017).

[6] See Martyn Lloyd-Jones, "The Battle for the Mind," https://www.mljtrust.org/sermons-online/1-peter-1-13/the-battle-for-the-mind/.

Some may object: Did Paul not warn that knowledge puffs people up and makes them arrogant (1 Cor 8:1)? However, the context of that passage makes it clear that Paul was not saying it is bad to pursue knowledge; rather, it is bad to pursue knowledge *apart from love*. Pursuing knowledge with a love for God and others leads to humility. Pursuing knowledge apart from love for God and love for others leads to arrogance. Paul was warning against the latter, not the former.

Jesus was not a philosopher in the same sense as Socrates or Plato, but few people appreciate how Jesus used logic and reason to explain his beliefs, to respond when people opposed him, and to educate others. Jesus is the model of what it looks like to love God with all your mind.

There are many reasons to love Jesus; he is gracious, kind, forgiving, and loving. But when you read the Gospels, another reason to love Jesus is that he models *intellectual faithfulness*. Jesus was not only gentle and meek, he was also a logical thinker.[7]

In one passage of the Bible (Luke 20:1–8, 27–40) Jesus was challenged by two different groups of religious leaders. One group challenged his authority, and another group challenged his logic. Jesus believed in the idea of resurrection (i.e., that a body can rise from the dead) and taught that he would die and rise again. To challenge his logic, his opponents asked him a question about life after death that intended to show that the idea of the resurrection was absurd. Jesus responded by challenging their assumptions about what life after death would be like, and in so doing, Jesus won the argument.

Jesus shows that loving God with all our mind means using reason and logic with faith and Scripture to challenge assumptions and to stand for what is true. He was capable of responding to his opponents with valid arguments and compelling metaphors rather than personal insult, physical force, or baseless emotional appeal.

The Impact of Ideas

How does philosophy affect you? After all, you are more likely to care about something the more it affects you directly. The reality is that ideas impact the world on a personal and societal level. Like it or not, we are largely at the mercy of our ideas.

For instance, the idea that humans have free will leads most people to think seriously about important decisions such as what classes to take, what career to pursue, who to date, and what politicians to support. The reason you take these decisions seriously is that you believe your choices are (in some sense) free, and that you are responsible for your choices.

---

[7] See Dallas Willard, "Jesus the Logician," https://dwillard.org/articles/jesus-the-logician.

Fatalism, on the other hand, is the belief that choices do not matter because we are bound to some predetermined future. If outcomes are determined, meaning we are not free, then it is a waste of time to research what classes you will take. If fatalism is true, just roll the dice or randomly select your courses and let the fates decide.

Ideas impact you personally, but they also have consequences that affect entire societies. The idea, for instance, that all humans are created by God and are equal led William Wilberforce to help lead England to abolish slavery. That is an example of how *good ideas* can have *good consequences*.

On the other hand, between 1958 and 1962, an estimated 45 million Chinese citizens died prematurely as the result of a foolish government policy (the Great Leap Forward) designed to speed up the country's pace of industrialization.[8] Mao's deadly idea was that humans were expendable, and that the millions of deaths were justified if it meant advancement and prosperity for the country as a whole. That is an example of how *bad ideas* have *bad consequences*.

Philosophy is not boring because it helps you to think and to advocate for good ideas and to combat bad ideas. In his book *The Republic*, Plato argued that societies should be ruled by philosopher kings: people who use reason and display virtue. Plato did not like democracy, because he was reluctant to trust the masses. He thought they would be governed by their desires and not by reason. Many have observed that Plato's view of humanity is quite elitist.

The Bible, however, says that wisdom is available to the common person. Wisdom cries out in the streets (Prov 1:20). You do not have to have a college degree to be wise, or a particularly high IQ. Some of the wisest people around have little education or formal philosophical training. Wisdom is practical knowledge, knowing what is true and how to live it out. Like the title character in the movie *Forrest Gump*, the most common people can exhibit the most profound wisdom.

Socrates is an example of a wise person because he seeks the truth, he asks questions, and he refuses to use big words just to sound smart. One way to do philosophy is to define words and then think about the definition. Plato's stories about Socrates are called dialogues because they are conversations between Socrates and other people; some real, and others fictitious.

Socratic dialogues generally unfold in three parts:

In part one, Socrates finds someone who seems to know the meaning of some important concept such as love, justice, or courage. Socrates pretends to be impressed that the person knows the

---

[8] See Frank Dikötter, *Mao's Great Famine: The History of China's Most Devastating Catastrophe*, 1958–1962 (London: Bloomsbury, 2011).

meaning or definition and the other person usually seems surprised that Socrates does not know the meaning or definition of the concept in question.

In part two of a Socratic dialogue, Socrates asks questions to the person with whom he is talking. The point of the question is to show that there is a problem with their definition of the concept. For instance, in *Laches*, Socrates asks a military man (named Laches) for the definition of courage, and Laches says that courage is standing your ground. But Socrates asks about instances where soldiers retreat in order to regroup and then fight from a different position. Is that courage, asks Socrates? Of course, says Laches. Here Socrates proves that courage is not as simple as standing your ground since sometimes the courageous thing to do is to retreat.

Part two of every Socratic dialogue is the process of exposing how people often do not know as much as they think they know. This is important for Socrates and to philosophical exploration. Knowledge, in many ways, starts with knowing what you do not know.[9]

In *Apology*, a friend of Socrates goes to the Oracle of Delphi and asks whether Socrates is the smartest man alive, and the Oracle says yes. The friend goes and tells Socrates that he is the smartest man alive, but Socrates refuses to believe it; how can he be the smartest man alive if he does not know anything? Eventually, Socrates realizes that he is the smartest man alive because he knows what he does not know, while others claim to know things they really do not know at all.

Knowing the limits of human knowledge is something the Bible also commends in the ancient story of Job, a man who suffers greatly without knowing why he is suffering. His friends suggest that he must have done something wrong because he has suffered so greatly. In reality, Job was a righteous man, and sometimes good people suffer for unknown reasons. After Job and his friends talk for most of the story, God speaks to Job and invites him to consider the limits of his knowledge. Job eventually puts his hand over his mouth and refuses to speak (Job 40:4–5).

The point of the story is not that questions are bad or that that it is wrong to pursue answers, but that wisdom requires an understanding of the limits of human knowledge. There are some things we know and (many) other things that only God knows. For instance, we know God uses suffering for good, but only God knows *how* he uses it for good (Rom 8:28). Wise people, therefore, limit themselves to what they know to be truth without pretending to know more than they do.

---

[9] In Christianity, this is the starting point for the apophatic tradition and of negative theology. According to this tradition, the best (or only) way to describe God is by negation because God is beyond human language and concepts.

Some people claim that since God is infinite, we cannot know him. However, just because you do not know something *fully* does not mean you do not know something *genuinely*. There are limits to our knowledge. We do not know everything about God, but we do have genuine knowledge of God. This simple philosophical distinction between "knowing fully" and "knowing genuinely" allows us to respond to those who say that since God is infinite we cannot know him.

Part three of a Socratic dialogue is the communal pursuit of knowledge. After asking the meaning of some important concept (part one) and then showing how the definition given does not quite capture the meaning (part two), Socrates and the person(s) with whom he is speaking pursue the matter together (part three).

The above summary of the way in which Socrates pursued truth is called the Socratic method. The Socratic method can be described as a cooperative argument because it involves at least two people helping each other arrive at truth by challenging each other on what they believe. The goal is not to show that one person is smarter than the other, but to arrive at a definition using critical thinking and challenging assumptions and presupposition. A presupposition can be understood as a belief that is assumed but not proven; for instance, a person who says, "I'm looking to talk to the nurse, is she around?" is making an assumption that the nurse is female.

There are some interesting similarities between Jesus and Socrates. Both men had disciples, often taught while walking, had no interest in earthly riches, used questions to provoke thought, went against the teaching of their societies, were condemned to die by leaders who felt threatened by their teaching, and chose to die when they could have escaped death.

Of course there are many dissimilarities between Jesus and Socrates as well. Jesus had answers, but Socrates claimed to only have questions. Jesus taught with such authority that even his opponents were astounded (Matt 7:29). Jesus did not just point to the truth, he claimed to be the truth (John 14:6). While Socrates was merely a good teacher, Jesus was God in the flesh. Socrates died, but Jesus died and then rose from the dead.

Despite the differences, the similarities are helpful to illustrate that faith and reason go together. Loving God with "all your mind" means that there is nothing about the Christian faith that requires you to abandon reason or intellect. On the contrary, Jesus asks us to think about God, to question what others assume, and to even choose to die for the truth rather than to live for lies.

Question 1.8

How does philosophy help us to exhibit integrity?

_____

_____

Question 1.9

True or false: Martyn Lloyd-Jones said that one problem with society is that we think too much.

Question 1.10

The way Socrates pursued truth through dialogue is referred to as the _____ _____. This is a _____ argument because it involves two people helping each other arrive at _____.

Question 1.11

Correctly order the parts of a Socratic dialogue:
_____ Socrates asks a question to challenge his partner's definition of the concept.
_____ Socrates pretends to be impressed by his partner's knowledge of a concept.
_____ Socrates and his partner join together in their pursuit of knowledge.

Question 1.12

Complete the chart, marking which elements apply to Socrates, to Jesus, or to both.

	Socrates	Jesus
Claimed to be the truth		
Condemned to die by leaders who felt threatened		
No interest in earthly riches		
Gave answers		
Only gave questions		
Resurrected after death		

Astounded his opponents with his teaching		
Used questions to provoke thought		
Chose to die rather than escape		

Question 1.13

Socrates realized he was the smartest man alive because
- a) he asked the right questions.
- b) he was persecuted for his beliefs.
- c) he knew his knowledge was limited.
- d) the Oracle of Delphi said so.

The Truth Will Set You Free

Jesus spoke often about the importance of seeking the truth and telling the truth: "If you continue in my word, you really are my disciples. You will know the truth, and the truth will set you free" (John 8:31–32). Philosophy is an exploration in search of truth. Socrates called the search for truth the "greatest improvement of the soul."[10]

In March 1968, Martin Luther King Jr. gave a speech titled "The Other America" in which he talked about freedom and human dignity. These, for King, were connected with eagerly searching for and discovering the truth, then just as eagerly admitting the truth. This, he believed, was the path to freedom because when one tells the truth, one experiences freedom as a plus.[11]

Philosophy is a search for truth. In the last years of his life, French philosopher René Descartes wrote an unpublished essay titled "The Search for Truth" in which he talked about

---

[10] Plato's *Apology*: "Men of Athens, I honor and love you; but I shall obey God rather than you, and while I have life and strength I shall never cease from the practice and teaching of philosophy, exhorting anyone whom I meet after my manner, and convincing him, saying: O my friend, why do you who are a citizen of the great and mighty and wise city of Athens, care so much about laying up the greatest amount of money and honor and reputation, and so little about wisdom and truth and the greatest improvement of the soul, which you never regard or heed at all? Are you not ashamed of this?" (http://classics.mit.edu /Plato/apology.html).

[11] See Martin Luther King, "The Other America," March 14, 1968, http://www.gphistorical.org/mlk /mlkspeech/index.htm.

having a zeal for truth.[12] In his book *Metaphysics* Aristotle talks about philosophy as "the investigation of the truth."[13]

Of course, not everyone in the history of philosophy has agreed that philosophy is a search for truth. Around the same time that Aristotle lived (384–322 BC) several groups of philosophers (the Stoics and the Epicureans) came to believe that the goal of philosophy was less about searching for the truth and knowing the truth and more about enjoying life. The Bible refers to these groups when describing Paul's interaction with the philosophers: "Some of the Epicurean and Stoic philosophers also debated with him" (Acts 17:18).

The Epicureans followed the teaching of the Greek philosopher Epicurus (341–270 BC). He believed that the goal of life was happiness, and he defined happiness as the absence of physical and mental pain. Unlike Plato, Epicurus did not believe in the soul, and therefore did not believe in the afterlife. Since this life was all you had, he reasoned, you had better get as much pleasure as possible. Epicurus taught people to avoid things that cause physical or mental pain (romance, politics, religion, etc.) and to focus instead on friendship; specifically, friendship among his followers who were committed to his teaching. These followers would live together, share possessions, and spend time talking. There are interesting similarities between Epicurean communities and the descriptions of early Christian communities in Acts.

The Stoics followed the teaching of Zeno who taught at a place called the *Stoa*, from which the school of thought (Stoicism) is named. The Stoics taught that only the physical world exists. Unlike Plato, they did not believe there is more to life than meets the eye. Stoics believe that this world was all there was and that nature was divine (i.e., pantheism). A wise person, therefore, focuses on what is (i.e., the natural world). Like the nineteenth-century German philosopher Friedrich Nietzsche, the Stoics believed that time was cyclical, so everything in this life happened over and over again. Since eternity is an endless loop, it is best not to get emotionally attached.

For both the Stoics and Epicureans, perception was more important than reason. The goal of philosophy was practical living, not ultimate truth. In the history of philosophy, others have agreed with this approach to philosophy. For instance, in contemporary philosophy, George Edward (G. E.) Moore thought that philosophy was about defining terms, not arriving at truth. This turn, from seeking ultimate truth to defining terms (i.e., linguistics), has been referred to as

---

[12] René Descartes, "The Search for Truth by Means of Natural Light," in Descartes, *The Philosophical Writings of Descartes*, trans. John Cottingham, Robert Stoothoff, and Dugald Murdoch (Cambridge: Cambridge University Press, 1984), 2:400.

[13] Aristotle, *Metaphysics*, trans. C. D. C. Reeve (Indianapolis: Hackett, 2016), bk. Little Alpha, 27.

the "linguistic turn" in philosophy. For those who took the "linguistic turn," philosophy is not the study of reality but of the way we talk about reality.

A Christian approach to philosophy is concerned with both ultimate truth and practical living. When Jesus said "the truth will set you free," he was talking about what it means to be a disciple. A disciple is someone who has a relationship with Jesus by faith and who also seeks to put into practice the teachings of Jesus. The truth sets us free from the bondage to sin to make it our goal to follow Jesus in joyful obedience.

Philosophy is not boring because it helps us to connect everyday decisions to timeless truth. For instance, if God is love, then we should love others. If God forgives us in Christ, then we should also forgive others. If truth sets us free, then we should want to live in a society where people are free to think, speak, and act according to their beliefs. Philosophy is both theoretical and practical.

Philosophy and Wisdom

The word *philosophy* is a combination of the Greek words *philo*, meaning "love," and *sophia*, which means "wisdom." The Greek historian Herodotus used the word to describe someone who had a "desire of knowledge."[14] A philosopher is someone who desires knowledge and pursues truth using reason and logic.

Aristotle was a student of Plato and the teacher of Alexander the Great. Aristotle wrote a book called *The Nicomachean Ethics* (so named because it was probably written as a guide for living to his son, Nicomachus). In this book, Aristotle defined happiness as living the good life. The idea of the good life connects knowledge with everyday decisions, or as Aristotle said, "living well and doing well."[15]

Philosophy is a love of knowledge that connects truth with right living. One person who embodies this idea of truth and action is Fredrick Douglass, an African-American who was born into slavery but eventually escaped. He later wrote several autobiographies describing his journey, one of which is titled *My Bondage and My Freedom*.

My Bondage and My Freedom, among other books, contains a letter Douglass wrote later in life to the man who had owned him as a slave, called "Letter to His Old Master; To my old master, Thomas Auld." In it, Douglass described being a young boy and realizing that slavery was an

---

[14] George Fullerton, *An Introduction to Philosophy* (London: Macmillan, 1906), 2.

[15] Aristotle, *Nicomachean Ethics*, bk. 1, pt. 4, http://classics.mit.edu/Aristotle/nicomachaen.1.i.html.

invention of sinful men and not of a good and loving God. This realization led him to determine, at the age of six, to one day run away and gain his freedom. His process of thought is an excellent example of the way in which truth, arrived at by reason and argumentation, has practical application for everyday life, which we call wisdom:

> From that time, I resolved that I would some day run away. The morality of the act, I dispose as follows: I am myself; you are yourself; we are two distinct persons, equal persons. What you are, I am. You are a man, and so am I. God created both, and made us separate beings. I am not by nature bound to you, or you to me. Nature does not make your existence depend upon me, or mine to depend upon yours. I cannot walk upon your legs, or you upon mine. I cannot breathe for you, or you for me; I must breathe for myself, and you for yourself. We are distinct persons, and are each equally provided with faculties necessary to our individual existence. In leaving you, I took nothing but what belonged to me, and in no way lessened your means for obtaining an honest living. Your faculties remained yours, and mine became useful to their rightful owner.[16]

Like anything else, philosophy can be used for good or bad. Knowledge has the tendency to lead to arrogance and pride. Paul said that knowledge (apart from love) makes you puffed up (1 Cor 8:1).

How do you grow in knowledge without getting puffed up? Jesus is the perfect example of someone who was knowledgeable but not sinfully arrogant. His life and teaching reveal three keys to the way in which he modeled intellectual humility. First, Jesus cared about people. If you care about people, you are more likely to possess knowledge in humility. Second, Jesus was thankful, as we see from all the times he stopped to give thanks to God. A person who realizes that God is the giver of all good things (including knowledge) will avoid being puffed up. Third, Jesus always wanted to glorify God. In fact, he said, "I do not seek my own glory" (John 8:50). Let God get the glory for whatever intellectual skills you develop. After all, whatever knowledge you possess is ultimately created by God.

Question 1.14

Matching (some answers used twice).

---

[16] Frederick Douglass, September 3, 1848, "Letter. To Thomas Auld," in Philip Foner, ed. *Frederick Douglass: Selected Speeches and Writings* (Chicago: Lawrence Hill Books, 1999), 111.

_____ Life is about happiness, understood as the absence of physical and mental pain.

_____ This philosophical outlook argues that the truth will set you free.

_____ Nature is divine.

_____ Argues for a theoretical *and* practical approach to philosophy.

_____ Philosophy is about defining terms, not about truth.

_____ A wise person, according to this philosophy, focuses on the natural world.

_____ Followers of this philosophy resembled early Christians in their communal life.

A. Christianity

B. Stoicism

C. Epicurean philosophy

D. G. E. Moore

Question 1.15

The word *philosophy* comes from which two Greek words? (Provide the Greek and English translation.)

_____

_____

Question 1.16

Complete this quote from the authors: "Philosophy is a love of knowledge that connects _____ with _____ _____."

Why Should You Study Philosophy?

There are different reasons someone may enroll in a philosophy class. It may be required for your degree program. You might have had an elective to fill and this class fits your schedule. It is possible that you have an interest in philosophy and have been wanting to take a philosophy course. Whatever the circumstances that led you to enroll in a philosophy course, what follows are four reasons why studying philosophy is worth your time (in addition to the benefits of philosophy already described):

First, God designed you to think. Part of being made in God's image is the ability to think critically, reflectively, and self-referentially (which means to think of yourself as a *self* in the world). God designed a world with logic so that humans can think *rightly*. Your body is equipped with senses (sight, touch, hearing) that provide generally accurate data to your mind so you can properly navigate the world around you. God designed you to think, and philosophy helps you do so by exposing you to categories, concepts, and questions that help you to love God with your mind.

Second, philosophy influences world history. Philosophers generate ideas, and these ideas influence everything in culture from movies, leadership trends, politics, and economics. You live in a culture saturated with ideas that are philosophical in nature, whether you realize it or not. For instance, you probably know that there is a national and global demand for justice. However, did you know that the idea of justice, and that it is good and worth fighting for, is deeply philosophical in nature and reflects a view of the world where there are moral facts about right and wrong?

Third, philosophy will help you in whatever future career you choose. Chances are that you are not studying to be a professional philosopher. Whatever your career ambitions, you will be a better employee if you are able to think critically and communicate clearly. Analytic philosophy, for instance, requires that words be defined and understood in their context. Developing philosophical skills will help you not only in your career but in your friendships and in other relationships.

Fourth, philosophy has broad application; you can be philosophical about anything. Consider for a moment the topic of superheroes. Have you ever wondered what is the definition of a superhero? That is a philosophical question. Must a superhero have an innate superpower (Superman), or can a person be a superhero if they simply know how to use resources to achieve super things (Iron Man)?

You can be philosophical about superheroes, and you can also be philosophical about sports. Do you like sports? I suppose that depends on what you consider to be a sport. You might not like the major team sports (baseball, basketball, football, hockey, and soccer), but perhaps you like chess. Is chess a sport? Well, again, that depends on your definition. Does participating in a sport require physical exertion? If so, does chess count, since it requires mental exertion? You might say that chess is a game and not a sport, but you would need to define the difference between the two.

The point is, you can be philosophical about anything. While superheroes and sports are somewhat trivial examples, there are far more substantial ways to prove that philosophy has broad application and is therefore worthy of your time and serious consideration. Take, for instance, the question of what it means to be a person. We will consider this question more in depth in chapter 6, but how you define a person affects your views on a variety of topics.

If you believe that being a person requires the ability to think and enjoy bodily health, for instance, then someone in a coma who is unconscious and unable to think is no longer a human person. If you take the view that someone who is unable to think is no longer a human person, then you may find yourself believing that it is okay to kill people with end-stage dementia, or to kill babies born with serious complications. This may shock you, and it should! Peter Singer, tenured professor of bioethics at Princeton University, has advocated such ideas in his widely read book *Practical Ethics*.[17]

Ideas have consequences, for good or bad. Philosophy applies to life, both in mundane and consequential ways. Philosophy can often be challenging and difficult, but it is not boring.

Question 1.17

In your own words, explain the author's four reasons for why you should study philosophy.

_____

_____

Philosophy and Happiness

One of the primary goals of philosophy is happiness. John Stuart Mill said in his book *Utilitarianism* that "happiness is the sole end of human action."[18] Blaise Pascal wrote in his book *Pensées*, "All men seek happiness. This is without exception."[19] Seeking happiness and finding happiness are two different things. As the English poet William Blake put it in his poem "London":

> A mark in every face I meet
> Marks of weakness, marks of woe.

---

[17] Peter Singer, *Practical Ethics* (Cambridge: Cambridge University Press, 2011).

[18] John Steward Mill, *Utilitarianism* (London: Longmans, Green, 1879), chap. 4, https://www.gutenberg.org/files/11224/11224-h/11224-h.htm.

[19] Blaise Pascal, *Pensées* (New York: E. P. Dutton, 1958), Project Gutenberg ebook, 113, https://www.gutenberg.org/files/18269/18269-h/18269-h.htm.

We can probably all agree that happiness is a good thing and worth pursuing, but we do not all agree on what happiness is or on what makes a person happy. From the beginning of Western philosophy, it has generally been understood that truth and happiness go together; right belief and right actions increase happiness. This basic idea—the connection between happiness and truth—has been agreed upon by everyone from Plato in his classic book *Republic* to Bertrand Russell in his book *The Conquest of Happiness*: Believing what is true will increase your happiness.

On the contrary, happiness generally decreases under the following conditions. You probably are not happy when you feel confused or unsure, and you definitely are not happy when someone has lied to you. Beliefs have an effect on happiness. Truth may be hard to hear, but in the end it is better than lies. Making wise decisions in light of what is true is a better path to happiness than lies, myths, and ignorance. The ancient Greek philosophers emphasized the importance of basing beliefs on *logos* (reason) rather than *mythos* (made-up stories that controlled beliefs).

Fredrick Douglass offered a powerful example of how a lie can steal your joy. As a boy, he heard people say that God created white people to own black people. After he achieved his freedom and wrote about his experiences, he reflected upon how the lie of slavery affected him: "I had, through some medium, I know not what, got some idea of God, the Creator of all mankind, the black and the white, and that he had made the blacks to serve the white as slaves. How he could do this and be good, I could not tell. I was not satisfied with this theory, which made God responsible for slavery, for it pained me greatly, and I have wept over it long and often."[20]

Your beliefs affect your happiness, and so, too, do your actions. Have you ever had a goal to do something that you knew was good for you, and then you did it? You probably were happy at this accomplishment. Conversely, we've all let ourselves (and others) down by not doing something we should have done, or by doing something we knew was wrong. Beliefs and actions directly affect happiness.

All of this begs the question, What is happiness? Down through the history of philosophy, there have been three main theories of happiness from which to choose. In what follows, we will look at these theories of happiness, briefly comment on their strengths and weaknesses, and argue for a particular theory of happiness.

Happiness is pleasure. Many philosophers, from Epicurus to John Stuart Mill, have taught the theory that happiness is pleasure (i.e., hedonism). Epicurus focused on individual happiness, while Mill focused on the greater good (i.e., the most happiness for the most people). In both cases, they defined happiness as maximizing pleasure and minimizing pain.

---

[20] Pascal, 397.

The hedonic theory of happiness (sometimes called the hedonic calculous) says that increasing pleasure and decreasing pain equals happiness (Pleasure > Pain = Happiness). The goal of life, according to hedonism, is to maximize pleasure and minimize pain.

If romantic relationships can lead to pain, then you should avoid romantic relationships. If sports can lead to pain, then you should avoid sports. Basically, avoid things that (on balance) lead to more pain than pleasure.

Take baseball, for instance. A great baseball player who bats .300 over the course of his career still gets out seven out of ten times. In case you have never played baseball or softball, striking out is no fun! In these sports, you do a lot more striking out (or getting thrown out at first base) than you do getting a hit and making it on base. Someone with a hedonic theory of happiness might conclude it is best to avoid baseball; while the thrill of a hit is pleasurable, there is (statistically) more pain in defeat.

The hedonic theory of happiness has some strengths. Pleasure can certainly be a good thing. On average, we would all prefer pleasure to pain. However, happiness seems to be something different than, or greater than, pleasure. While pleasure can lead to happiness, some people enjoy loads of pleasure but are unhappy, while others suffer physically and yet are happy. In fact, there seems to be a paradox in regard to pleasure and happiness. The more you pursue your pleasure, the unhappier you often become. On the other hand, embracing discomfort for a greater purpose (volunteering at a homeless shelter, for instance) often leads to more happiness than avoiding discomfort. The people of Finland (a nation known for happy citizens) have a popular concept called *sisu*, which means embracing discomfort and being determined as a means to ultimate happiness through character development (e.g., grit and determination).

Happiness is life satisfaction and well-being. Another theory of happiness is that to be happy is to be satisfied with your life in terms of circumstances. You might call this the "bucket list" theory of happiness. You have probably heard of people having a list of things they want to do before they die: see the Eiffel Tower, visit the pyramids in Egypt, run a marathon, and so on. The idea is that having goals and being able to achieve them is what it means to be happy. Positive circumstances result in a state of happiness.

Every year since 2012, the United Nations has published the *World Happiness Report*. Countries are ranked according to factors such as life expectancy, political corruption, charitable giving, and economic growth. These factors are combined to generate a happiness score, reflecting the varying levels of positive or negative circumstances in which citizens live, based upon the idea that if your circumstances are positive then you will be happy.

The strength of the life satisfaction theory of happiness is that setting goals and improving lives is a noble cause. A person with no goals in life is probably not very happy. It stands to reason that people living in societies with higher levels of corruption and lawlessness would experience higher levels of sadness.

However, there are serious problems with this theory of happiness. On an individual level, for instance, it is possible to set bad goals. Imagine a person making it their goal to steal more cars than any other person in history. Such a person could achieve their goal but it probably would not, and definitely should not, make them happy.

On a societal level, people who live in countries that score high on the happiness index (e.g., Iceland and Canada) often use antidepressant medication at higher rates than those living in countries that score lower on the happiness index (e.g., Estonia and Hungary), for instance. Also, in some countries it is culturally acceptable to talk about being happy, while in other cultures it is considered immodest and bragging. Checking off lists and measuring statistics seems scientific and therefore objective, but it does not seem to capture what we mean by happiness.

Here's the problem: meeting goals and improving conditions does not equate happiness. Some people have thought that if they could lose weight then they would be happy; however, after losing the weight they wanted, they found they were still unhappy. Other people have thought that finding a romantic partner will lead to happiness, and they make it their goal to find that "special someone," only to feel disappointment that romance does not always (or even usually) lead to lasting happiness. There is nothing wrong with getting in shape, romance, or goals in general. However, these things do not equate with happiness.

Happiness is goodness. This theory of happiness has its roots in both ancient philosophy and is compatible with Christianity. Aristotle rejected the idea that happiness was about physical pleasure. Instead, he argued that happiness was living the good life. In other words, if you align your life with what is good, you will be happy, regardless of whether you experience physical pleasure, achieve your goals, or are satisfied with the circumstances of your life.

The theologian and philosopher Augustine wrote a book called *Confessions* in which he argued that happiness is about love: if you love the right things in the right ways, then you experience happiness. For Augustine, misplaced love is the primary reason why people are not happy. Like Aristotle, Augustine believed that happiness was more about goodness and truth than pleasure and circumstances.

To be truly happy, Augustine said, you must first love God. Human love for God is a response to God's love for humanity. Once you love God, then you are able to love everything else properly (i.e., in the right way and in the right order); this includes love for others, love for all the good things in life, love for creation, and so on. Even people who do not believe in God can agree that priorities matter. If you love money more than you love people, you are probably going to be miserable.

Augustine said God is the true source of happiness and our love for God should exceed all other loves. If you love God above everything else, then you can be happy in this life, even if you experience physical pain or never achieve satisfaction with your life. Happiness is about knowing God who is the source of goodness and love.

For Augustine, there is an afterlife that offers the greatest happiness. A person who loves God is able to be with God in the next life, and in that life (eternal life) one experiences true and lasting happiness. In this life, loving God requires self-sacrifice and self-denial, but it pays off in the next life. Philosopher Blaise Pascal made a similar argument in his book *Pensées*, saying, "there is an eternity of life and happiness" in relationship to God in Christ.[21]

For Augustine, as with Plato and Aristotle, happiness was more about the soul than the body. The word *eudaimonia* is sometimes translated as happiness or flourishing, but can also mean blessing. In the Sermon on the Mount, Jesus said "blessed are the poor" and "blessed are the pure in heart." Some Bible translations use the word "happy" in place of "blessed," but Jesus seems to be talking about *eudaimonia*: soul happiness that results from having faith, hope, and love.

Philosophy is not boring, because it is a pursuit of truth using reason and logic in order to experience *eudaimonia*—deep and lasting happiness rooted in something that cannot be taken away (i.e., a relationship with God).

Question 1.18

Which of the following is *not* a major historical philosophy of happiness?
   a)   Happiness is life satisfaction and well-being.
   b)   Happiness is emotional stability.
   c)   Happiness is pleasure.
   d)   Happiness is goodness.

---

[21] Pascal, *Pensées*, sec. III, 233.

Question 1.19

What does the word *eudaimonia* mean, and how does it contribute to a Christian philosophy of happiness?

_____

_____

The Four Main Branches of Philosophy

You can be philosophical about anything, but philosophy as a *subject* contains four main branches. Each of these four branches of philosophy introduced below make use of logic and reason, which will be discussed in chapter 4. Additionally, political philosophy applies insights from the four main branches of philosophy to human government, individual liberties, and concepts of justice that you will read about in chapter 8. The four main branches of philosophy are metaphysics, epistemology, ethics, and aesthetics.

Metaphysics is the branch of philosophy that deals with reality. In metaphysics, you ask questions such as what kinds of things exist, and what they are made of. Many of these questions will be covered in subsequent chapters. In Shakespeare's play *Hamlet*, the title character says to another, "There are more things in heaven and earth, Horatio, than are dreamt of in your philosophy."[22]

The word *metaphysics* is derived from Aristotle's book *Metaphysics*, which means "after physics." He wrote *Metaphysics* after he wrote *Physics*, which is why he named it as he did. In *Physics*, Aristotle dealt with the physical world. In *Metaphysics*, he addressed questions about what caused the physical world and what, in the physical universe, does not change.

Today, metaphysics is a branch of philosophy that deals with questions such as: Do humans have free will? Is the mind distinct from the brain? Does God exist? What is the meaning of life? Why is there something rather than nothing?

Epistemology is the branch of philosophy that deals with knowledge. What does it mean to say you *know* something? Many of these questions will be covered in chapter 3. Epistemology investigates the difference between knowledge and belief. You believe everything you know, but you do not know everything you believe. So, what turns belief into knowledge?

---

[22] William Shakespeare, *Hamlet*, 1.5.174–75. References are to act, scene, and line.

In the history of epistemology, there are two main schools of thought about what is the surest path to knowledge. Plato believed that reason was the best foundation for knowledge; this is called rationalism. His student Aristotle believed that observation was a better foundation for knowledge; this is called *empiricism*. In Raphael's famous painting, *The School of Athens*, Plato is pointing up to the invisible world of forms known by reason, and Aristotle is pointing down to the physical world, which he believes to be "the most authoritative knowledge."[23] This basic debate between rationalists and empiricists continues today in epistemology.

Ethics is the branch of philosophy that deals with morality. In ethics, you ask questions like: Is there such a thing as right and wrong (i.e., moral facts)? If there are moral facts, what in the universe makes them moral facts? Does morality change as people change their minds, or are moral facts like mathematical facts—fixed in the universe and true at all times and in all places? Ethics will be addressed in chapter 5.

In Book Two of Plato's *Republic*, a story is told of a young shepherd named Gyges who served the king of Lydia. One day, there was an earthquake, and an opening appeared in the ground. Gyges descended into the earth and found a gold ring. He took the ring and ascended back to the surface of the earth. Back with the other shepherds, Gyges realized that the ring gave him the power of invisibility. Once invisible, Gyges killed the king and seduced the queen.

What would you do with the power of invisibility? Sociologists have observed that given the choice between the power of flight or the power of invisibility, whichever you choose says something about attitudes and personality traits.[24] Psychologists have called this the superpower dilemma, and suggested that those who choose invisibility do so to indulge some shameful desire, or what Karl Jung called the "Shadow" (i.e., one's dark side).[25]

Plato's myth of the ring of Gyges raises an important question: Why be good? Plato believed that if people could get away with being bad (such as with an invisible ring) they would, like Gyges. Philosophers have debated what motivates good behavior. Do we do what is right out of

---

[23] Aristotle, *Metaphysics*, trans. W. D. Ross, bk. 1, pt. 1, http://classics.mit.edu/Aristotle/metaphysics.1.i.html.

[24] See Joseph Folkman, "Which Superpower Would You Choose?" *Forbes*, August 17, 2005, https://www.forbes.com/sites/joefolkman/2015/08/17/which-superpower-would-you-choose-to-fly-or-to-be-invisible/?sh=a13d6b61a7d9.

[25] William Berry, "What Your Superpower Might Say About You," *Psychology Today*, May 29, 2015, https://www.psychologytoday.com/us/blog/the-second-noble-truth/201505/what-your-superpower-might-say-about-you.

self-interest (egoism), pleasure (hedonism), concern for others (altruism), the greater good (utilitarianism), or noble character (virtue)?

Aesthetics is the branch of philosophy that deals with beauty. What does it mean to say something is beautiful? Is beauty merely in the eye of the beholder (subjective), or is beauty an attribute that exists independent of opinion and perspective (objective)? If there were no humans on earth to behold Leonardo da Vinci's *Mona Lisa*, would it still be beautiful? Aesthetics is the subject of chapter 9.

When film critics debate which movie was the best movie of the year, or when literary critics discuss what book should win a Pulitzer Prize, they do so by appealing to qualities of the film or the book they believe make it more pleasing (i.e., more beautiful). The concept of beauty can apply to all physical objects (e.g., people, movies, food, music) but also to qualities of character as well (e.g., love, compassion, kindness). The Bible talks about inner beauty (character) and outer beauty (physical) but puts the emphasis on what is inside: "Don't let your beauty consist of outward things like elaborate hairstyles and wearing gold jewelry or fine clothes, but rather what is inside the heart—the imperishable quality of a gentle and quiet spirit, which is of great worth in God's sight" (1 Pet 3:3–4).

Aesthetics helps to define what it means to say that something is art. You might not consider yourself an artist. Perhaps, for instance, you are more of an athlete and enjoy playing sports. Consider this: Have you ever seen an athlete do something in a game that you considered to be artistic? Perhaps the way they made a catch in football, served a ball in tennis, or scored a goal in soccer? In those moments you believe that you are watching something more than competition; you are witnessing something beautiful. We generally consider sports and art to be two different things, but beauty is a bridge between realms of human activity. To say that something (like beauty) is not confined to a specific context (art or sports) is to say that it is transcendent.

The main branches of philosophy (metaphysics, epistemology, ethics, and aesthetics) address the three things that make life worth living: goodness, truth, and beauty. When ancient philosophers such as Aristotle spoke of the good life, they had in mind these three pillars of human flourishing that promote happiness, enrich culture, and strengthen societies.

Question 1.20

Complete the chart:

Branch of Philosophy	Deals with:	Explain:
Metaphysics		
	Knowledge	
Ethics		
	Beauty	

Philosophy and Worldview

Another way of thinking about philosophy is as a worldview. Put together, your view of goodness, truth, and beauty is your worldview. The German word for "worldview" (*weltanschaüung*) is the sum total of your views about humanity's three most important relationships: our relationship to God, to one another, and to the world.[26]

Abraham Kuyper referred to one's worldview as a life system. Your beliefs are connected, and what you believe about God affects what you believe about yourself and the world around you. Only Jesus lived out his worldview with perfect integrity and absolute consistency; the rest of us struggle with varying levels of hypocrisy (i.e., failure to live up to our own standards). Every worldview has standards, and everyone fails to live up to the standards of their worldview and is therefore guilty of hypocrisy.

---

[26] See Abraham Kuyper, *Lectures on Calvinism* (Grand Rapids: Eerdmans, 1994), 16.

Christianity is a religion that offers to explain what is wrong with the world (sin) and what God (in Christ) has done to fix the problem. The story of Christianity unfolds like a play in four acts.

- Act 1 is creation: God created a world that was good, where humans enjoyed life in God's presence without sin, shame, or death.
- Acts 2 is the fall: Humans are tempted by Satan, disobey God, are banished from Paradise (God's presence), and all of creation is cursed by sin and death.
- Act 3 is redemption: God promises a Savior (Gen 3:15) who will defeat sin and death. This promise unfolds through the Old Testament as the concepts of covenant, sin, redemption, sacrifice, and blessing are developed. Act 3 climaxes in the life of Jesus, God's long-promised Messiah, who dies for sinners as the perfect sacrifice and then rises from the dead on the third day.
- Act 4 is restoration: The resurrection proves that all of God's promises come true and guarantees that all believers will follow Jesus into eternity by faith, and all who reject Jesus will be judged and condemned. In the end, there is perfect restoration: a new heaven, a new earth, sinless existence in God's presence, and an end to suffering, temptation, sin, and death.

Theologian Herman Bavinck wrote a short book titled *Christian Worldview*. This book is important because it shows that Christianity offers a way of looking at the world that makes sense of the various subjects explored in philosophy, which philosophy (apart from God) cannot properly understand nor adequately explain. Think of Christianity like a magnet in a compass. A compass points north, south, east, and west. If you are lost, a compass can you get you home. However, for a traditional compass to work, there must be a magnet inside. Without the magnet, the compass is worthless.

In the same way that a traditional compass only works with a magnet, so too the ideas of truth, goodness, and beauty only work if Christ is risen. Christianity as a worldview makes sense of the world and of human experience. As Paul said to the philosophers in Athens, "In him we live and move and have our being" (Acts 17:28). Jesus is not just the center of Scripture, he is the center of the universe. Everything is from him, through him, and to him (Rom 11:36).

Question 1.21

A person's worldview consists of his or her view of what three things?

Question 1.22

Order and briefly describe the four acts of the Christian worldview.

　　Act ＿: Redemption—

　　Act ＿: Fall—

　　Act ＿: Creation—

　　Act ＿: Restoration—

Philosophy as Punk Rock

Punk rock is a disruptive music genre. It is inclusive, since anyone can learn to play the simple chord structures of most punk songs. Punk rock shows usually involve a low stage that limits the separation between "band" and "audience" and emphasizes equality. Punk rock is also contrarian, breaking conventions (for instance) by featuring songs that are short and to the point. Punk rock cares more about being honest than appearing cool; watch an old video of Fugazi playing "Waiting Room" and you will see a group of people who demonstrate a certain fearlessness and courage.

　　Philosophy is not boring because, in many ways, it is the punk rock of subjects: it is inclusive, contrarian, and courageous. Philosophy is like a party where everyone is invited, not just the cool kids. As twentieth-century philosopher Mortimer Adler says, "Philosophy is everybody's business."[27] Aristotle talked about the inclusive nature of philosophy in his book *Metaphysics*: "The investigation of the truth is in one way hard, in another easy. An indication of this is found in how no one is able to attain the truth adequately, while, on the other hand, we do not collectively fail, but everyone says something true about the nature of things, and while individually we contribute little or nothing to the truth, by the union of all a considerable amount is amassed."[28]

---

[27] Mortimer Adler, quoted in https://www.deseret.com/1993/5/31/19049404/socrates-helps-remind -us-philosophy-is-for-everyone, source taken from the prologue to *The Four Dimensions of Philosophy* (Macmillan Publishing Company, 1993).

[28] Aristotle, *Metaphysics*, trans. W. D. Ross, bk. 2, pt. 1, http://classics.mit.edu/Aristotle/metaphysics .2.ii.html.

While philosophy has not always lived up to its ideals, there is something inherently inclusive and communal about a discipline whose primary requirement is the willingness to ask good questions in conversation with others, to be open to criticism, and to employ reason. Philosophy is also inherently disruptive. Doing philosophy requires a fair dose of skepticism and a certain contrarian spirit; evident even in the titles of such famous philosophy books as *Critique of Pure Reason* by Immanuel Kant. There is nothing boring about endeavoring to critique what others consider to be common sense.

In the field of philosophy, what matters most about you are the arguments you make. In the twentieth century, some of the most celebrated philosophers show the inclusivity of philosophy. G. E. Anscombe, for instance, was a British philosopher whose essay "Modern Moral Philosophy" almost singlehandedly revived serious academic interest in virtue ethics (see chapter 7). She begins her essay by saying (in essence) that modern moral philosophy is mostly worthless and should be ignored.[29]

Anscombe continues what is an ancient philosophical tradition of *moxy*, which means a force of character. This punk-rock attitude that permeates philosophy dates back to Socrates, whose last words were: "The hour of departure has arrived, and we go our ways—I to die, and you to live. Which is better God only knows."[30] This same fearlessness and hubris is seen in René Descartes's introduction to his classic book *Meditations on First Philosophy* in which he argued for the existence of God and of the human soul, as separate from the body. He said, "These proofs are such that I do not think that there is any way open to the human mind by which it can ever succeed in discovering better."[31]

The Place of Philosophy in Higher Education

Of all the subjects you will study in college, philosophy has a particularly rich history. Consider, for a moment, that few subjects taught in colleges and universities existed before colleges and universities. Plato started a school called the Academy, and his student Aristotle started a school called the Lyceum. Both the Academy and the Lyceum were influential to the establishment of the modern college or university.

---

[29] See G. E. Anscombe, "*Modern Moral Philosophy*" in *Philosophy* 33, no. 124 (January 1958), https://www.pitt.edu/~mthompso/readings/mmp.pdf.

[30] Plato, *Apology*, http://classics.mit.edu/Plato/apology.html.

[31] René Descartes, ed. Stanley Tweyman, *Meditations on First Philosophy in Focus* (New York: Routledge, 2002), 36.

Philosophy is sometimes regarded as the queen of all sciences. For many people, if there were a hierarchy of subjects, philosophy would be at the top. How did it get this royal reputation?

First, philosophy is foundational to other subjects. There is philosophy of science, philosophy of history, philosophy of education, and so forth. Since you can be philosophical about anything, philosophy is often understood to be foundational to all other disciplines. Every other subject has to address, or assume, what exists (metaphysics), what is good (ethics), what can be known (epistemology), and what is beautiful (aesthetics). Even if you do not want to be a professional philosopher, philosophy will be an important part of your educational and professional development.

Second, philosophy helps to bring unity. In college you study different subjects, but it is not always clear if, or how, they relate to each other. Modern education is highly specialized; the further up you go, the more specialized you become. Historically, philosophy was seen as a unifying subject, bringing cohesion to education. Famous philosophers like George Berkeley were also scientists, poets, theologians, humanitarians, and more. Philosophy is able to foster a holistic and interdisciplinary approach to education that enables you to be well read and well rounded. We often hear people claim that philosophy is not practical. Nothing could be farther from the truth. As the "queen of all sciences," philosophy touches all of life and thought. In this way, it is the most practical branch of learning there is.

Philosophy is coloring outside the lines. You get to follow the questions across disciplines in pursuit of truth, wherever they lead. Unlike in other disciplines, philosophy does not require you to "stay in your lane." At once both ancient and punk rock, philosophy is anything but boring.

Chapter Review

Question 1.23

The authors give Jesus as an example of someone who exhibits intellectual humility. Imagine a scenario in which you are conversing with a new friend. This friend presents a point of view on a particular topic that you think is blatantly wrong. Briefly describe the scenario and how you might demonstrate intellectual humility in this conversation.

Question 1.24

Match the philosopher/philosophy with their respective views.

A. Epicureans

B. Fredrick Douglass

C. Martin Heidegger

D. Christianity

E. Stoicism

F. Socrates

G. Aristotle

H. Augustine

_____ It's best not to get emotionally attached, since time is cyclical.

_____ Pursued truth through dialogue, challenging and redefining concepts.

_____ God is the source of true happiness; our love for God should exceed all other loves.

_____ Life is about the pursuit of pleasure.

_____ Defined happiness as living the good life.

_____ "You cannot be outside philosophy looking in; human beings always stand within philosophy."

_____ A lie can steal your joy.

_____ This approach to philosophy is concerned with both ultimate truth and practical living.

Question 1.25

The authors claim that "The goal of this book is to help you understand philosophy in a way that connects with your interests (and passion), helps you discover and cultivate new ones, and minimizes boredom." Can you locate any connections between philosophy and some of your interests? Describe these connections.

_____

_____

Meet the Philosophers

British philosopher Simon Critchley wrote an essay for the *New York Times* titled "What Is a Philosopher?" Critchley opens the article saying, "There are as many definitions of philosophy as there are philosophers—perhaps there are even more."[1] Somewhat ironically, attempts to define philosophy are themselves philosophical! Philosophy is unique in that while you usually need a law degree to practice law, or a medical degree to practice medicine, you do not need a philosophy degree to practice philosophy. While you usually need a philosophy degree to *teach* philosophy, anyone can be philosophical.

Ironically, it is often the least likely characters who are the most philosophical. In popular culture, there are Socratic characters who embody the pursuit of truth and wisdom through logic and reason. For instance, the character of Doc in the Disney film *Cars* is a Socratic character who helps Lightning McQueen realize that in order to go left, you sometimes have to turn right. Similarly, in the film *Finding Nemo*, the laid-back turtle Crush helps the uptight character Marlin to realize that maturity and development require freedom. Lastly, in Quentin Tarantino's *Django*

---

[1] Simon Critchley, "What Is a Philosopher?" *New York Times*, May 16, 2010, https://archive.nytimes .com/opinionator.blogs.nytimes.com/2010/05/16/what-is-a-philosopher?/.

Unchained the wise character of Stephen (played by Samuel L. Jackson) sees the truth of things before his slave owner.

In literature, there are other examples of Socratic characters who defy stereotypes of what it means to be philosophical. In Ransom Riggs's novel *Miss Peregrine's Home for Peculiar Children* the main character of Jacob Portman is philosophical in how he insists on the reliability of his memory and experience despite all of the authority figures in his life (parents, counselor, etc.) doubting what he claims because they deny the possibility of the supernatural. Similarly, in Marilynne Robinson's novel *Gilead*, character John Ames is a Congregational minister in Gilead, Iowa, who models the pursuit of truth and practical wisdom in the face of doubt and uncertainty.

It might interest you to know that in the history of philosophy, most of the famous philosophers discussed in this chapter were not vocational or professional philosophers; in other words, they were philosophical because they loved the truth, not because they made a living doing philosophy. For most of these individuals, philosophy was a labor of love. Blaise Pascal, for instance, was a mathematician and inventor by trade. Philosophy was essentially his hobby.

Why is this important? Just because you never get a degree in philosophy or get paid to teach or write on the subject of philosophy, does not mean you should not aim to be philosophical. No matter what your profession or vocation, you can and should use logic and reason in pursuit of truth by defining terms and analyzing argument. Loving God with all your mind and being wise are traits that will bless others, help you succeed, and make a positive impact on your community in the process.

The Beginning of Philosophy

Every story has a beginning. In one sense, the history of philosophy is the history of humanity. Humans are philosophical by nature (*homo cogitans*). As Aristotle explained in the opening line of his book *Metaphysics*, "all men by nature desire to know."[2]

Since the dawn of time, humans have contemplated the meaning of life and their purpose in the universe. For instance, as recorded in the Old Testament, King David looked up at the night sky and pondered his own existence:

> When I observe your heavens,
>   the work of your fingers,

---

[2] Aristotle, *Metaphysics*, trans. Ross, bk. 1, pt. 1.

the moon and the stars,

which you set in place,

what is a human being that you remember him,

a son of man that you look after him? (Ps 8:3–4)

Humans have always asked questions about where we come from, the purpose of life, and what happens after we die. Romanian philosopher and historian Mircea Eliade observed in his book *The Sacred and the Profane* that in traditional societies humans are *homo religiosus*; by nature, humans long to know about deeper meaning and ultimate truth.[3] Humans are by nature *homo religiosus* and *homo cogitans*: beings who think, reason, and believe in unseen realities that give meaning to this life and hope for the next. To deny these truths is to deny humanity.

You can see traces of this pursuit of deeper meaning and ultimate truth in Native American spirituality, African traditional religion, and ancient Vedic writing (modern-day India and Pakistan). While philosophy is different (as a subject) in that it seeks to answer questions using reason and analysis without needing to appeal to sacred texts, it has historically been the case that philosophical questions and religious questions overlap. Not surprisingly, some of the greatest philosophers (Thomas Aquinas, René Descartes, George Berkeley, and William James) were genuinely religious.

Before we look at famous philosophers, do not miss the philosopher staring at you in the mirror: you are a philosopher. You use reason and logic in pursuit of what you consider to be the good life. You have questions about truth, goodness, and beauty. You wonder about things that are currently unknown. Philosophy is not just about a bunch of people who died a long time ago, or people who teach at universities with fancy offices and long titles; it is about everyday people all around the world who think, reason, and dream about a better world. Since you are already a philosopher, we hope that by reading this book, you will become a better one!

Question 2.1

Provide an example from pop culture of a Socratic figure (i.e., a character who embodies the pursuit of wisdom and truth through reason and logic).

_____

_____

---

[3] See Mircea Eliade, *The Sacred and the Profane* (New York: Harcourt, 1987), 15.

Question 2.2

True or false: Philosophy is only worth studying if you intend to make a career out of it.

Question 2.3

Explain in your own words what the author means by, "the history of philosopy is the history of humanity."

_____

_____

Question 2.4

Mircea Eliade describes man as *homo cogitans* and *homo religiosus*. Can you think of any ways philosophy and religion might overlap?

_____

_____

Some of the First Philosophers

The story of Western philosophy begins in ancient Greece. In the sixth century BC, a group of thinkers appeared who tried to answer questions about the origin or unifying principle of existence (*arche*) and order (*logos*). Early philosophers stood out and drew attention to themselves because they appealed to reason rather than popular myths to explain the nature of reality. Like modern figures such as Elon Musk and Mark Zuckerberg, early philosophers were disrupters who rejected the traditional way of doing things and taught others and wrote down their ideas. In the same way that doctors practice medicine or lawyers practice law, philosophy was begun by people who practiced the use of reason and logic.

Why did philosophy as a subject emerge in Greece? One theory is that Greece was at the crossroads between East and West. People living in Greece in the sixth and fifth centuries BC would have had access to traders from ancient civilizations like Persia (modern-day Iran) and Egypt. As people traded goods and did business, they probably would have also gotten into conversations and exchanged ideas. There was no priestly class in Greece, so people were more free than in other societies to question what everyone else believed.

One of the goals of the early Greek philosophers was to understand the nature of the world (cosmology). The basic idea was that the universe (cosmos) had a unifying principle that provided permanence in a world of change. In ancient myths, there were thought to be four basic elements: air, fire, water, and earth. The first philosopher, Thales of Miletus (c. 580 BC) thought that the world was made of water. He declared, "The first principle and basic nature of all things is water."[4] This is one of only four surviving sentences from Thales's book. It goes to show that what you say matters more than how much you say.

Of course, we know now that Thales was wrong; not everything is made of water. However, considering that Thales was working without any modern scientific tools or the Internet, it is amazing that he chose water because it actually composes so much of reality. Consider for a moment that roughly 50–75 percent of the human body is composed of water and 71 percent of the earth's surface is covered in water.

Other ancient philosophers, often called pre-Socratic philosophers because they lived before Socrates (c. 470–399 BC), thought that something else was the ultimate stuff that the world was made from, and they got very creative! Anaximander (c. 610–546 BC) reasoned that whatever is the stuff behind the physical world must itself not be a part of the world. He called this other-worldly substance "the boundless" and thought that the four basic elements (air, fire, water, and earth) were created from the boundless.

Pythagoras (c. 570–500 BC) thought that all things were numbers. Democritus (c. 460–370 BC) thought the universe was made of invisible, eternal, and indestructible bits of matter called atoms. Parmenides (c. 515–440 BC) believed that only reason and thoughts exist and that change is an illusion, whereas Heraclitus (c. 540–480 BC) held the opposite view, that reality is change ("you cannot step in the same river twice").

The pre-Socratic philosophers are important for at least four reasons: First, early philosophers used reason and logic to explain the world and not myths. Second, they introduce a division in philosophy between those who think that reason is the best way to arrive at knowledge (rationalism) and those who think that the senses (or observation) is the best way to arrive at knowledge (empiricism). Third, the pre-Socratic philosophers believe that reality is somehow unified; that there is something that explains everything else (what modern physicists call the *theory of everything*). Fourth, the pre-Socratic philosophers introduced *reductionism* as a method

---

[4] Phillip Wheelwright, ed. *The Presocratics* (New York: Odyssey Press, 1966), 44.

of reasoning. Reductionism is the process of explaining something by showing how it can be reduced to a more basic kind of thing. Understanding the world in smaller and smaller parts is one way that science advances.

Question 2.5

Matching:

A. Democritus   _____ Believed the world was made of water.

B. Cosmology   _____ All things are numbers.

C. Anaximander   _____ Change is an illusion.

D. Heraclitus   _____ The nature of the world.

E. Thales of Miletus   _____ Believed that something called "the boundless" was behind all things.

F. Pythagoras   _____ All things are made of atoms.

G. Parmenides   _____ Reality is change.

Question 2.6

Which is *not* a reason for the pre-Socratics's importance?
   a) They used logic and reason to explain reality.
   b) They believed in something that unified all reality.
   c) They contributed greatly to Greek social and military prowess.
   d) They distinguished between rationalism and empiricism.
   e) They introduced reductionism.

The Four Eras of Philosophy

It is helpful to think of philosophy as unfolding in four main eras: ancient, medieval, modern, and contemporary. An era is a period of history that overlaps with other historical events, people, and trends. The more you know about history in general, the better your understanding will be of philosophy. Philosophy is a great subject because you get to interact with history, politics, art, and so forth when you explore the history of philosophy and philosophical questions.

Each of these eras of philosophy is like a chapter in a book or an act in a play. New figures emerge (characters), new problems arise (conflict), new solutions are offered (resolution), old ideas reemerge (flashbacks), and future concepts begin to take shape (foreshadowing).

The first era of philosophy is known as the ancient era. We have already introduced the first era: ancient philosophy begins with Thales in the sixth century BC. In this same century, the Jews are taken into captivity in Babylon, Confucius teaches practical philosophy in the Zhou Dynasty of China, and the trans-Saharan trade route emerges in Africa.

The ancient era of philosophy spans roughly 800 years ending in the third century AD. During this time, the most important characters are Socrates, his student Plato, and Aristotle, the student of Plato.

There are three main reasons these ancient philosophers are important. First, they are important because they took a more systematic approach to philosophy, which means that they attempted to explain and connect all the main branches of philosophy (as we will discuss later). Second, they are important because they focused on metaphysics (the study of reality) and ethics (the study of right living). Third, they are important because they handed down their teaching and mentored others.

While these three ancient philosophers did not agree on everything, they all agreed that there was more to life than meets the eye and that living the good life required people to think for themselves. They wanted others to learn how to do philosophy (i.e., define terms, analyze concepts, and use logic), so Plato started a school (the Academy) and Aristotle also began a school (the Lyceum) to teach students. Ancient philosophers laid the foundation for the modern university.

In the ancient era, one of the most important problems was understanding the relationship between change and permanence. A philosopher named Heraclitus had thought that permanence was an illusion and that everything was constantly changing. Parmenides believed the opposite. Parmenides believed that change was an illusion and reality was fixed.

Plato tried to solve this problem by saying that there were two worlds: the physical world and a world of ideas, which he called *forms*. The world of forms is eternal and unchanging and can only be known through reason. The world of physical objects is temporary and changing and is known by observation. Plato reasoned that since the invisible world of forms gives rise to the visible world of objects, a wise person would spend their time contemplating the forms.

Plato told a famous story called the "Allegory of the Cave." In it, a group of slaves are chained underground facing a wall. Against the wall, all can only see shadows of figures passing in front of a fire behind them. At some point, a slave frees himself and sees that the shadows are only a glimpse of objects behind him. Even when he turns around, the cave is dark because the fire provides little light. Climbing out of the cave, the freed slave sees all things clearly in the light of the sun. The lesson of the allegory is that a person who only thinks about the physical world is like the slave chained to the wall of the cave. Philosophers ascend by reason into the light of unchanging ideas (i.e., the real world), which explains the physical world: Plato believes that the world above makes sense of the world below.

Plato's most important book is *Republic*. In it, Plato tries to understand the idea of justice. He thought that justice was a difficult concept to define. How would you define justice?

In order to understand justice at a large level (i.e., society), he tried to understand justice at a small level (i.e., individual). Each person has a soul, and the soul is divided into three parts: the rational, the spirited, and the appetitive. Each part has a virtue: the virtue of the rational soul (mind) is reason, the virtue of the spirited soul (heart) is courage, and the virtue of the appetitive soul (stomach) is self-control. Since a wise person is governed by reason, Plato thought that a wise society should be governed by a small group of philosopher kings. Plato did not believe most people to be reasonable, so he was afraid of democracy (i.e., the rule of the many). Justice is therefore a kind of harmony between parts both in the soul and in society.

Aristotle thought that there was only one world: the one we see. He believed in forms, like Plato. However, he did not think that the forms (ideas) that gave rise to this world existed in some other invisible realm, but rather they existed in objects themselves. Each object contains form (purpose) and matter (individual properties) and together this created a substance (form + matter = substance).

Since Aristotle believed the physical world contained the world of forms, he emphasized empirical observation (that is, observing the world through the senses: sight, touch, smell). Plato, on the other hand, had emphasized reason as the surest path to knowledge. This division foreshadows an ongoing debate between empiricists and rationalists about whether the senses, or reason, are the better path to truth. In fact, a famous painting by sixteenth-century artist Raphael called *The Academy* features, at its center, Plato pointing up (to the invisible world) and Aristotle pointing down (to the physical world).

Aristotle wrote *Metaphysics* and *Nicomachean Ethics*. In *Metaphysics*, Aristotle explained there are four kinds of causes: material, final, formal, and efficient. A material cause is the stuff something is made from (e.g., a computer is made of plastic and other composite material). An efficient cause is the action that brings an object into being (e.g., a computer is produced on an assembly line by machines, with its final touches done by humans). A formal cause is the design in the mind of the creator (e.g., a computer is designed by engineers who envision what it should look like and how it should function). A final cause is the purpose of the machine (e.g., the things it should be used for, such as typing papers, watching videos, and listening to music).

The *Nicomachean Ethics* was written to help people understand how to be virtuous. Virtue is an important word that will be explored more in chapter 5. Aristotle taught that virtue was excellence of character. Virtue could be discovered by reason, but you learn it by imitating others who already have virtue. In other words, if you lack kindness, hang out with someone who is kind and follow their example.

Aristotle also taught the *Golden Mean* (sometimes called the *Golden Middle*). Virtue is found between deficiency and excess. Kindness, for instance, is the virtue between being mean and being a pushover. A kind person is not mean, nor are they a pushover. Kindness is somewhere in the middle. This has been a helpful way for people to think about character ever since.

In summary, the ancient era was the beginning of philosophy as a formal discipline. People started using logic and reason to answer questions about the nature of reality and constructed systems of thought in an effort to understand how the visible world of sensation related to the invisible world of ideas. The pursuit of truth was connected to the idea of living the good life and having good character.

Question 2.7

Complete the quote: "In the ancient era, one of the most important problems was understanding the relationship between _____ and _____."

Question 2.8

_____ believed that the forms existed in a separate realm, while _____ believed that the forms existed in the objects themselves.

Question 2.9

According to Aristotle, what might be the material, efficient, formal, and final cause of a table?

_____

_____

The second era of philosophy is known as the medieval era. The medieval era of philosophy takes place from about the third century AD to the beginning of the Renaissance period. During this time that is also known as the "Middle Ages," medieval philosophers tried to understand and explain the relationship between Christianity and philosophy. One of the main themes of medieval philosophy is the relationship between faith and reason. Not all medieval philosophers were Christian. Muslim philosophers, such as Avicenna, made important contributions to logic. It is historically mistaken to call this period the "Dark Ages." Nothing could be farther from the truth. Medieval philosophy bristled with great thinkers who developed important ideas with great skill and reflection

Many of the philosophers during the medieval era were committed Christians. Augustine wrote about the role of affections (love, desire, etc.) in directing human actions in his book *Confessions*. Augustine believed that in order to truly change, you need a change of heart (i.e., different affections). Augustine also taught that human governments and rulers were temporary, but that Christians belonged to a heavenly city. Therefore, though they should be good citizens on earth, their ultimate loyalty is to God.

Another medieval philosopher was named Boethius. His most famous book was *Consolation of Philosophy*. Before dying in his forties, Boethius raised important philosophical problems, such as the problem of evil and the problem of universals. The problem of evil questions how God can exist in a world with lots of evil and suffering. If God is good why does he allow evil to exist? We will look at this problem in chapter 3.

The problem of universals has to do with how something can be unique and distinct from other things (i.e., particulars) and yet have qualities that are shared with other particular objects (i.e., universals). For instance, your car may be red. Red is universal since there are many things that share the color red, and there are many red cars. But your red car is unique and distinct. It is particular. So how does your particular red car share a property or attribute (being red) with all the other red cars, and all the other red things, in the world? That may not seem like a problem to you, but medieval philosophers like Boethius tried to understand the relationship between universals and particulars in regard to substance.

Such problems reflect the close relationship between Christianity and philosophy during the medieval era. The word *theology* comes from the Greek words *theos*, meaning "God," and *logia*, which means "words." So theology refers to thinking, writing, or speaking about God. Theology refers to the study of God and things related to God.

In the medieval era, theologians like Thomas Aquinas thought deeply about faith and reason. In his famous book *Summa Theologica*, Aquinas wrote about the doctrine of the Trinity, which explains how God is one eternal substance in three eternal and distinct persons. Using reason to think deeply about Scripture and doctrine (i.e., beliefs) is called *philosophical theology*.

Aquinas also made several arguments for God's existence in his book *Summa Theologica*. Published in 1485, the *Summa* (as it is known) contains several famous arguments for God's existence. The cosmological argument, for instance, says that something caused the universe to come into existence. Since the universe cannot be the cause of itself, there must be something outside the universe that caused the universe to come into existence. God is the "first cause" who caused the universe to come into existence. This, and other arguments for God's existence, will be explored in the next chapter.

Another question raised during the medieval era had to do with whether humans have free will. If God knows everything that will happen in the future (i.e., divine foreknowledge), then how can humans be free? What does it mean to be free? In his book *On Free Will*, Augustine argued that human freedom and divine foreknowledge are compatible, which means they both exist. Humans are free and God is omniscient, so it follows that God knows what humans will freely choose.

In summary, philosophers in the medieval era explored the relationship between faith and reason. Theology and philosophy were seen as allies in the battle against ignorance and unbelief. Arguments for God's existence demonstrated the rationality of belief in God, and philosophical theology reasoned that Christian doctrine made sense of the world. The medieval phrases that capture this sentiment come to us from Augustine ("I believe in order that I might understand") and Anselm ("faith seeking understanding").

Question 2.10

True or false: The medieval era is accurately called "the Dark Ages," especially when it comes to philosophy.

Question 2.11

The _____ argument from _____ argues that God is the "first cause" of all things.

Question 2.12

"I believe in order that I might understand" captures Augustine's understanding of the relationship between _____ and _____.

Question 2.13

Matching (some used twice):

A. Avicenna

___ Raised questions about the problem of evil.

B. Problem of universals and particulars

___ Wrote about the Trinity in his *Summa Theologica*.

C. Augustine

___ Died early in his forties.

D. Aquinas

___ In order to change, you need a change of heart.

E. Boethius

___ A notable Muslim philosopher from the medieval era.

___ Asks how things can be unique while sharing qualities with other things.

___ Argued for the compatibility of free will and God's omniscience.

___ Christians, members of a heavenly kingdom, are good citizens on earth but ultimately loyal to God.

The third era of philosophy is known as the modern era. The modern era of philosophy starts with French philosopher René Descartes (AD 1596–1650) and the publication of his book *Meditations on First Philosophy*. During the medieval era, philosophers generally reasoned about the world from the foundation of commonly held beliefs such as that God exists, the senses are reliable, and mathematics helps us to understand realities both seen and unseen. During the modern era, a significant shift occurred. Philosophers began to tear down previously held beliefs and to reason from the starting point of doubt and skepticism rather than principles and faith.

Descartes illustrated this shift when in the opening section of *Meditations* he wrote:

Some years ago I was struck by how many false things I had believed, and by how doubtful was the structure of beliefs that I had based on them. I realized that if I wanted to establish anything in the sciences that was stable and likely to last, I needed—just once in my life—to demolish everything completely and start again from the foundations . . . Today I have set all my worries aside and arranged for myself a clear stretch of free time. I am here quite alone, and at last I will devote myself, sincerely and without holding back, to demolishing my opinions.[5]

Notice what Descartes said in the first sentence. He is right, of course. We've all gotten answers wrong on a math or history test. We've all misremembered something. You may *think* that you had pizza for lunch yesterday, but in reality, you had a chicken salad for lunch and pizza for dinner. Everyone's eyes have deceived them. Have you ever seen the picture that, depending on how you look at it, can either be a duck or a rabbit (Google "duck or rabbit" and you will see)? Ideas based on memory, perception, and reason can be faulty. So, how do we know anything when we can be so wrong about so many things?

These questions about the nature of knowledge are a part of the branch of philosophy called *epistemology*. To answer these questions, Descartes thought that he should base all of his beliefs on something that could be known beyond any doubt. Descartes popularized the idea that in order to know something, it must be known with certainty. Even though Descartes believed in God and in mathematics, for instance, he was able to doubt these things and therefore believed they could not be the foundation of knowledge. Finally, he arrived at something that could not be doubted: his own existence.

---

[5] René Descartes, *Meditations on First Philosophy, with Selections from the Objections and Replies*, trans. John Cottingham, 2nd ed., Cambridge Texts in the History of Philosophy (Cambridge: Cambridge University Press, 2017), n.p.

Descartes realized that he could doubt everything except his own existence. If he were to doubt his own existence, then he would be doubting. If he were doubting, he would be thinking; and if he were thinking, he would exist. This led to Descartes's famous declaration, usually translated "I think therefore I am" (*cogito ergo sum*).

With this declaration, Descartes ushered philosophy into the modern era, which has at least four distinctives. First, just as Descartes pursued truth on his own (and not in community) the modern era of philosophy tends to be quite individualistic. Second, just as Descartes employed doubt as a method of arriving at his conclusion, the modern era tends to start from a position of doubt and skepticism. Third, just as Descartes saw his own existence (and perspective) as a surer foundation than traditional starting points such as God, the world, morality, and mathematics, the modern era can be described as emphasizing the role and importance of perspective and experience. Fourth, Descartes made *certainty* the standard of knowledge, so in the modern era, philosophers spend a lot of time discussing epistemology (the study of knowledge) and place a high value on the physical sciences and how the mind interacts with the physical world. These four developments summarize what made the modern era of philosophy different than either the ancient or medieval eras.

Descartes introduced a division between the mind and the body that started a debate that continues today. He believed that there are two kinds of substances: mind (or soul) and body. According to Descartes, a substance is something that does not depend on anything else for its existence.[6] Substances are known by their attributes. Minds (i.e., mental substances) are known by the attribute of thought, and bodies (i.e., physical substances) are known by the attribute of extension.[7] It is important to understand that for Descartes, minds are nonphysical and bodies are physical. Descartes, like Plato, believed that humans have a soul. He raised an important question: How does the nonphysical you (the mind or soul) control the physical part of you (the body)?

This question opened a can of worms and modern philosophers spent a lot of time seeking to understand and explain the relationship between the mind and the physical world, in general. Many people today make the mistake of thinking that their mind is the same as their brain. But you can lose some of your brain and not lose any of your mind. The you that is a mind (or a soul)

---

[6] See René Descartes, *Principles of Philosophy*, ed. Jonathan Bennet, https://www.earlymoderntexts .com/assets/pdfs/descartes1644part1.pdf, p. 13.

[7] Descartes, 13.

is greater than, and not reducible to, your physical body. To put it another way, you are more than the sum of your physical parts.

Plato, Aquinas, and Descartes all agree that humans are souls that will never die. But how does something that is nonphysical control something that is physical? Try moving something physical with just the power of your mind. You can't do it. But every day your immaterial self, including your will, thoughts, and desires actually move your physical body. The body has a complex neurological and physiological process of turning your thoughts into actions, but the mystery raised by Descartes is how something like the soul that is nonphysical controls something that is physical, such as the body (brain, muscles, etc.).

In the modern era, the issues raised by Descartes resulted in some interesting positions. Eighteenth-century Irish philosopher (and pastor) George Berkeley rejected the idea that there are two kinds of substances (minds and bodies) and argued instead there are only minds and ideas. This position is called *idealism*. German philosopher Immanuel Kant argued that all we can know is the way the world appears to us after the distorting filters of our mind and senses have done their work. We cannot know reality as it is in itself. Modern philosophy tends to distance the self from the world, and the self from others.

David Hume wrote a book called *An Enquiry Concerning Human Understanding* in which he argued against miracles and traditional arguments for God's existence. Hume believed that the laws of nature are based on normal patterns of experience that always count against anything that goes against the laws of nature, such as a miracle.[8] He also believed that while we can know that God exists from the existence of the universe, we cannot infer anything about God from the universe itself.[9]

The isolation, uncertainty, and unraveling of meaning that resulted from philosophy in the modern era was exposed by German nihilist philosopher Friedrich Nietzsche. In his book *The Gay Science* he declared, "God is dead."[10] Nietzsche did not mean that God once existed and actually died. He meant that God, as a theory to explain the world (existence, morality, etc.), was no longer believable by modern man. In the absence of God, and with him any inherent value of existence, humans would need to create their own values.

---

[8] See David Hume, "On Miracles," sec. 87.

[9] See *David Hume, Dialogues Concerning Natural Religion*, ed. Dorothy Coleman (Cambridge: Cambridge University Press, 2007), 142.

[10] Friedrich Nietzsche, *The Gay Science: With a Prelude in Rhymes and an Appendix of Songs*, trans. Walter Kaufmann (New York: Vintage, 1974), 167.

Question 2.14

What is epistemology?

_____

_____

Question 2.15

Explain Descartes's conclusion, "I think therefore I am."

_____

_____

Question 2.16

What four distinctives of the modern era does the author give?

_____

_____

Question 2.17

Matching (some answers used more than once):

A. David Hume   _____ Claimed that "God is dead."

B. Descartes   _____ There are only minds and ideas.

C. Friedrich Nietzsche   _____ We only know reality through filters, but not as it really is.

D. Immanuel Kant   _____ Inaugurated the modern era of philosophy.

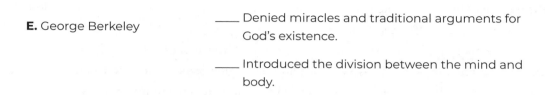

E. George Berkeley

_____ Denied miracles and traditional arguments for God's existence.

_____ Introduced the division between the mind and body.

The fourth era of philosophy is known as the contemporary era. In many ways, the contemporary era of philosophy begins in the rubble of all that modern philosophy destroyed. Consider the state of philosophy after Nietzsche by each branch of philosophy. Metaphysics had largely been reduced to naturalism, which means that only physical objects exist. If naturalism is true, then nonphysical things (e.g., God, souls, and angels) do not exist.

Epistemology had limited the scope of knowledge either to personal sensations and experience to the deliverances of the hard sciences. By the end of the modern era, philosophers tended to isolate and alienate the individual from community, from the world, and from God. These themes of alienation and isolation are evident in postmodern literature such as Albert Camus's *The Stranger*, which explores the legacy of modernity in the twentieth century.

In the absence of God or the soul as a starting point for morality, utilitarianism became the reigning paradigm for ethics. Utilitarianism (which will be discussed in chapter 5) is the view that something is good if it produced the best outcomes for the most people. Rather than discussing right and wrong in the terms of God's character or commands, philosophers such as Jeremy Bentham and John Stuart Mill focused instead on the pragmatic outcomes of actions and beliefs. In philosophy, pragmatism is the view that to say something is true simply means that it works.

What about aesthetics? The influence of ancient philosophy is evident in classical art, for instance, with its emphasis on symmetry, realism, heroism, and elegance. Medieval art focused on the role of faith and religion and on the tension between good and evil. Modern art (much like modern philosophy) gave attention to sensations over detail (impressionism) leading to art forms in the contemporary era that embraced the deconstruction of order and meaning. Art in the contemporary era favors action over contemplation and reaction over reality (abstract expressionism).

During the contemporary era, philosophy became highly specialized in the academic context of the modern research university. As a result of this trend, combined with the rise of secularism and the increasingly limited influence of Christianity, philosophy has tended to focus on language and technical arguments (called *analytic philosophy*). The shift to philosophy as an analysis of language is sometimes called the *linguistic turn* of philosophy. Philosophers such as Gottlob Frege, Ludwig Wittgenstein, Bertrand Russell, and Saul Kripke helped to focus philosophy on the meaning of terms and the relationship of ideas. Thus, science studies reality and philosophy studies how we talk or conceptualize reality.

Contemporary philosophers have tried to find a new foundation for philosophy. In the ancient era, philosophers such as Plato had an unchanging reality called the Good as a basis of reality. In the medieval era, philosophers tended to view God as the ultimate reality and meaning of life. In the modern era, although philosophers still tended to believe in God (with Nietzsche as one of the few exceptions), independent reason and experience became the foundation of philosophical exploration, highlighting the debate between the rationalism and empiricism.

For some philosophers, the new foundation in contemporary philosophy for understanding reality and analyzing knowledge is called *phenomenology*. Founded and practiced by such philosophers as Edmund Husserl, Martin Heidegger, and Jean-Paul Sartre, phenomenology is "the study of human experience and of the ways things present themselves to us in and through such experience."[11] While ancient and modern philosophers sought to understand reality from an ultimate or objective perspective (reason, logic, God, etc.), phenomenology embraced the idea that what humans call reality is inherently subjective because it is limited to personal consciousness and a first-person point of view.[12]

Question 2.18

Briefly describe contemporary philosophy's approach toward the different branches of philosophy (metaphysics, epistemology, ethics, and aesthetics).

_____

_____

The Complex Founding Fathers of Philosophy

One way to look at philosophy is by analyzing the eras discussed above. There are developments that any student of philosophy should consider. However, another way to become interested in philosophy is by considering the complex lives of the philosophers themselves, and

---

[11] Robert Sokolowski, *Introduction to Phenomenology* (Cambridge, UK: Cambridge University Press, 1999), 2.

[12] See Shaun Gallager, *Phenomenology* (New York: Palgrave MacMillan, 2012), 56–59.

in doing so, realizing that they share many of the same interests, experiences, and passions to which you may relate.

The Broadway musical *Hamilton* made a lot of people interested in an obscure "founding father" when they realized that behind the image on the ten-dollar bill was a complex orphan and immigrant who died in a dual. Similarly, the more you study the people behind the ideas, philosophy comes to life. In what follows, we sample but a few of the Hamiltonian stories found in the history of philosophy to humanize the subject and to cultivate interest.[13]

Augustine. Augustine is probably the most influential philosopher of the medieval era. He is known by many as "Saint Augustine." In his book *Confessions*, Augustine argued that human beings are fallen (i.e., sinful) and totally dependent upon God for everything.

Augustine was born on the continent of Africa in a small town called Thagaste, in modern-day Algeria.[14] Growing up in this small rural farming community meant Augustine grew up poor.[15] His mother (Monica) was a loving Christian but is described by Augustine as being somewhat overbearing.[16] His father (Patricius) was an angry man who cheated on Monica and did not seem to understand Augustine. Patricius died when Augustine was a young man, and he became a Christian some time before his death.[17] Augustine had a brother (Navigius) and maybe two sisters; Augustine was probably not close to his siblings.

Augustine also experienced loss. He shared in *Confessions* a period of grief and depression following the death of a close childhood friend: "My heart grew dark with grief, and wherever I looked, I saw only death. My own town became a torment to me and my own home a grotesque abode of misery. All we had done together was now a grim ordeal without him. My eyes searched everywhere for him, but he was not to be seen. I hated all places we had been together, because he was not in them, and they could no longer whisper to me, 'here he comes!'"[18]

---

[13] Since little is known about the early life of most philosophers in the Ancient Era, our survey will begin in the Medieval Era of philosophy.

[14] See Peter Brown, *Augustine of Hippo; A Biography* (Berkeley, CA: University of California Press, 2000), 7.

[15] Brown, 8.

[16] See Augustine, *Confessions*, bk. 5, trans. E. B. Pusey (Edward Bouverie), https://www.gutenberg.org/files/3296/3296-h/3296-h.htm: "For she loved my being with her, as mothers do, but much more than man." In addition, Monica attempted to influence control over Augustine in regard to his relationships with women, family, and so on.

[17] Brown, *Augustine of Hippo*, 18–19.

[18] Augustine, *Confessions*, chap. 4, 4.9.

Conflict followed sadness. His mother had to kick Augustine out of the house for becoming a heretic. He came to believe what is called Manichaeism (named after a religious teacher named Mani), which says that good and evil are in eternal conflict. Manichaeism is heretical because it denies the absolute goodness, holiness, and sovereignty of God. Based upon this false teaching, Augustine came to believe that he was a conflict of absolute good and uncontrollable evil.[19] As a consequence, he embraced lifestyle choices that went against his Christian upbringing and alienated him from his beloved mother.

Augustine left his hometown and became a teacher, had a son (named Adeodatus), and moved to Milan (in modern-day Italy). Despite a successful career and growing family, Augustine was miserable. He described that in his soul there was a "mighty storm bringing mighty shower of tears."[20] Sitting outside one day, he heard a child's voice saying, "Take up and read! Take up and read!" So he picked up a Bible and read the first passage he opened: "Let us walk with decency, as in the daytime: not in carousing and drunkenness; not in sexual impurity and promiscuity; not in quarreling and jealousy. But put on the Lord Jesus Christ, and make no provision for the flesh to gratify its desires" (Rom 13:13–14).

Augustine's heart was changed as he came to personal faith in Jesus. He wrote of this experience: "Instantly at the end of this sentence, by a light as it were of serenity infused into my heart, all the darkness of doubt vanished away."[21]

Augustine's upbringing is probably relatable to many of us who have experienced hardship, lost loved ones, dealt with depression and grief, and experienced hope through a change of heart through faith in Jesus. Augustine went on to become a leader in the church as the bishop of Hippo. His writings and views influenced medieval scholastics and Protestant Reformers such as Martin Luther, and his books continue to influence people today.

Berkeley. Did you know that the notoriously liberal town in the East Bay of California, which serves as home to one of the most world-renowned research universities, is named after Irish philosopher George Berkeley?

George Berkeley was born in 1865 in County Kilkenny, Ireland. The oldest child, Berkeley went to Trinity College in the city of Dublin, about one day's journey from his rural hometown. Very little is known about his upbringing, but he went on to marry Ann and together they had six children, four of whom survived infancy, and one of whom (his son, William) died only a short

---

[19] Augustine, 22.
[20] *Confessions*, chap. 12, https://www.ccel.org/ccel/augustine/confess.ix.xii.html.
[21] *Confessions*, chap. 12.

time before Berkeley's own death at sixty-seven. On the occasion of William's death, he preached what is believed to be his last sermon, titled "Thy Will Be Done."

Berkeley is known today as a leading figure in a unique form of idealism: the view that only minds and ideas exist. God communicates ideas of sense to our human minds directly, so the whole world of senses is God's communication to humanity declaring his existence (often called Berkeley's Divine Language Argument). Berkeley thought that any view of the world in which everything did not depend entirely on God was inherently atheistic; in other words, either humans need God for everything, or we do not need him at all.

So how did an Irish philosopher with such a radically theocentric (i.e., God-centered) philosophy end up with a progressive city in California named after him? Berkeley came to America because he wanted to start a college in Bermuda to train people to think clearly and love God. He wanted to train missionaries and pastors for the "New World." He was going to call his new college St. Paul's, but despite promises from the British government, funding never came through; Berkeley returned home to England as a failure.

While still in America, Berkeley wrote a letter to his friend George Percival dated 1726. In it, Berkeley included a poem that he had written titled "America as the Muse's Refuge; A Prophesy." The poem, containing only six short stanzas, concludes:

> Westward the Course of Empire takes its Way,
> The four first Acts already past.
> A fifth shall close the Drama with the Day,
> The world's great Effort is the last[22]

In the Capitol Building in Washington, DC, by the western staircase of the House of Representatives, there is a painting by a nineteenth-century German immigrant named Emanuel Leutze, best known for his painting *Washington Crossing the Delaware*. The painting hanging in the Capitol Building is called *Westward the Course of Empire Takes Its Way*, and it depicts American settlers and the San Francisco Bay. Berkeley, California, is named after George Berkeley because when the city of Berkeley was founded, Berkeley's poem was read: "The world's greatest Effort is the last."

Berkeley experienced his share of tragedy. St. Paul's College was never built. He moved his family across the ocean on the basis of an empty promise, lost a child while in America, had to

---

[22] G. Berkeley, "America as the Muse's Refuge," in *The Works of George Berkeley, Bishop of Cloyne*, 9 vols., ed. A. A. Luce and T. E. Jessop (London: n.p., 1948–57), 7:369–70.

return home embarrassed and heartbroken, and spent his later years combatting a pandemic among the poor to whom he ministered.[23]

Yet, Berkeley himself is no tragic figure. In addition to philosophy, he published essays on medicine, vision, physics, political science, and theology. On the night he died, he was lying on the couch and asked his wife to read to him from 1 Corinthians 15, where Paul speaks of death: "Listen, I am telling you a mystery: We will not all fall asleep, but we will all be changed" (v. 51). When she finished reading, Ann looked up, and her husband had died.

The *Irish Times* quoted a newspaper article from 1744 that summarizes perfectly Berkeley's intelligence and faith: "Whether he teaches, reasons, prescribes, or analyses, he does all with the humanity of a gentleman and to crown it all, with a good Bishop's piety and leaves us uncertain whether to admire in him the chemist, physician, philosopher or divine."[24]

Pascal. Imagine a person who creates what is believed to be Europe's first mass transportation system, invents one of the first (if not *the* first) calculating machines, discovers mathematical properties in order to have a triangle named after him ("Pascal's triangle"), and is regarded as the father of modern-day game theory. Blaise Pascal did all of this (and much more) even though he died before his fortieth birthday.

Pascal was raised by a single father name Etienne after his mother died when he was only three. Pascal had two sisters, one older and one younger. The family was close, and Pascal would go to work with his father, who collected taxes. Pascal observed that if there was a machine for counting time (a clock) there should be a machine for counting money. Since one did not exist, Pascal invented it.

Pascal obtained a patent for the calculating machine that he invented (called the Pascaline) then started a business selling his new invention. Like all visionary inventors, Pascal faced production challenges and supply chain disruptions. As a small business owner, Pascal did everything from fixing machines to making sales calls: Pascal was an entrepreneur.

During his youth, geometry was fashionable. People would gather in pubs and listen to papers and presentations on mathematics. Pascal was so fascinated by geometry that his father feared he would ignore his other subjects! In order to keep Pascal from becoming obsessed, his father locked away the geometry books. It was not until Pascal himself presented a paper on

---

[23] See Berkeley's later work *Siris* on the subject of tar water.

[24] "A Man of Every Virtue under Heaven," *Irish Times*, January 14, 2003, at https://www.irishtimes.com/culture/a-man-of-every-virtue-under-heaven-1.345301.

geometry that was brilliant beyond his years that a family friend convinced Etienne to unlock the books and allow his son to study geometry.

Despite his brilliance and creativity, Pascal knew that something in his life was missing. When he was thirty years old, Pascal had a life-changing experience. For two and a half hours, Pascal had something like a terrifying vision or dream that he recorded in his work titled *Memorial*:

> Fire
> GOD of Abraham, GOD of Isaac, GOD of Jacob
> not of the philosophers and of the learned.
> Certitude. Certitude. Feeling. Joy. Peace.

Pascal wrote down the events on this night of fire and sowed the writing into his coat pocket as a reminder of his conversion experience. Pascal did not come to believe in God because of abstract arguments (i.e., not of the philosophers and of the learned). He was converted by a personal experience that first produced fear and then confidence, joy, and peace.

Pascal is probably most famous for an argument for God's existence that he makes in his book *Pensées* called simply "the wager." This argument will be explored in the next chapter, but Pascal basically says: *You have to choose whether or not you believe that God exists, and you stand to gain more from believing that God exists than you do from believing that God does not exist.*

Pascal's wager is famous not only as an argument for belief in God based upon a cost/benefit analysis, but also because he does not believe that agnosticism is an option. Agnosticism is the view that there is not enough evidence for or against God's existence. Theists believe God exists, atheists believe God does not exist, and agnostics believe there is not enough evidence one way or another. Pascal thinks you have to choose (i.e., wager).

The wager is an argument for God's existence, but it is also foundational to what is today called probability theory, which is used in gaming. Probability theory is the study of uncertainty and how to make decisions given our uncertainty about outcomes. Despite his radical conversion, Pascal knew that faith in God made sense even in the presence of doubt and uncertainty.

Pascal is a brilliant sceptic who believed that faith makes sense but requires commitment and persistence. In one section of his book *Pensées*, he gives advice to someone who has not yet come to faith but would like to be a believer:

> Endeavour then to convince yourself, not by increase of proofs of God, but by the abatement of your passions. You would like to attain faith, and do not know the way; you would like to cure yourself of unbelief, and ask the remedy for it. Learn of those who

have been bound like you, and who now stake all their possessions. These are people who know the way which you would follow, and who are cured of an ill of which you would be cured. Follow the way by which they began; by acting as if they believed, taking the holy water, having masses said, etc. Even this will naturally make you believe, and deaden your acuteness.—"But this is what I am afraid of."—And why? What have you to lose?[25]

Pascal's advice is timeless. Faith makes sense because you stand to gain more than you stand to lose. Faith may be a gift from God, but once received, it is active and not passive (i.e., "endeavor to convince yourself"). Pascal is advocating for a kind of faith where a thoughtful person speaks the truth to himself and argues against his own unbelief. He also says you should learn from people who believe: Listen to their stories of how they came to faith, imitate those who believe (i.e., "follow the way"), and this will usually lead a person to personal faith (i.e., "even this will naturally make you believe").

Despite his own supernatural conversion experience, Pascal wanted people to take ownership of their faith and to be active (not passive) in regard to their relationship with God. Pascal shows that a person can be intellectual, skeptical, realistic, scientific, *and faithful*. There is no need to choose between being passionate about God and being a logical realist. Never forget that the father of probability theory who invented a calculator also walked around with his conversion experience sown into his coat pocket. If you were to ask Pascal, "Why should I believe in God?" he would probably respond by asking you, "What do you have to lose?"

Question 2.19

Matching (some answers may be used more than once):

A. Augustine   _____ Offers a wager between believing in God or agnosticism.

B. George Berkeley   _____ Before his conversion, he adopted Manichaeism.

C. Blaise Pascal   _____ A leading figure of idealist philosophy.

---

[25] Pascal, *Pensées*, 68 (see chap. 1, n. 19).

_____ A brilliant student of geometry.

_____ Became bishop of Hippo.

_____ Moved to America to found a Christian college.

_____ Converted upon reading Paul, encouraged by a voice to "take up and read."

_____ Invented a calculating machine (arguably the first).

_____ Argues that God communicates sense directly to our minds.

Conclusion

There are so many more stories that could be told. Philosophy is not just about arguments and ideas; it is about people. People are not boring, and neither is philosophy.

Hopefully you have seen in the lives of Augustine, Berkeley, and Pascal something that is true for everyone. Faith and reason are meant to go together. Your intellectual life and spiritual life are both an important part of who you are. Personal hardships and struggles are part of the work that God is doing in your life. God wants us to love him with all that we are: heart, soul, strength, *and mind*.

Chapter Review

Question 2.20

This chapter talks about philosophy in two ways. First, it takes you through a timeline of different philosophical eras. Second, it tells you stories of the lives of individual philosophers. Why are both methods helpful for understanding philosophy?

_____

_____

Question 2.21

Which era of philosophy interests you most? Why?

_____

_____

3

Questions That Matter

Peter Theil, the founder of PayPal and an early investor in Facebook, wrote a book called *Zero to One: Notes on Startups, or How to Build the Future*, in which he shares what he calls the "contrarian question." The contrarian question is something that Thiel asks whenever he is interviewing someone for a job: "What important truth do very few people agree with you on?" Thiel says, "This question sounds easy because it's straightforward. Actually, it's very hard to answer. It's intellectually difficult because the knowledge that everyone is taught in school is by definition agreed upon. And it's psychologically difficult because anyone trying to answer must say something she knows to be unpopular. Brilliant thinking is rare, but courage is in even shorter supply than genius."[1]

Few people possess true genius, but everyone can cultivate courage. Courage will be to your competitive advantage in education and in the workforce. Further, courage enables Christians to stand firmly against the cultural majority without being angry or defensive. When everyone else is putting their energy into trying to be (or appearing to be) smart, you will be focused on being courageous. Intellectual courage requires that you ask important questions and that you develop

---

[1] Peter Thiel, *Zero to One: Notes on Startups, or How to Build the Future* (New York: Crown Business, 2014), 5.

the ability to distinguish between significant questions (i.e., questions that matter) from trivial questions (i.e., questions that do not matter). And intellectual courage grows as you become more proficient at knowing what and why you believe as you do. This is why in addressing the fear Christians were experiencing in the face of hostility, the apostle Peter urged them to learn how to defend their faith intelligently (1 Pet 3:15). As you grow in your intellectual capabilities, intelligence combined with courage is a powerful force for good in the world. It is critical for preserving a bold witness to an increasingly secular, hostile culture.

Great philosophers possess the courage to ask important questions. In this chapter we will explore questions that matter. In most cases, these questions have been asked for thousands of years. Across generations and cultures, they have resonated in the minds and hearts of people just like you. Long after we are gone, others will summon the courage to ask these same questions. Like two people looking at the same moon in the sky from across oceans from on different continents, we look at these questions in intellectual comradery with others across time, language, religion, and culture. Important questions are transcendent.

Question 3.1

In an increasingly hostile, secular culture, Christians will need _____ combined with _____ to ask important questions.

Question 3.2

Important questions are transcendent questions. What does this mean, and why is it important specifically for Christians?

_____

_____

The Practical Benefits of Philosophical Questions

British R&B and soul artist Seal lyrically opined that getting a little "crazy" was the only way for us to survive.[2] Having the courage to ask important questions raises our awareness above

---

[2] Check out the song "Crazy," by Seal and Guy Sigsworth from the album *Seal*, produced by Trevor Horn (ZTT, Warner Music UK, and Sire, 1991).

the petty and trivial aspects of life that can be disappointing and lead to depression and anxiety. There is a great practical benefit to learning to appreciate important questions. As one Christian philosopher put it, believers spend way too much time thinking about things that do not matter.

You may be wondering, "Why should this matter to me?" The questions we will consider in this chapter, when honestly asked and carefully considered, can be tremendously life giving. Important questions reveal timeless truth and can infuse meaning into the mundane. As the apostle Paul wrote, "Set your minds on things above, not on earthly things" (Col 3:2).

Paradoxically, the more we focus on things above, the more meaning there is on earth. Conversely, the less we focus on things above, the less meaning we find on earth. Those who do not believe in a world above, no reality beyond the immediate, struggle to find meaning on earth. It is no accident that as culture has increasingly abandoned theism, the search for true meaning has been replaced by the quest for the immediate satisfaction of desire. Purpose is replaced by pleasure.

If you think about some of the worst things that have happened in human history, like slavery and genocide, they share something in common: human life is devalued. The first step toward great evil is dehumanizing your enemy.

The great questions of philosophy reveal something important about human beings: we are not as different as we think. Ideas that are new to us are often recycled from generations ago, repackaged, and relabeled. As a wise ancient king once wrote:

> What has been is what will be,
> and what has been done is what will be done;
> there is nothing new under the sun. (Eccl 1:9)

These ideas, born on other continents in other centuries, find new homes in classrooms, on social media feeds, in art and poetry, and thus are eternal. We do not own these questions; we are only stewards of them.

When you, as a student, connect with the value and meaning of these questions, you will find a common humanity with the countless other humans who have wondered the same things that you wonder. Through them you connect with others, and these connections help good people to work against social evils predicated upon the process of dehumanization.

Asking good questions will help you be successful in life. If you are put in charge of running a meeting at work, for instance, it is good to start the meeting by asking those in attendance, "What is the problem we are trying to solve?" This question brings clarity and purpose to the meeting. Answering the question invites participation and creates a shared sense of purpose.

Questions communicate interest. In a job interview, when the person interviewing you asks, "Do you have any questions?" the answer should be "yes!" You should have questions prepared beforehand about the job, the company, the mission of the organization, and the person interviewing you. Asking questions projects interest and communicates value.

Philosophy asks questions about life. In so doing, these questions project your interest in life and in the value of living. Philosophical questions are therefore both humanizing and life affirming.

Lastly, learning to appreciate philosophical questions is humbling. Generally speaking, to ask a question is to exercise humility because in so doing you are admitting that there is something you do not know. To ask the questions in this chapter is to acknowledge that you need other people to think rightly about your life, and there are things you do not know.

American novelist Jack Kerouac once dismissed certain questions by saying, "I don't know. I don't care, and it doesn't make any difference."[3] It is tempting to dismiss difficult questions. After all, it takes time and energy and people disagree! But something that you do not think will make a difference in your life may end up making a tremendous difference. Just because something does not seem like it should matter to you now does not mean it will not matter to you later.

Sadly, many contemporary Christians do not know how to think philosophically or explain why they believe important Christian ideas. Many dismiss these issues as irrelevant. Why is this? Because it takes too much effort to learn these things, so it is easier not to try. One can justify this lack of effort by adopting the view that these issues do not really matter, so it is useless to waste time reflecting on them.

Question 3.3

True or false: The more we set our minds on things above, the less meaning things on earth have.

Question 3.4

Philosophical questions are both _____ and _____ _____.

---

[3] Jack Kerouac, "Quotes," The Official Website of Jack Kerouac, accessed July 7, 2022, http://www.cmgww.com/historic/kerouac/about/quotes/.

Question 3.5

For each situation, provide a meaningful question that offers a new way of seeing the problem.

    a)   Your friend offers you a cheat sheet to an online quiz, assuring you that "everyone cheats on these online quizzes anyway."

    b)   You are part of a fraternity/sorority council in charge of advertising your annual charity event. None of the proposed marketing ideas seem to be working.

    c)   Your roommates are arguing (again) about whose dishes are whose and who is responsible for cleaning them.

Does God Exist?

Whether or not God exists is not only an important question, it is *the* most important question. Every other question discussed in this chapter inevitably refers back to the question of God's existence. In regard to morality, for instance, Dostoevsky says in *The Brothers Karamozov* that if God does not exist then everything is permissible.

There are several options in regard to God's existence. A person who believes that God exists is called a theist. A person who believes that God does not exist is called an atheist. An agnostic is someone who does not think there is enough evidence to know if God exists; they are undecided.

So does God exist? The first thing to do is define God. In his book *Proslogion*, Anselm of Canterbury defines God as the being *than which no greater can be conceived*. The shorthand for this definition is simply the greatest conceivable being. To conceive of something is to think about it, so Anselm is saying that God is the pinnacle of human thought. In *Confessions*, Augustine similarly says that God is the highest good. Plato never talked about God, but he similarly taught that life is comprised of something called The Good. Theists believe that God is the object of our highest thought, the greatest good, the source of value and meaning.

This definition of God is the basis for one of the oldest arguments for God's existence. It is called the ontological argument. The word *ontology* refers to the branch of knowledge dealing with being itself. So the ontological argument is based simply on God's being.

The ontological argument is a deductive argument. It is based on the definition of God. The conclusion of a deductive argument (if the premises are sound and the form of the argument is valid) is necessary and we know the conclusion with certainty. The other arguments mentioned in this section (moral and cosmological) are inductive arguments. The conclusion of an inductive argument (if the premises are sound and the form of the argument is valid) is probable and we can know the conclusion with confidence but not certainty. Inductive arguments tend to be based on observations. The conclusion of an inductive argument (if true) is known with probability, which means it is more likely to be true than false.

If God is the greatest being you could possibly think of, then he is everything good to the maximal degree of perfection. He is perfectly loving, just, kind, forgiving, powerful, and so on. He does not lack anything that would make him perfect.

Now ask yourself: Is it better to exist or not to exist? Obviously, if something is good, it is better to exist. If I am hungry and imagining the greatest possible hamburger, it would be better for that hamburger to exist in reality and not just in my imagination.

Back to God. You can think about God and the idea of a perfect being. Even atheists can think about God; otherwise, they wouldn't be able to say they do not believe in God. After all, it would be silly to say you do not believe in something you cannot even think about.

If you can think about a perfect being (God), then God must exist. If God did not exist, then he would lack something: existence. We already said that God, by definition, is perfect. A perfect being does not lack anything good, and existence is good, so God exists.

You might think that unfair. After all, just because I can imagine a perfect hamburger does not mean that it exists in reality. Of course, no one agrees on what makes a perfect hamburger. In fact, if you talk to your friends, you probably all disagree on what toppings would go on a perfect hamburger. Your vegetarian friends have different opinions as well.

The idea of God is different, however. People generally agree on what God would be like if God did exist. Even atheists sometimes argue that God does not exist because there is evil in the world. This argument against God assumes that, if God existed, God would be perfectly good, and a perfectly good God wouldn't permit evil. Sometimes people say they do not believe in God because people who claim to believe in God can be so unloving. This implies they know that God by definition is perfectly loving. The disconnection between the way they conceive of God, and the way Christians sometimes behave, is what they claim is the source of their unbelief.

All this to say that God is not like hamburgers, islands, bands, or movies. People disagree about those things and what makes them good, but usually agree (generally speaking) about what God would be like if God exists. After all, when theists and atheists debate God's existence, they have to be using the same concept of God. Otherwise, they would not be debating; they would be talking about different things. God is truly one of a kind and exists in a category all by himself. From medieval philosophers like Anselm to contemporary philosophers like Alvin Plantinga and William Lane Craig, the ontological argument has been a resilient proof for God's existence.

Another argument for God's existence is the cosmological argument that comes in different forms. This argument is also ancient, going back to ideas found in Plato (*Laws*) and Aristotle (*Metaphysics*) in the fourth century BC.[4] The Muslim philosopher Al-Ghazali and the Christian philosopher Thomas Aquinas both made cosmological arguments.[5]

The word *cosmological* refers to the cosmos, or the universe. Most scientists agree that the universe had a beginning, sometimes called the Big Bang. Regardless of how you think the universe came into existence, it did come into existence.

Things that come into existence have a cause—that's pretty basic. Looking for causes is what science does, so the start of the universe is beyond the scope of science. Since whatever started the universe is outside the universe, scientific tools and instruments cannot settle the questions.

Whatever caused the universe would need to possess enough power to cause the universe to come into existence. Since the universe is filled with information, whatever caused the universe would have to be capable of embedding information within the universe. A smart universe requires a smart cause.

Many scientists believe that information could be the building blocks of the universe.[6] Raphael Bousso, a professor of physics at UC Berkeley and member of the Berkeley Center for Theoretical Physics, has argued that the universe is an information system.[7] Every cell is coded with information, and cells are the building blocks of life. Without information there is no life and no universe.

Belief in God is supported by these conclusions. The universe did not cause itself. Whatever caused the universe to come into existence had to exist independently of the universe and has to be powerful and smart enough to have caused the whole universe to come into existence. That describes God.

The final argument for God's existence is the moral argument. This will be explored more in chapter 5, but in summary, the moral argument says that if moral facts exist then God exists. The idea is that moral facts require something that makes them moral facts. Take genocide. Any rational person knows that genocide is morally wrong. But what makes it wrong? If everyone on earth voted and decided that genocide was okay, would that make it so? Of course not!

---

[4] See Plato, *Laws*, 893–96; and Aristotle, *Metaphysics* XII, 1–6.

[5] See William Lane Craig, *The Kalam Cosmological Argument* and Thomas Aquinas, *Summa Theologica.*

[6] See Robert Lawrence Kuhn, "Forget Space-Time: Information May Create the Cosmos," https://www.space.com/29477-did-information-create-the-cosmos.html.

[7] See Kuhn, "Forget Space-Time."

So, moral facts are universal and objective. Universal means that something is true regardless of time or place. Objective means that something is true regardless of what you (or anyone else) might think. Mathematical facts are also universal and objective.

But what in the universe makes moral facts universally and objectively true? And how could there be such facts? Surely, they did not come from the Big Bang! There is nothing in the universe that makes genocide wrong. The phrase "genocide is wrong" is not something we observe in the universe, and the word *genocide* itself does not contain the idea of "wrong" within its definition like the word *bachelor* contains the meaning of "unmarried man."

The moral argument says that something outside the universe must account for the moral fact within the universe. Whatever accounts for the moral facts in the universe must itself be the source of moral truth about genocide and other distinctions between good and evil. The moral argument says that God is the basis and explanation of moral facts and without him, there simply would be no way to explain why moral facts exist or why they are universal and objective.

What if God did not exist? German philosopher Friedrich Nietzsche was an atheist who famously declared that "God is dead" in a section called "The Madman" in his book *The Gay Science*. After making this declaration (in very poetic fashion) he described the implications of God's nonexistence:

> The madman jumped into their midst and pierced them with his eyes. "Whither is God?" he cried; "I will tell you. *We have killed him*—you and I. All of us are his murderers. But how did we do this? How could we drink up the sea? Who gave us the sponge to wipe away the entire horizon? What were we doing when we unchained this earth from its sun? Whither is it moving now? Whither are we moving? Away from all suns? Are we not plunging continually? Backward, sideward, forward, in all directions? Is there still any up or down? Are we not straying, as through an infinite nothing? Do we not feel the breath of empty space? Has it not become colder? Is not night continually closing in on us? Do we not need to light lanterns in the morning? Do we hear nothing as yet of the noise of the gravediggers who are burying God? Do we smell nothing as yet of the divine decomposition? Gods, too, decompose. God is dead. God remains dead. And we have killed him.[8]

---

[8] Friedrich Nietzsche, "The Madman," in *The Gay Science*, https://sourcebooks.fordham.edu/mod /nietzsche-madman.asp.

What is important about this passage is the consequence of God's nonexistence. Nietzsche knew that the question of God's existence was central to meaning itself. He described life without God as "infinite nothing."

While there are many arguments for God's existence, there is one primary argument against God's existence called the Problem of Evil. According to the Problem of Evil, if God existed and was perfectly good, perfectly powerful (omnipotent), and all-knowing (omniscient), then evil would not exist. Of course, evil does exist, so God does not exist. What problems can you see with this argument?

First, it ignores the good reasons God might have for allowing evil. We sometimes see glimpses of the good that is accomplished through evil. Of course, good coming from evil does not make bad things any less bad; it simply means that God can use bad things for good. God uses evil to develop character and teach us to rely upon him.

Take war, for example. War is a mixture of moral evil and natural evil. Moral evil is when people do bad things (kill others unjustly, for instance). Natural evil is the bad things that happen just in the course of living in a world in which sin exists, such as disease and starvation.

War inevitably comes with death and a wide range of suffering from both moral and natural evil. Sometimes fighting in a war is just and necessary, for instance, in the case of self-defense or in the aid of other people suffering under tyranny. In such a case, God uses the evil things about war (tyranny, suffering, disease, and death) to effect good things such as deliverance from tyranny and the expansion of freedom. The evils of war also showcase human resilience, courage, sacrifice, and compassion. These things are noble and good. Something evil like the suffering and death of war can lead to something good like freedom and courage.

Most of the time we do not know the ultimate reasons why God allows evil. It requires humility to recognize that just because we do not know the reasons does not mean those reasons do not exist. At the very least, evil in the world makes us look for a lasting solution to evil and suffering, which God provides through faith in the death and resurrection of Jesus who defeated sin and death for us. Evil in the world should also lead us to look forward to the next life, to a new world without evil that the Bible describes as heaven.

Second, the Problem of Evil fails to appreciate the matter of human freedom. We will look at this issue in more depth later in this chapter. For now, it is important to remember that God created humans with a certain level of freedom, including the freedom to obey or disobey. Sin inclines our hearts to disobedience, which is why God promises to give believers a new heart, with new desires to honor and serve him (Jer 32:39–40; Ezek 11:19; Heb 8:10). God could have created a world with no evil, but human freedom would have been limited.

Third, the Problem of Evil is actually a bigger problem for atheists. If God does not exist, then what exactly makes evil and suffering bad? No one likes to suffer, and sane humans do not like evil, but saying you do not like something (e.g., murder) is not the same thing as saying it is wrong. If God does not exist, evil and suffering do not magically go away, but we lose the foundation for calling something evil. We will explore this more in chapter 5.

In summary, there are many arguments for God's existence, and some of them (such as the ontological and cosmological arguments) are quite good. You may not need an argument for God's existence to believe in God, but if someone ever claims that there are no good reasons to believe in God, you will know that is not true. The primary argument in the history of philosophy against God's existence is called the Problem of Evil, and there are several reasons this argument is unconvincing.

Question 3.6

A theist believes . . .
An atheist believes . . .
An agnostic believes . . .

Question 3.7

Matching:

A. Anselm of Canterbury

B. St. Augustine

C. Plato

_____ Did not believe in God per se, but thought that life was composed of The Good.

_____ God is the highest good.

_____ God is that than which no greater can be conceived.

Question 3.8

Explain briefly the ontological, cosmological, and moral arguments in your own words.

_____

_____

Question 3.9

The primary argument against God's existence is the Problem of _____. Give at least one response to this challenge.

What (If Anything) Can We Know?

Another foundational question in philosophy has to do with knowledge. What, if anything, can be known? Is everything just a matter of opinion, or is it possible for humans to know anything? In the science-fiction movie *Inception* a group of people travel between realities, struggling to maintain a distinction between reality and fantasy. In the end, the characters (and viewers) are left in a state of suspended belief.

What can we know? A philosopher named Pyrrho lived from about 360 to 270 BC. He was a painter and a world traveler, accompanying Alexander the Great on his Indian expedition. As with most people, world travel made Pyrrho realize that people in other places believed many different things. As is common, this realization had the effect of causing Pyrrho to doubt whether anything could be known.

Remember that for Plato, knowledge requires three things. First, to know something you must believe it to be true. Second, to know something you must have a good reason for believing it to be true. Third, to know something, what you believe must actually be true.

Pyrrho claimed that knowledge was impossible and everything was just a matter of opinion. For instance, instead of saying, "I know that the earth revolves around the sun," you should say, "It appears that the earth revolves around the sun." Every statement should be prefaced with some acknowledgment of uncertainty.

The views of Pyrrho came to be known as skepticism. A skeptic is someone who does not believe that humans can attain knowledge, at least in the sense that Plato meant it. The question that we should ask is: Why did Pyrrho reject knowledge of things that common people know to be true, such as that 1+1=2 or that something cannot be true and false at the same time (i.e., the law of non-contradiction)?

The answer has to do with happiness. Pyrrho (like most ancient Greek philosophers) believed that happiness was the ultimate goal of philosophy. You want to know the truth because the truth will make you happy. But think about times when you have been wrong. Does being wrong make you happy? Probably not. So to avoid being unhappy, you should avoid being wrong, and to avoid being wrong, you should just say "I think" rather than "I know." Skepticism, in some ways, is a big defense mechanism against the unhappiness that accompanies the humility of being corrected.

You have probably experienced a conversation where people are talking about something serious, like politics or religion. In the conversation, people often start their sentence by saying "I think . . ." or "To me . . ." This can be an effort at politeness or genuine humility, but it can also be a way of avoiding the conflict over truth claims.

You may remember that epistemology is the study of knowledge. In epistemology, the two main camps are rationalism and empiricism. Rationalism is the view that knowledge is based on reason and empiricism is the view that knowledge is based on experience or sensation. You may recall from the previous chapters that Plato can be described as a rationalist and Aristotle an empiricist.

Toward the end of the modern era of philosophy, David Hume argued in his books *A Treatise on Human Nature* and *An Enquiry Concerning Human Understanding* that human knowledge is limited to experience. Rationalist philosophers such as René Descartes had argued that humans come into the world with innate ideas that are somehow built into their soul, conscience, or essence. Like migratory birds that somehow know how to fly thousands of miles innately, humans have certain innate ideas about right and wrong, logic, language, and so on.

Both John Locke and David Hume rejected the idea of innate ideas. Locke argued that humans are born into the world as blank slates (*tabula rasa*) and all knowledge is based upon experience. Hume agreed, but limited knowledge to what can be experienced directly and only to what can be experienced, not inferred.

Direct knowledge is what you see, touch, taste, smell, or otherwise experience by your physical senses. Inferential knowledge is what you conclude based upon your observations. Hume even rejected things like cause-and-effect since this is inferred from what is observed but is never *itself* observed.

Hume argued against miracles on the basis that human knowledge is based on regular observations (i.e., the laws of nature). Since a miracle would violate what we regularly observe, and since a wise man proportions his beliefs to the evidence of experience, Hume argued that it is never wise or justified for a person to believe in miracles on the basis of evidence. In other words, for Hume, there could never be enough evidence to justify belief in a miracle.[9]

---

[9] See David Hume, "On Miracles" in *An Enquiry Concerning Human Understanding*, sec. 87.

So Hume leaves no room for any beliefs that would go against what is regularly observed. Is this a good way to evaluate beliefs about miracles? Let's set religion aside for a moment, and apply this logic to a different subject: Alexander Hamilton. According to Ron Chernow's biography *Alexander Hamilton*, which served as the basis of the Broadway musical, the historical events of Alexander Hamilton's life are staggeringly improbable.

If true, we are to believe that a person born in poverty on a remote island grew to become a founding father of the most powerful nation in the history of the world. To do this, Hamilton needed to overcome the death of his mother, the abandonment of his father, a hurricane, multiple plagues, combat in war, and a host of other physical, emotional, and financial obstacles. Have you ever known or heard of anyone else overcoming these obstacles only to create the Treasury Department, Coast Guard, and at the same time be a self-taught lawyer who never graduated from college?

If Hume is right, then our not observing such things makes it unreasonable to believe in the story of Alexander Hamilton, such as it is told. While Hamilton's life is not miraculous in a religious sense (i.e., a violation of natural laws), that we do not regularly observe such improbable accomplishments makes it unreasonable to believe that they actually happen—if Hume is right.

But there are good reasons to believe that Hume is wrong, that people like Alexander Hamilton do overcome great obstacles and rise to historic heights, and that miraculous events like the resurrection of Jesus Christ or Moses's parting of the Red Sea are things that rational people who believe in the laws of nature can believe based upon sufficient evidence. If reasonable people can read a biography about Alexander Hamilton and conclude that he did almost unbelievable things, then reasonable people should also be able to read the Bible and hear historically reliable testimony about miraculous events.

All of this suggests that human knowledge is not just based upon human observation, but about testimony, authority, inference, and reason. The Scottish philosopher Thomas Reid argued against Hume's limited scope of human knowledge (which leads to skepticism), suggesting instead a common-sense approach to knowledge.

Reid's book *Inquiry and Essays* explores such things as beliefs based on memory, sensation, abstraction, and judgment. Think of these things as tools. God gave us all these tools to know about the world around us. Common sense tells us that knowledge based upon these tools enables us to make decisions and live our lives. Reid makes the point that the goal of philosophy is to build upon common sense, not cause people to doubt what is obviously true: "It is a bold philosophy that rejects, without ceremony, principles which irresistibly govern the belief and the conduct of all mankind in the common concerns of life; and to which the philosopher himself must yield, after he imagines he hath confuted them. Such principles are older, and of more authority, than Philosophy; she rests upon them as her basis, not they upon her."[10]

Reid is right. We can know things about the world around us. God has given us tools for knowledge, and it is wise to trust these tools in the light of who he is and what he has done in Christ. Philosophers who traffic in skepticism undermine their own project. After all, if I can't trust my own senses or reason, then why should I trust anyone else's?

Question 3.10

Who of the following would *not* be considered an empiricist?
 a) Hume
 b) Plato
 c) Aristotle
 d) Locke

Am I Free?

In the young adult novel *Miss Peregrine's Home for Peculiar Children*, author Ransom Riggs tells the story of a group of children with special talents. These peculiar children live under the protection of an equally peculiar adult in something called a loop. A loop is a place in time that resets every day so that time never passes and nothing ever changes. While the characters have some freedom within the loop, their place of safety is actually a kind of prison.

Though most have only thought of time as linear—with a beginning, a middle, and an end—the idea that time is cyclical is ancient. Several Native American cultures symbolize the eternality of time with circular imagery indicating both unity and eternality. Nietzsche also argued that time was cyclical and recurring.

What does time have to do with human freedom? In Miss Peregrine's loop, the children are safe but not free. Their journey of development requires that they leave the loop in order to survive. The larger point that Riggs seems to be making is that freedom is essential to human flourishing. Better to be free and in danger than safe in captivity.

---

[10] Thomas Reid, *Inquiry and Essays* (Indianapolis: Hackett, 1983), 9.

Are humans free? Philosophers have wondered about this question since ancient times. While we tend to think about freedom in terms of physical movement, the ancient Greeks thought about freedom primarily in terms of thought and civic participation. To be free was a matter of debating things that mattered and having a thriving thought life. By contrast, a slave spent their time working so that those who were free could pursue intellectual pursuits.

Socrates emphasized that right thoughts would lead to right actions. Freedom of thought, therefore, preceded freedom of action. A person who was enslaved in her thinking would inevitably but unknowingly be enslaved in her actions. Your acts are therefore determined by your thoughts. For both Socrates and Plato, a person pursues what he believes to be good.

Aristotle took a slightly different approach. He observed that people sometimes do what they know is bad; acting contrary to known interests. The apostle Paul said something similar: "I do not understand what I am doing, because I do not practice what I want to do, but I do what I hate" (Rom 7:15).

In *Nicomachean Ethics*, Aristotle called this "incontinence." An incontinent person's actions are determined not by belief but by impulse or desire. Aristotle said that an incontinent person is (in the moment) not in control of themselves.[11] No wonder both Aristotle and the apostle Paul argued for self-control.

To what extent are you in control of yourself? Most of us like to think of ourselves as being free. Human freedom relates to human dignity. A person is least free during childhood. To be free is to be mature and in charge of one's own decisions. For students, college is usually an exciting time of exploring increasing freedom. For parents, college can be a frustrating time of coming to terms with decreasing influence over young adult children. For both college students and parents, freedom can be scary.

There is something called the paradox of choice. Sociologists have observed that a total lack of choice leads to decreased happiness. However, too many choices also leads to decreased happiness, such as when one is overwhelmed at all the choices in the cereal aisle. Too many choices can be debilitating.

Humans want to be free, but freedom is scary. A free person is responsible. No wonder it is common for a person who is caught doing something bad to basically blame someone or something else for their actions. This is as old as the garden of Eden, when Adam blamed Eve for breaking God's command.

---

[11] See Aristotle, *Nicomachean Ethics*, 3.2, http://classics.mit.edu/Aristotle/nicomachaen.3.iii.html.

Then what is freedom? There are a few options. Freedom is sometimes defined as the ability to do otherwise. This is called libertarian freedom. Libertarian freedom is the ability to choose between doing X or refraining from doing X, doing X or doing Y. If a person does not have a choice, then according to libertarian freedom, that person is not free.

Augustine argued for a slightly different idea of freedom called *compatibilism*. He thought that freedom was not so much about choice as it was about desire. Freedom is getting what you want. Imagine being at a restaurant and being told by the waiter that everything on the menu was sold out, except banana cream pie. Whether or not this is good news depends on what you wanted to eat. If you came to the restaurant for banana cream pie, you would happily order the pie because you got what you wanted. So for Augustine, freedom is about desire and getting what you want, not having choices.

To explore these concepts of freedom, think about arranged marriage. Imagine for a moment that you are single but that one day you want to get married. The thought of meeting someone, dating, proposing, being engaged, and all the work involved in each of these steps may seem overwhelming. In some cultures, even today, people do not date to find a spouse but their parents arrange for their marriage. In most cases, the adult child has input as the parents make the arrangements and retains final approval over who the parents choose.

Imagine you live in a culture that practices arranged marriage. You tell your parents what you desire in a spouse. They work with other communities or villages to find a suitable partner. You meet the person the day of your wedding. As they walk down the aisle, you see the embodiment of all the things you have ever wanted in a spouse. Your parents did an amazing job!

Now ask this question: Are you free in regard to marriage? Your answer to this question will depend on your definition of freedom. If you believe in libertarian freedom, then the lack of choices or options means that you were not free. If you believe in compatibilism, then your new spouse meeting all your desired criteria means that you are free. Thinking about arranged marriage (done well) is a good way to think about your definition of freedom.

Of course, in the history of philosophy, many people simply have not believed that humans are free. In general, determinism is the view that humans are not in full control of their will, behavior, or choices. Hard determinism, in particular, is the view that actions are determined and humans are therefore not free. Democritus (fifth century BC) is probably the first known determinist. He believed that all reality was comprised on physical particles called atoms. All outcomes in the world are determined by these atoms.

Today, two popular kinds of determinism are biological determinists and psychological determinists. A biological determinist believes that actions are determined by biology. The Lady Gaga song "Born This Way" is an anthem of biological determinism.[12]

This view that actions are determined by biology might seem like a good way to advocate for inclusion, but let's apply this logic to something else. A kleptomaniac is said to have been born with a desire to steal. Would it work for a kleptomaniac to sing that same Lady Gaga song? Was he or she in fact "born" that way?

Aside from the empirical question of what is actually determined by genetics and birth, determinism seems problematic for several reasons. First, it robs humans of the dignity of choice. If you give money to a charity, is not the freedom of the act what makes it so dignified? If the action of giving to a charity or helping a stranger is psychologically or biologically determined, then it is not really good in the same way these things are if you do them freely.

Second, determinism eliminates responsibility. If we are not free (in some sense) then we are not responsible. A person who is insane at the time a crime is committed is able to defend themselves, and be acquitted, on the grounds that they were not in control of their actions and therefore not culpable (i.e., responsible) based on mental illness.

Modern technology has raised new questions about human freedom. Imagine purchasing something online. You may think that you freely ordered a new pair of shoes online, but your choice may have been in response to a pop-up digital advertisement. Companies run data analytics based on search history and data analytics to run ads with the shoes you like, in the colors you prefer, from the brands you have searched, at the times of day you are most likely to make an online purchase.

So, when you bought those shoes, were you free? Why does it matter? Of course, in regards to things like shoes and ordering at a restaurant the choices may be trivial. The stakes get higher when we talk about marriage by dating or parental arrangement or criminal culpability. Now think about the implications of choice in regard to religious belief and the prospect of where you spend eternity. The questions of human freedom are important and have a wide range of implications.

---

[12] Stefani Germanotta (Lady Gaga) and Jeppe Laursen, "Born This Way" (New York: Germano, 2010), studio album.

Question 3.11

True or false: For the Greeks, the most important freedom was the ability to think freely, rather than freedom to go wherever and do whatever they wished.

Question 3.12

Which Greek philosopher was closer to Paul in his view of freedom—Plato or Aristotle?

_____

_____

Question 3.13

Aristotle's word for lack of self-control is _____, which means your decisions are based on _____ or _____.

Question 3.14

What is the paradox of choice, and how does it relate to a discussion of human freedom?

_____

_____

Question 3.15

Imagine you sign up for a literature class next semester. On the first day of class, the professor announces, "I am willing to let you each choose a list of whatever books you would like to read, and then we will vote as a class on which ten books make it into the syllabus." After the second class period, your top two books are on the list, along with eight other books that were not, but that you are still interested in reading. In this scenario, explain some different ways of understanding human freedom.

_____

_____

What Is the Difference Between Right and Wrong?

In one Socratic dialogue, Plato tells the story about a young man named Euthyphro. The exchange raises a question about the essence of goodness:

> *Socrates:* And what do you say of piety, Euthyphro? Is not piety, according to your definition, loved by all the gods?
> *Euthyphro:* Certainly.
> *Socrates:* Because it is pious or holy, or for some other reason?
> *Euthyphro:* No, that is the reason.
> *Socrates:* It is loved because it is holy, not holy because it is loved?[13]

The above is called the "Euthyphro dilemma," after the young man to whom Socrates is speaking. A dilemma is a choice between two things that cannot both be true. In this case, either something is good in itself or because some external authority (i.e., "the gods") says it is good. To put it another way, the labels "good" and "bad" are either assigned or inherent.

If assigned, then who (or what) does the assigning and for what reason? If inherent, then what makes something good? Both options have problems. If goodness is assigned, then the things assigned good could have been assigned bad, or vice versa, which seems to imply that goodness (or morality) is arbitrary. If goodness is inherent, then there is some unknown source of goodness external to any known authority (i.e., the gods) and goodness is subjective.

All of this has a practical purpose, which is to provide a reason for why anyone should bother being good.[14] Like the old saying goes, nice guys finish last. Have you ever been in a situation where everyone was doing something wrong and enjoying themselves while you did the right thing and received no obvious benefit? Like Plato's myth of the ring of Gyges mentioned in chapter 1, philosophers have tried to explain the difference between good and bad.

You might be tempted to say that there is no difference and good and bad are just terms we use to describe things we either like or do not like. Some have argued that moral facts are simply statements of personal preference. To say "cheating is wrong" is to say "I don't like cheating."

---

[13] Plato, *The Dialogues of Plato*, translated by J. Harward, Robert Maynard Hutchins, ed., vol. 7 of *Great Books of the Western World* (Chicago: Encyclopedia Britannica, Inc., 1952), 195.

[14] See John E. Hare, *Why Bother Being Good?: The Place of God in the Moral Life* (Eugene, OR: Wipf and Stock, 2002).

Others have argued that moral truth claims are culturally relative. The ancient historian Herodotus said, "Culture is king."[15] His observation about different cultures leads some to conclude that because cultures disagree about morality, then there must not be any real (i.e., objective) difference between right or wrong. Is morality simply a matter of personal taste or cultural preference?

However, there are serious problems with moral anti-realism (i.e., the view that there are no objective and universal moral facts). First, just because people disagree about the facts does not mean there are no facts. Imagine being in a car with friends and disagreeing about the fastest route to your destination. Your disagreement does not imply that all routes are equally fast and there is no best route. It simply means you disagree.

Second, moral anti-realism and moral relativism ignore the agreement and commonality among diverse cultures in regard to morality. C. S. Lewis points this out in *Mere Christianity* when he says, "The human idea of decent behavior [is] obvious to every one."[16] If morality was culturally specific, there could be no UN Declaration of Human Rights or Geneva Convention. Such cross-cultural agreements and declarations assume that there is moral common ground and that morality is not culturally relative.

Third, when a person says "X is wrong," they mean something more than "I don't like X." In fact, depending on what "X" is referring to, such a statement could be quite offensive and obviously wrong. What if "X" stood for sexual assault? Can you imagine believing that the statement "sexual assault is wrong" only means "I/we don't like sexual assault"? This one example proves the falseness and offensiveness of equating morality with personal or societal preferences.

Often, we soften our statements about moral disagreements out of a desire to be conciliatory or polite. However, we should never confuse a desire not to offend someone needlessly over moral disagreement with the belief that there is no objective reality about moral facts.

Moral realism says that moral truths are objective and universal. Historically, moral truth claims have overwhelmingly been grounded in the character and commands of God. It makes sense that if morality comes from God, and if God is transcendent (i.e., exists in all places and at all times) that morality would also be transcendent, as we have observed above.

---

[15] James Dreier, "Moral Relativism and Moral Nihilism" in *The Oxford Handbook of Ethical Theory*, ed. David Copp (New York: Oxford University Press, 2006).

[16] C. S. Lewis, *Mere Christianity* (New York: Macmillan, 1958). Full text available at http://lib.ru /LEWISCL/mere_engl.txt.

The branch of philosophy that deals with morality is ethics. The discipline of ethics is usually divided into three sections: metaethics, normative ethics, and applied ethics. Metaethics deals with the questions we have been addressing, such as whether moral facts exist, and if so, what makes them true. Normative ethics seeks to set a standard for ethical behavior. In other words, how should people know what is right or wrong *in general*? In turn, this issue of standards is associated with another task of normative ethics: the search for the best overall system of ethics (e.g., virtue ethics, moral relativism, utilitarianism, deontological ethics, ethical egoism). Lastly, applied ethics gives specific ethical guidance in specific situations in regard to specific ethical questions. Is abortion wrong? Should Christians fight in war? These are issues addressed in applied ethics.

In normative ethics, there are three basic approaches or theories about moral behavior: virtue, deontology, and consequentialism. Virtue theory says that something is right or wrong depending on whether a person's character was virtuous. For virtue theory, ethics is not so much concerned with what you do as it is the kind of character you have. Of course, good character leads to good behavior, so the two are always connected.

Deontology refers to the theory of ethics related to moral duty. According to deontology, ethics is about knowing what is required of you (i.e., the moral rules) and being duty-bound to following the rules. If children are to obey their parents and you obey your parents, then (according to deontology) you have done your job. The benefit of deontology is that it provides clear moral directives. The problem is that sometimes moral directives are contradictory. For instance, "children obey your parents" is not absolute. If your parent told you to rob a bank, the moral thing to do here is to disobey your parents. A moral dilemma is where one or more moral commands are in conflict. In the context of religious commands, deontology is sometimes called divine command theory because it focuses on God's laws or commands.

Lastly, consequentialism focuses not on character (as in virtue theory) or on duty or laws (as in deontology) but on outcomes. The consequentialist theory of ethics says that the outcome of an action is what determines whether it is good or bad. If the outcome is good, then the act is good. If the outcome is bad, then the act is bad. So determining the difference between good and bad is about calculating the outcomes.

Historically, Christian ethics have tended to focus on virtue and commands. It is generally agreed that right and wrong are determined by God's character. This is one answer to the Euthyphro dilemma. Something is not right simply because God says it is right or because it is right in itself. Rather, good and bad are relative to God's character. For instance, God is love and God is just. So love is good when expressed in holy ways. It is God's character that keeps morality from either coming arbitrarily from God or being outside of God (i.e., random). God could not have said that lying is good because God himself is truth and cannot lie (Num 23:19; Titus 1:2; Heb 6:18).

The Bible does contain lots of commands, but those commands reflect the character of God and help us to know how to reflect his character as those made in his image. Jesus made it clear that the essence of morality is not in merely following rules, but in possessing God's character, saying: "Love the Lord your God with all your heart, with all your soul, with all your mind, and with all your strength. The second is, Love your neighbor as yourself. There is no other command greater than these" (Mark 12:30–31).

From a Christian perspective, there is no conflict between character and duty. Our duty is to reflect God's character. We are commanded to love. However, the Bible also talks at great length about outcomes. Heaven and hell, blessing and curse, life and death; these are all ways the Bible encourages us to consider the outcomes of our beliefs and actions. However, in chapter 5 we will see that the Bible's view of the role of outcomes or consequences in morality is quite different from the way consequentialism/utilitarianism depict that role.

How do we know how to live our lives in a way that is right and good? God gives us his Word, the Bible, to direct our thoughts and actions. It is a lamp to our feet and a light to our path (Ps 119:105). God also gives believers his Spirit to counsel and to convict. Christian morality is a matter of being empowered by the Spirit to reflect God's character and follow his commands. Lastly, wisdom is required to navigate the tough decisions of life. Sometimes there is not clear guidance on decisions in life, but God gives wisdom to those who ask in faith (Jas 1:5).

Question 3.16

Describe the Euthyphro dilemma.

_____

_____

Question 3.17

The branch of philosophy that deals with morality is called _____.
Its three branches are _____, _____ _____ and
_____ _____.

Question 3.18

You have a friend—let's say Regan—who has maintained a perfect GPA so far. She needs to keep her GPA up in order to get into law school. However, there is one class in which she is really struggling. She is tempted to cheat on the final, since this would give her the score she needs. Her parents actually encourage her to cheat, since getting into law school is a greater good than an elective class (entirely unrelated to her major). How should Regan respond according to each view: virtue ethics, deontology, and consequentialism?

Question 3.19

How does Christianity incorporate all three ethical views (virtue ethics, deontology, and consequentialism)?

What Is the Meaning of Life?

Perhaps the ultimate philosophical question pertains to the meaning of life. Whether life has meaning relates to the other questions addressed in this chapter (and others) about happiness, God's existence, right and wrong, human freedom, and the like. These other questions relate to, or inform, the ultimate question about whether life has meaning or is meaningless.

Those are the only options: life is either meaningful or meaningless. To say that something is meaningful is to say it has objective value or purpose. Meaning can also refer to intelligibility. If something is gibberish or nonsensical, then it is meaningless. If something communicates and tells a story, then it has meaning.

The question at hand is whether life has value, purpose, meaning, and intelligibility, or if life is simply gibberish. The view that life is meaningless (or gibberish) is called nihilism. If life is meaningless, then whether or not to go on living or die is a legitimate question. French philosopher Albert Camus poses this question forcefully in the opening paragraph of his book *Sisyphus and Other Essays*: "There is but one truly serious philosophical problem, and that is suicide.

Judging whether life is or is not worth living amounts to answering the fundamental question of philosophy. All the rest—whether or not the world has three dimensions, whether the mind has nine or twelve categories—comes afterwards. These are games; one must first answer."[17]

The question of meaning relates to the question of living. Camus says one must first answer. This means that if life has no meaning then every other philosophical or academic question is meaningless. If life has no meaning, then all the subjects in school have no meaning, because all of them relate (in some way) to life. On the other hand, if life has meaning, then everything else in life also has meaning.

Shakespeare raises the question of whether or not life has meaning in the play *Macbeth*. When Macbeth learns about the death of his wife, Lady Macbeth, he says:

> She should have died hereafter.
> There would have been a time for such a word.
> Tomorrow, and tomorrow, and tomorrow
> Creeps in this petty pace from day to day
> To the last syllable of recorded time.
> And all our yesterdays have lighted fools
> The way to dusty death. Out, out, brief candle.
> Life's but a walking shadow, a poor player
> That struts and frets his hour upon the stage,
> And then is heard no more. It is a tale
> Told by an idiot, full of sound and fury,
> Signifying nothing.[18]

To say that life is "full of sound and fury, signifying nothing" is to say that life is meaningless and gibberish. Such a life, Camus would say, is not worth living. Nietzsche explained in *The Madman* that most people are afraid to consider life without meaning. Plato suggested in *The Republic* that rulers tell people a "Noble Lie" to keep them from believing that life is meaningless.

In one corner is nihilism, which says that life has no inherent meaning. The only meaning is what you assign to it. Each person assigns different meaning. In such a society, life is an endless conflict between people and groups and the meaning they try to project upon life. Imagine

---

[17] Albert Camus, *Sisyphus and Other Essays*, https://postarchive.files.wordpress.com/2015/03/myth-of-sisyphus-and-other-essays-the-albert-camus.pdf.

[18] William Shakespeare, *Macbeth* (act 5, scene 5, lines 16–27), http://shakespeare.mit.edu/macbeth/full.html.

going to a movie theater and having five different projectors and sound systems playing multiple movies at the same time. The result would be chaos. So, too, is the result of nihilism on modern secular society.

In deciding what value to project on life, each person must in essence become a god. After declaring the death of God in *The Madman* Nietzsche went on to ask, "Must we not ourselves become gods simply to be worthy of it?"[19] The result of atheism is nihilism, but ironically, in getting rid of one God you end up with a society of little gods, all competing to project their own values and meaning onto the screen of life, apart from which (as Camus says) life is simply not worth living.

If not for the meaning we project, what meaning could life have in itself? What constitutes the value of life? What story does it tell? In his book *The Meaning of Life: A Very Short Introduction*, author Terry Eagleton says, "Philosophers have an infuriating habit of analysing questions rather than answering them."[20] To avoid infuriating the reader, the following is an answer to the question at hand, "What is the meaning of life?"

Every good story has a beginning, a middle, and an end. Characters are introduced and developed, conflict and tension arises, then the story brings resolution and conclusion. Christianity offers a story about the meaning of life that echoes the great themes of philosophy and ties together the great questions of this chapter.

In the beginning God created the heavens and the earth (Gen 1:1). The universe had a beginning and it has a Creator. Among all that was created, humans alone were given the privilege of bearing the image of God. They have a noble and unique purpose: to glorify God by enjoying relationship with him.

Despite God's love and compassion, humans broke the relationship with God by going against God's commands (i.e., sin). Death enters the world with sin. Immediately, God promises to send someone to rescue humans and to defeat sin and death for them (Gen 3:15). Despite their ongoing sin and rebellion against him (Rom 3:23), God still loves humans (Gen 1:1; 3:1–16).

Over time, it becomes clear that God requires faith (Gen 15:6). Humans have to trust God and follow him. Since God is holy, sin requires sacrifice (Isa 6:3–5; Heb 9:22). Nothing on earth is perfect and pure enough to cover the sins of humans. God's people will need an ultimate

---

[19] Friedrich Nietzsche, *The Gay Science*, ed. Walter Kaufmann (New York: Vintage, 1974), par. 125.

[20] Terry Eagleton, *The Meaning of Life: A Very Short Introduction* (Oxford: Oxford University Press, 2007), 1.

sacrifice, and someone to lead them (king), speak to God for them (prophet), and cover their sins (priest) (Heb 1:1–3).

One night in Bethlehem a young virgin gave birth to a boy and named him Jesus (Matt 1:18–25). Everything about his birth fulfilled all that God had promised for thousands of years, going back to the garden of Eden. The seed of the woman came into the world to save sinners (Matt 5:17). Jesus was sinless and perfect (Heb 4:15). He was also fully human (Isa 9:6). Unlike every other human, Jesus existed before he was born (John 8:58). He was with God. He was God. God came to earth to accomplish the rescue of the humans he still loved (John 15:13).

Jesus proved in many ways that he was the promised Savior (Acts 1:3). Eventually, Jesus sacrificed himself for our sin—the just for the unjust (1 Pet 3:18). He died, but he did not stay dead. Three days after he died, he rose from the dead (1 Cor 15:4). By faith in his death and resurrection anyone can take part in his eternal victory, be forgiven, and receive eternal life (Eph 2:8–10). A soul of a person who dies goes immediately into the presence of God (2 Cor 5:8). One day, everyone who dies will rise physically from the dead in a resurrected body that will never again die; either to eternal life through faith in Jesus or to eternal judgment for rejecting the free offer of salvation through faith in Jesus (Heb 9:27).

In essence, knowing, loving, serving, and becoming like God is the meaning of life. Apart from God, one must embrace that life is gibberish. In the words of atheist philosopher Bertrand Russell, life apart from God is built upon "the firm foundation of unyielding despair."[21] You have the choice. There is meaning and purpose in relationship with God and there is unyielding despair apart from him. Camus is right; there is only *one truly serious philosophical problem.*

Question 3.20

Why is the question of meaning such a serious philosophical problem? How does Christianity answer this problem?

_____

_____

_____

_____

---

[21] Bertrand Russell, "A Free Man's Worship," in *Why I Am Not a Christian*, ed. P. Edwards (New York: Simon & Schuster, 1957), 107.

Chapter Review

Question 3.21

Matching:

A. Macbeth

_____ Right *action* comes from right *character*.

B. Dostoyevsky

_____ Believed that right thought would lead to right actions.

C. Libertarian freedom

_____ Claimed that "culture is king."

D. David Hume

_____ Life is "full of sound and fury, signifying nothing."

E. Lady Gaga

_____ Claimed that without God, everything is permissible.

F. Rationalist philosophers

_____ Right action is bound to duty.

G. Virtue ethics

_____ Expressed *biological determinism* in a hit song.

H. Nietzsche

_____ True freedom means getting what you desire.

I. Euthyphro

_____ A skeptic philosopher who accompanied Alexander the Great on his Indian expedition.

J. Determinism

_____ Claimed that we are born as a "*tabula rasa*" (blank slate).

K. Thomas Reid

_____ There is no true freedom; everything is determined.

L. Socrates

_____ Claimed that life without God is an "infinite nothing."

M. Consequentialism

_____ True freedom means meaningful choice related to anticipated outcomes.

N. John Locke

_____ Claim that we are born with innate ideas.

O. Herodotus

_____ Advocated for a "common sense" approach to knowledge.

P. Compatibilism

_____ An interlocutor (dialogue partner) who discussed piety with Socrates.

Q. Pyrrho

_____ Distinguished between direct and inferential knowledge.

R. Deontology

_____ Right action is determined by _consequence._

Question 3.22

This chapter asks a series of great philosophical questions. Find passages in Scripture where these questions are asked, and passages where these questions are answered.

    a)   Does God exist?
    b)   What (if anything) can we know?
    c)   Am I free?
    d)   What is the difference between right and wrong?
    e)   What is the meaning of life?

4

How to Win an Argument in the Right Way

Every subject in college has its tools. In medicine you use a stethoscope, in math you use a calculator, and in astronomy you use a telescope. Logic, reason, and argumentation are the tools of philosophy.

The tools of philosophy will help you inside, and outside, the classroom. Relationships require friends, spouses, and coworkers to argue (which is quite different from being argumentative), persuade, and compromise. Further, these provisions will help you be a better listener. Why? By giving you confidence, you will become less defensive. By giving you new ways to think and observe, you will discern more in a conversation. The simple fact is that the more you know about logic and reasoning, the more effectively you will understand, analyze, and advocate. You do not have to fight, but you do have to argue. If you are going to argue, you might as well win! The tools of philosophy will help you flourish in your relationships by enabling you to communicate with clarity and empathy.

An argument is simply a competition of ideas. Arguments need not be heated or contentious. Imagine being at dinner with friends and discussing what movie to see after dinner. Imagine there is a difference of opinion among you and your friends about what movie you should see after dinner. A conversation follows in which you (and your friends) debate what movie to see, each of you giving reasons why the group should agree to see a certain movie. A conversation that involves a competition of ideas is an *argument*, even among friends.

In this chapter, we will look at three aspects of argumentation. First, we will look at Aristotle and the art of persuasion. Second, we will explore common ways that people violate the laws of logic (called logical fallacies). Third we will look at different ways of reasoning so that when you get into an argument, you know the different ways to reach your conclusion.

Keep in mind that logic and reason apart from love and grace are not effective and will not honor the Lord. The Bible makes this clear in at least two places:

> If I have the gift of prophecy and understand all mysteries and all knowledge, and if I have all faith so that I can move mountains but do not have love, I am nothing. (1 Cor 13:2)

> Let your speech always be gracious, seasoned with salt, so that you may know how you should answer each person. (Col 4:6)

As you approach the subject of logic, it is wise to remember that grace and love will make people more likely to hear your argument, follow your reasoning, and consider your conclusion. As the old saying goes, you attract more flies with honey than vinegar. However, as important as grace and love are, they are not sufficient for presenting a good argument or solid line of reasoning in advocating for what you believe. Sadly, we live in a culture that makes important decisions not on the basis of reason, logic, and argumentation, but on emotion, image, and satisfying one's desires. The makeup artist is more important than the speech writer. By learning the contents of this chapter, Christians can become a part of the solution to this sorry situation.

Question 4.1

The three tools of philosophy are _____, _____ and _____.

Question 4.2

An argument is a conflict between (choose one)
__ people
__ ideas

Question 4.3

To avoid hostile argumentation, Christians must argue with _____ and _____.

Aristotle and the Art of Persuasion

The word *persuasion* means to help someone see the reasons why they should believe something. Of course, no one can believe for you, and you cannot believe for anyone else. The act of persuasion is inherently respectful because it honors the will and belief of the individual. The opposite of persuasion is indoctrination, manipulation, or coercion (i.e., pressure).

Persuasion is different than pressure. Most people do not like to feel pressured. If you feel pressure, you are likely to resist the person pressuring you and whatever it is being pressured upon you. Giving in to pressure can result in anger and resentment because you have acted against your will or desires.

Persuasion, on the other hand, results in a change of mind that results in a change of action. Persuasion works with the will and not against it. Being persuaded of the reason or logic of something endears you to the person who has acted as the agent of persuasion. Persuasion is not always easy, but it is a hallmark of healthy and respectful communication.

The failure to recognize these truths about genuine persuasion is a major factor in our society's inability to engage in civil discourse and disagreement. Genuine persuasion has been replaced with rhetorical manipulation, group think, emotional shaming of politically incorrect views, and downright bullying and the employment of power to force others to conform. It should be obvious how disrespectful of persons these forms of "communication" really are.

Aristotle was the first to study logic and persuasion. *The Organon* is a collection of Aristotle's writing on logic. In the introduction he wrote, "Logic furnishes the rules on which all reasoning is constructed."[1] That's a good place to start: logic is the set of rules for reasonable conversation.

In sports, there are people on the field who govern the rules of play. In football, we call them referees. In baseball, they are called umpires. Think of logic as the referees or umpires governing the rules of play for reason and argumentation. Later in this chapter we will look at logical fallacies. A logical fallacy is a violation of the rules of logic.

---

[1] Aristotle, *The Organon*, translated by Octavius Owen (London: George Bell and Sons, 1889), 5.

Aristotle gave us what has come to be known as the rhetorical triangle. In *Rhetoric*, Aristotle laid out three proofs of persuasion. Each of these three proofs constitutes a point on the rhetorical triangle.

The first point of persuasion is logos. Logos refers to the argument being made by the person speaking. In order to be persuasive, you must make an argument that appeals to truth using reason.

The second point of persuasion is pathos. Pathos refers to emotion, or the ability of the speaker to relate to the emotional state of the audience. In modern psychology this is referred to as "emotional intelligence" (sometimes referred to as EQ). Successful people are often not the smartest person in the room in terms of IQ or GPA, but they know how to relate, connect, and motivate (i.e., they have high EQ).

The third point of persuasion is ethos. Ethos refers to the character of the speaker. A person who makes a good argument but lacks ethical credibility is unlikely to be persuasive. The character of the speaker matters to the impact of the message on the audience.

Aristotle called his book *Rhetoric* the counterpart of his book *Dialectic*. The book *Dialectic* deals with the internal thoughts of the speaker prior to public speech. Aristotle made the point that a person should think before they speak. The Bible puts it this way: "My dear brothers and sisters, understand this: Everyone should be quick to listen, slow to speak, and slow to anger" (Jas 1:19).

How can we summarize Aristotle's rhetorical triangle? We can say in conclusion that a person will never be a persuasive public speaker unless they have thought through what they intend to say, organize their thoughts, make reasonable arguments, guard their character (i.e., virtue), and understand the emotional state of the audience. A person equipped with reason, character, and emotional intelligence is likely to be capable of effective communication.

Aristotle's analysis of rhetoric is helpful because it gives hope to those who do not feel like naturally gifted speakers. Logos, ethos, and pathos are things you can work on and improve. Anyone who is open to feedback, suggestions, and critique can be a persuasive public speaker.

Unfortunately, many today claim that "Aristotelean logic" is a Western invention of white males and, as such, has become an expression of cultural imperialism and pride. Nothing can be farther from the truth. By adding pathos and ethos to logos, Aristotle provided safeguards for just this sort of thing. Further, we challenge anyone to make any claim at all without presupposing the truth of the basic laws of logic. This will become evident as we press on in this chapter.

Question 4.4

Define *persuasion*, distinguishing it from *pressure*.

_____

_____

Question 4.5

The three points of persuasion are:
- a) Logos, ethos, bathos
- b) Pathos, ethos, logos
- c) Ethos, pathos, mythos
- d) Pathos, psyche, logos

The Socratic Method

Winning an argument requires more than reason, emotional intelligence, and character. Arguments are oftentimes stalled out because individuals or groups talk past each other. Have you ever been in a conversation where you did not think people were actually listening to each other? You probably found it to be frustrating and unproductive.

You cannot win an argument if it is never clear what you are arguing about. In this section, you will learn some basic tactics from what is called the Socratic method to give you a better chance of having a productive conversation and getting somewhere in everyday arguments.

Socrates's first tactic was mentioned in chapter 1. Start by defining your terms. If you are debating whether the death penalty is just, ask the group how they define *justice*. Once you arrive at a definition, make sure everyone agrees and is on the same page. During the conversation, you may have to remind people how you defined the concept in question (justice, equality, beauty, etc.); because oftentimes in a conversation people will, intentionally or unintentionally, change the ideas or reasons being debated (what is called "moving the goalposts").

Second, identify common ground. Once you agree with a definition of *justice*, for instance, say something like: "I think we agree that justice is a good thing and that it has something to do with having a right relationship with authority, ourselves, and others. I also think we agree that every society fails, in some way, to live up to this ideal and that it is our job to seek ways to promote justice. Do I have that right?"

This is an important step in the argument because it shows that you are listening, and also because it establishes common ground. Even in an argument, you and the other person agree about something. Appealing to common ground helps establish empathy. Republicans and Democrats disagree about how to stimulate the economy and promote prosperity, but they both want what is best for the economy and they both want to promote prosperity. They simply differ on the best way to achieve these shared goals. By identifying common ground, the two sides can focus their attention on exactly where they differ. It may seem either trivial or basic, but failing to establish definitions and common ground is probably the most common reasons why arguments are lost or are unproductive.

After you have defined terms and established common ground, ask what reasons a person has for believing what it is they believe. If you are having an argument about if recreational marijuana should be legal, ask the person with whom you are speaking the reasons they hold their position. You will be surprised how often a person is used to stating their position but not giving their reasons.

If a person gives their reasons, it is good to repeat them back. Say something like: "Okay, so you gave two reasons for believing that marijuana should be legal. First, it's no more dangerous than other substances that are legal. Second, legalizing marijuana would save money currently used to arrest, prosecute, and imprison marijuana users. Is that a fair summary?"

Again, you are building empathy. You are showing respect to the person with whom you are speaking by making sure you address their reasons and do not misrepresent their position. Getting your opponents' position wrong and then arguing against something other than what they believe is called the straw man fallacy.

A position is the conclusion of an argument. A conclusion is a declarative statement about a subject or topic. "Abortion is wrong," "Marijuana should be legal," and "Pornography is bad" are all examples of conclusions of commonly debated topics.

Oftentimes in both written and verbal communication the communicator will indicate when they are giving their reasons and are about to summarize their conclusions by using the word "therefore . . ." or the phrases "for these reasons . . ." or "this is why I believe that . . ." These (and other) cues notify the listener or reader that the reasons have been given and the conclusion is coming next. In your communication, these are helpful cues to let others know where you are in your presentation. But these cues are not enough. To be effective in rational persuasion, one needs to grasp the basic structure of an argument.

Question 4.6

Imagine a discussion between yourself and a friend on the topic of free speech. Write a brief section of this dialogue in which you employ the Socratic method.

_____

_____

The Basic Structure of an Argument

Think for a moment about airplanes. There are lots of different types of airplanes, but they all have a basic structure. If I asked you to draw an airplane, I would probably see two wings, some kind of propeller or jet (i.e., something to give it propulsion), a tail, and a cockpit. A person who draws a square box is not drawing an airplane. You would look at a box and say, "That's not an airplane!"

Here is the problem. In many conversations, people fail to make arguments. They are essentially drawing a box and saying, "Check out this airplane." So how do you distinguish between an argument from a non-argument in the same way you can distinguish between an airplane and a box?

The basic structure of an argument is a set of premises and a conclusion. We discussed earlier the need to ask a person for the reasons for their conclusion. Another word for *reasons* is *premises*. Premises are the reasons for a conclusion. The former provide rational support for the latter.

A premise is usually a statement that is either true or false. In an argument, a premise cannot be in the form of a question. The idea is that you are building an argument like you would build a house. The first premise is the foundation. The second premise is the walls. The third premise is the conclusion, like the roof on top of a house. The roof goes on last.

A premise can be particular or general. For example, consider the following examples of premises based upon particular observation:

1. John is a sad astronaut.
2. My dog always barks at the mailman.
3. My philosophy teacher usually prefers coffee over tea.

Each of the above premises is based upon limited observation. In order to make these statements, it is presumed that you (or someone) has observed, or could observe, what has been reported.

Another kind of premise is based not upon observation but on definition. While the premises above are about particular people, the premises below are universal and make statements about categories of persons or things. Consider the following:

1. Astronauts are sad.
2. Dogs bark at mailmen.
3. Philosophy teachers prefer coffee over tea.

These premises apply to groups or categories. They are universal. If true, they apply to all astronauts, all dogs, and all philosophy teachers.

Arguments based upon limited or specific propositions are called inductive arguments. An inductive argument leads to a conclusion that is *probably* true or false. Probability refers to the likelihood that something will occur. If something is known probabilistically, it is known by observation and is inherently uncertain, because past observations cannot guarantee future outcomes.

Arguments based on general or universal propositions are deductive arguments. Deductive arguments often start with some definition and work their way to a conclusion that is certain because the conclusion is contained in the premise. Consider the following argument:

1. All astronauts are sad.
2. John is an astronaut.
3. Therefore, John is sad.

If it is true that all astronauts are sad, and if it is true that John is an astronaut, then John (by definition) is sad. The conclusion is certain if premises one and two are true. This is a deductive argument.

An inductive argument looks similar but is different. Consider the following inductive argument:

1. John is a sad astronaut.
2. Sad astronauts adjust well to life in space.
3. Therefore, John should adjust well to life in space.

This argument is inductive. It is based upon a specific observation about a specific astronaut (John), and its conclusion is based upon what is probable or likely given the observations in premise (1) and (2). Most arguments are inductive because they are based on limited experience and lead to conclusions that are likely but not certain. The more we observe something, the more likely the outcome and the more confident the conclusion.

Deductive and inductive arguments are the two primary forms of argumentation. Recognizing whether an argument is based on premises that are specific or universal will help you to evaluate the conclusion. In the inductive argument above, the conclusion includes the qualifying word *should*. Avoid the common mistake of making a conclusion stronger than your premises will support. And remember this: In a deductive argument, the truth of the premises *guarantees* the truth of the conclusion. In an inductive argument, the truth of the premises *supports to one degree or another* the truth of the conclusion.

Question 4.7

In your own words, describe the basic structure of an argument.

_____

_____

Question 4.8

Identify the following as general or particular premises:

Premise	General	Particular
All red dogs are named Clifford.		
My new car is a sedan.		
All apples come from trees		
No snakes have legs.		
Sarah's dog doesn't feel well.		

Question 4.9

Arguments based on observations are _____ arguments, while arguments based on definitions are _____ arguments. Only a _____ argument guarantees the truth of the conclusion.

Question 4.10

Provide an example of an inductive argument and an example of a deductive argument.

_____

_____

Evaluating an Argument

Once you have listened carefully to the argument a person is making, you should understand both the reasons and the conclusion they have for holding their position. You will now be in a position to evaluate the argument. In this section, we will consider how to determine whether an argument is a *good* argument.

When evaluating an argument, first consider the individual premises. A premise in an argument should be clear and have a definite truth value. A vague premise should be a point of contention. For instance, if someone says, "War movies often include unnecessary violence," you might ask some qualifying questions. What is meant by "often"? Is the opposite not also true: War movies often do not include unnecessary violence? What do they mean by "unnecessary violence"? Seeking clarity about what is meant by a premise will help you analyze the argument.

Second, make a judgment about the truthfulness of the premise. In logic, we say that a premise is either true or untrue. In order to accept an argument, each premise must be true.

Third, ask yourself: Does the conclusion follow from the premises? If a conclusion does follow from the premises, and if the premises are true, then the argument is sound. Be careful, though. An argument can be valid even though its premises are untrue. Such arguments are unsound. They appear good but under closer inspection and consideration should be rejected.

If you do not believe that a conclusion follows from the premises, then you will need to say something such as, "I don't think you've quite proven your case," or simply, "That doesn't follow." The conclusion may not follow because it violates some formal law of logic. There are formal and informal laws of logic. Formal laws of logic have to do with the form of the argument. Informal laws of logic have to do with the content of the argument.

Question 4.11

Which of the following is *not* provided by the author as a means of evaluating an argument?

    a)   Ask whether the conclusion follows from the premises.
    b)   Judge whether a premise is sound or unsound.
    c)   Judge whether the source of the argument has a good reputation.
    d)   Clarify definitions in any vague premise.

Eleven Informal Fallacies

In this section, we will look at eleven informal fallacies. Knowing these common mistakes in reasoning will help you identify bad arguments and avoid making them yourself. Everyone makes mistakes in reasoning. The key is not to become the "fallacy police" but to love God with all your mind by thinking more clearly and knowing how to lovingly guide others to more clear lines of reasoning.

The first informal fallacy is called *ad hominem*. This Latin phrase means "against the person." An argument against the person is easy to remember because it means that rather than directing your criticism against an argument you direct it against the person making the argument.

Ad hominem arguments are common on political cable television stations. When you hear someone dismissed as a conservative, liberal, fascist, left-wing, right-wing, and so forth, you are likely witnessing the ad hominem fallacy. Rather than addressing an argument, the person (or group) is attacked with dismissive language meant to stop reasonable conversation and argumentation. Ad hominem is the equivalent of name-calling.

The second informal fallacy is *hasty generalization*. Just like the name implies, this fallacy is committed when sweeping statements are made without nuance or qualification. Consider the following examples that are common in household arguments:

"You always leave your shoes on the floor."
"You never listen when I talk."
"No one understands me."

These statements may all contain a level of truth, but they exaggerate for effect. The exaggeration makes the statement false and makes the argument (and person making the argument) less credible. Rather than saying "you always leave your shoes on the floor," try to say "you have the habit of leaving your shoes on the floor" or "lately, you've been leaving your shoes on the floor."

Emotional appeal **is another informal fallacy**. Appealing to emotions can be a powerful way to strengthen a speech or presentation and is often utilized in advertisement and marketing. However, when emotions are evoked without reason, argument, or evidence, the emotional appeal fallacy has been committed.

Consider the following:

Humans should not eat other animals. Imagine a chicken that spends its entire life in a small and filthy cage without ever enjoying fresh air or sunlight. Is it worth torturing an animal just so that you can eat chicken?

This argument starts with the conclusion "Humans should not eat other animals." There may be good reasons why humans should not eat other animals, but in the argument above, none were given. Instead, a sad story is told about chickens living in squalid conditions. The paragraph ends with a question intended to pull at the heartstrings: Is it worth torturing animals just so you can eat chicken?

The point of the question is to create a false dilemma. Either I am an evil person and eat chicken or I am a good person and give up chicken. But are there not other options? For instance, there are cage-free organic farms where chickens live their lives pecking away in fresh air and are never confined to cages. Such farms provide chicken for human consumption and do not torture chickens.

Another common fallacy is an *appeal to the masses***, or sometimes called** *appeal to the majority*. In this fallacy, someone argues that something is true because the majority of people believe it is true. Parents sometimes ask their kids, "If everyone jumped off a cliff, would you?" The sentiment here is that just because everyone does something does not mean you should do it too. What is true for jumping off cliffs is also true for beliefs. Just because everyone else believes something does not mean you should too.

Imagine someone makes the following statement: "The majority of doctors agree that adults over sixty should take baby aspirin every day to minimize the risk of heart attacks." This statement was, in fact, common advice for decades. Until recently, the majority of doctors did agree that baby aspirin was a safe and effective preventative practice for all adults. Recently, however, studies showed that the potential negative side effects of daily aspirin for many adults outweighed the potential benefits. While some adults still benefit from a daily aspirin regimen, most are now being advised to reconsider this practice.

Sometimes the experts are wrong. Just because the majority of doctors, or scientists, or pastors, or economists believe something does not (by itself) mean they are right. Galileo stood against the majority of scientists of his day when he believed the earth revolved around the sun. One should never casually dismiss the majority opinion. However, one should never accept the majority position simply because it is the majority position.

The *straw man fallacy* is another way that arguments can violate the informal laws of logic and reason. This fallacy is committed when a person argues against a position that their opponent does not hold. If you have ever been in an argument and said, "That is not what I'm saying!" then you have probably been a victim of the straw man fallacy.

Consider the following example:

Capitalists believe that money is the most important thing and that poor people don't matter. As far as they are concerned, profits are all that matter. Capitalism is a dehumanizing economic system.

In this argument, the conclusion (capitalism is a dehumanizing economic system) is predicated upon the characterization that capitalists (1) only care about money and profits and (2) are not concerned with any ill effects on people. While the conclusion may or may not be true, both premises are mischaracterizations of capitalism.

A person may believe in capitalism because they believe it provides the most people with the best chance of prosperity and freedom. Adam Smith, for instance, argues in his classic text *The Wealth of Nations* that capitalism leads to the improvement of human living conditions. According to capitalism, caring about profit and caring about people can be coterminous (i.e., they can go together).

Also, is it really fair to say that capitalists believe that money is the most important thing? You can probably imagine that both capitalists and socialists believe their families or religious beliefs are more important than their beliefs about economics. Avoid dehumanizing your opponent by ascribing to them beliefs they do not hold.

Another informal fallacy is called the *genetic fallacy*. The genetic fallacy has to do with the origins of a belief or position, as indicated by the word *genetic* (meaning origins). Simply because the origin of a belief or position is good (or bad) does not mean the position itself is good (or bad).

Consider for a moment the history of the space program in the United States. It is true that the space program benefited in the 1950s from former Nazi scientists who were brought to the United States after World War II to help America develop its rocket program. Does this mean that the space program is bad because some of its early scientists formerly helped the Nazi rocket program?

Of course not. There are other ways you could argue against the space program. For instance, you could argue that going to space is a waste of money, that space exploration has not advanced human well-being, or that there are bigger problems to solve on earth. Any of these arguments would avoid the genetic fallacy. However, arguing against the space program because of its history violates reason by inferring that rightness or wrongness depend upon origin.

The *"no true Scotsman" fallacy* **is another common error in logic**. The funny name gives away the meaning of this fallacy. Whenever someone argues on the basis of what is authentic or genuine, they are probably committing the "no true Scotsman" fallacy.

Consider the following hypothetical conversation between Gary and Robbie:

Gary: My mom is a Republican.
Robbie: Doesn't she believe in gun control?
Gary: Yeah, she believes in some forms of gun control.
Robbie: She must be a R.I.N.O. [i.e., a republican in name only] because no *real* Republican would be in favor of gun control.

In this conversation, Gary's mom is under suspicion because she is a Republican who believes in gun control. While it might not be common for a person to be a Republican and believe in gun control, Robbie has not proven that it is impossible (or even problematic). Robbie is simply arguing based upon some unproven idea of purity or genuineness.

When someone uses the "no true Scotsman" argument, they intend to shut down the conversation by appealing to purity. If someone says, "No real American would dodge the draft," they are implying that there is no reason to argue based upon the assumption that any real American agrees. In fact, real Americans disagree on all kinds of things, including the military draft.

Another fallacy is the *causation/correlation fallacy*. To cause something is to bring about a state of events. Correlation, on the other hand, means that two things happen in proximity to each other without being causally related. Confusing causation and correlation is a common fallacy.

Consider for a moment the two facts that more ice cream is sold over the summer and acts of murder increase during the summertime as well. To commit the causation/correlation fallacy would be to imply that there is a connection between ice cream and murder.

You probably realize that ice cream does not cause murder, and murder does not drive ice cream sales. But often in arguments people imply causation by suggesting that since two things go together that they must somehow be causally related.

Another common example is when politicians take credit for lower crime or economic gains by simply saying, "Since taking office six months ago the economy has grown and crime is down!" A wise person will recognize that no reason, evidence, or argument has been given as to why the politician's policies are responsible for the decrease in crime or the increase in profit. It is simply assumed that since there is correlation there must be causation.

Oftentimes, there are other explanations for why things go together. Murder and ice cream go up in the summer because it is hotter and the days are longer. Politicians often benefit from normal rises in the stock market following an election cycle and normal decreases in crime related to season of year or other factors unrelated to public policy. It is more difficult to prove causation than it is correlation, but make sure there is evidence given for causation and that it is not implied from correlation.

***Tu quoque* is another fallacy**. *Tu quoque* is Latin and means "you too." In this fallacy, a person argues against something by pointing out that the person talking (or the group being represented) is guilty of whatever offense is in question. Consider the following example:

> Chinese government officials were recently condemned by the United States government for injustices committed against Uyghur minorities. Chinese officials responded that the United States is actually the unjust government for economic inequity and social injustice.

Did you catch the fallacy? While there may be social injustice and economic inequity in the United States, this does not absolve Chinese officials of injustices against Uyghur minorities. The *tu quoque* fallacy is an attempt to avoid dealing with accusations by leveling the same accusations against your opponent. It is the adult version of saying, "I know I am but so are you!"

How do you respond to an accusation without committing the *tu quoque* fallacy? Imagine you work as a communications director for a senator. Now imagine that the senator you work for has been accused of lying. You are tempted to say, "The senator didn't lie! His political opponents are the liars!" However, you remember that you would be committing the *tu quoque* fallacy. So, you could say something like this:

> The senator has been accused of lying by her political opponents. In fact, the senator did not lie, and in time, this will be proven. The senator was misunderstood, and this misunderstanding has been used to imply that she lied, which she did not. I think the

citizens of our state are reasonable enough to withhold judgment until the facts emerge and a fair investigation is conducted. Until then, the senator is remaining focused on the pressing issues that affect us all.

This response shows the nuance that is sometimes needed in an argument to avoid committing a fallacy. In the above statement, a misunderstanding is admitted. It is always a good idea to admit when you have done something wrong; as the saying goes, "confession is good for the soul." Admitting you have done something wrong also helps establish one of Aristotle's three points of effective rhetoric: pathos. Admitting to miscommunication is perceived as a lesser offense than lying, and miscommunication is a common mistake that leads to conflict. The point is that you can avoid the *tu quoque* fallacy even when coming to your own defense.

The tenth common informal fallacy is called the *ambiguity fallacy*. The ambiguity fallacy uses words or phrases loosely or without definition. A person may leverage the confusion created (intentionally or unintentionally) by ambiguity to advance their argument.

The ambiguity fallacy is easy to avoid and address. Make sure to define your terms so that the person to whom you are talking understands your meaning. It is reasonable to ask others to define what they mean by certain words, terms, or phrases so that you can understand their meaning.

See if you can spot the ambiguity in the following example:

Michael Jordan is the most dominant professional athlete who has ever lived. He led his team to six NBA championships and was voted league MVP five times. Polls consistently show that Michael Jordan is regarded as the greatest basketball player who has ever lived.

Did you catch the ambiguity? The first sentence claims that Michael Jordan is the most dominant athlete who has ever lived, and the last sentence claims that Michael Jordan is the greatest basketball player who has ever lived. The evidence given (numbers of championship won, times voted MVP, and poll results) all perhaps prove that Jordan is the greatest basketball player of all time, but does this mean he is the most dominant professional athlete who has ever lived?

If you were talking to someone making this argument about Michael Jordan, you would want to ask for clarification. What do they mean by dominant? Are they limiting the conversation to team sports, or do individual sports count as well? What about non-traditional sports like rock-climbing or skateboarding? Are dominance and greatness the same, or can a person be great for reasons that do not make them dominant?

For instance, Rodney Mullen is a professional skateboarder who is personally responsible for creating many of the tricks you see in skateboarding today, but he does not have as many competition wins as other professional skateboarders. Serena Williams has twenty-three Grand Slam tournament title wins. If number of championships makes a person "great," then she is probably the greatest athlete of all time. While Michael Jordan had teammates around him to aid in his championship victories, it can be argued that he did not change basketball like Mullen changed skateboarding nor did he win championships alone like Williams.

Questions and counter-examples help to bring clarity to a conversation. Ambiguity is the enemy of good reasoning and of truth. Among ancient philosophers, Sorites Paradox (or, the paradox of the heap) shows the nature of ambiguity. When does a heap of sand become a heap of sand? Is one grain a heap of sand? No. Are two grains of sand a heap of sand? Probably not. So, when exactly does a heap of sand become a heap of sand? This paradox shows the danger of ambiguity. Failure to define terms can lead to misunderstanding and unproductive conversations.

It can sometimes become clear that there is no point in arguing about something because there is no agreed-upon definition. For instance, imagine you were arguing with someone about what percentage of Americans were bald. Baldness, like heaps of sand, is ambiguous. How much hair does a person need to lose before they are bald? If someone chooses to shave off all their hair, are they bald, or does baldness only refer to people who unwillingly lose their hair? These questions may produce an agreed-upon definition of baldness (such as the unwilling loss of a notable amount of hair) or it may end the argument because the concept under discussion is vague.

The final informal fallacy is *the slippery slope*. A slippery slope argument is one in which a conclusion appears to follow from an undesirable chain of assumptions. Consider the following:

You don't want to get married?
If you don't get married, you won't have kids.
If you don't have kids, you'll grow old alone.
If you're old and alone, you'll end up dying early of something preventable.
So, you should get married.

This line of reasoning is comical because the conclusion is obviously not true. Deciding to get married does not ensure you will have kids. There are many other ways to be cared for in old age that do not require you to have kids. While marriage and kids can be great, it does not follow that a person who decides not to marry is doomed to a life of loneliness and to an untimely death.

The impact of the slippery slope argument is implied by the name itself. If you imagine yourself hiking on a mountain, you want to avoid going over any steep ledge for fear that nothing will stop you from landing at the bottom. A slippery slope argument incites a similar fear. The best way to stay away from the bottom is to never go over the ledge in the first place.

Imagine you tell your parents that you want to be a musician and they communicate the following to you:

> You shouldn't pursue a degree in music.
> Musicians don't have stable jobs.
> Without a stable job, you will never have reliable income.
> Without reliable income, you won't enjoy life (travel, be independent, etc.).
> So, you should not become a musician.

This type of conversation is common. Fears of landing at the bottom (i.e., not being able to enjoy life) lead people to avoid pursuing their dreams and passions. While it is true that not all musicians have stable jobs, many of them do find meaningful employment. What does "stable employment" mean anyway? People in many industries get laid off or face economic uncertainty. Having a stable job is a good thing, but are there not other things more important?

People change careers all the time. It is not easy, but it does happen. One way off the "slippery slope" is perhaps to double major in business and music. You will have something to fall back on, and avoid the economic mistakes that other independent artists have made.

A slippery slope is a fallacy because it assumes that certain outcomes are inevitable. You will never enjoy life if you pursue music. You will die early and alone if you do not get married. There are good things to consider, but not inevitable outcomes that need to determine your decisions.

Question 4.12

Identify the fallacy associated with each argument, and offer a brief explanation.

Argument	Fallacy	Explanation
I got sick last time I ate rice, so I must be allergic to rice.		
Sure, I don't like your cat. Cats are all just selfish, obnoxious creatures.		

You can't trust that article. That came from a journal from Berkeley, which is a wildly liberal school.		
Look, there's nothing wrong with getting drunk every so often. Everyone has gotten drunk at some point in their life.		
If we allow students to have service dogs, then they will want all kinds of service animals. Pretty soon, this campus will be a zoo of all kinds of exotic creatures.		
Stephen told me the test was on Thursday. But he is a bad student, so I'm not going to trust his opinion.		
Sure, I may have cheated on my exam. But I saw you cheat on your quiz, so what's the difference?		
Churchill led England to resist the Nazi regime, which led to the end of the war. He is undoubtedly the most influential man in history.		
You should not discipline your children. Think of how sad it makes them when they think you are angry with them.		
I don't agree with Catholics. They all wear robes in church and chant strange music.		

Jerry claims that he is libertarian, but he voted for a candidate who supports gun control. Obviously, he is not a libertarian.	(No true Scotsman fallacy)	

Question 4.13

_____ is the enemy of good reasoning and truth.

The Square of Opposition

In the fourth century BC, Aristotle offered a way of thinking about what it means to affirm or deny something. In any argument, whether it is serious or silly, some proposition is affirmed or denied. Aristotle offered a way to visualize how affirmations are opposite negations. In other words, saying "yes" to something is the opposite of saying "no" to something. In between "yes" and "no" are words like "maybe" and "perhaps." In between words like "always" and "never" are words like "sometimes" or "occasionally."

The following is a simplified version of Aristotle's Square of Opposition:

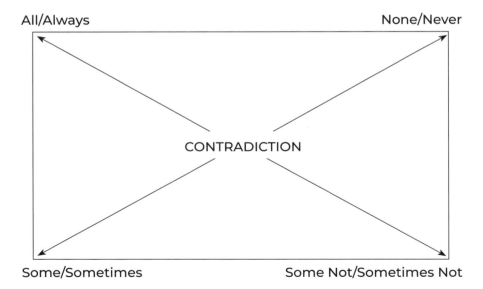

The Square of Opposition is a helpful tool for three reasons. First, it shows the logical relationship between propositions. Words matter, and we should be truthful when we speak. Second, it highlights the concept of contradiction. In logic, the law of non-contradiction states that something cannot be both true and false in the same way at the same time. If God is always loving, then it would be a contradiction to say that God is sometimes not loving. Third, the square of opposition shows that a proposition's truth value is often inferred in relation to other propositions. For instance, the truth value of the proposition "God exists" may relate to the truth value of other propositions such as "the universe came into existence" or "the Bible is a reliable book."

While this all may sound complicated, Aristotle's Square of Opposition is used on a daily basis. Suppose you message three friends and ask them to meet up for dinner. One friend says "no"; she will not be joining you for dinner. Another friend says "maybe"; it is possible he will be joining you for dinner. A third says "yes"; she is definitely available to join you for dinner.

Given the above scenario, if someone asked you, "Do you have plans for dinner?" you would say "yes": At least one friend is meeting you for dinner and another friend may be joining you as well. In a matter of minutes, the truth value of the proposition "I have dinner plans with friends" is affirmed.

The Square of Opposition also helps us identify two concepts in logic that are important in arguments: universal and particular truth claims. When we say X is always P (or X is never P), we are making a universal affirmation. If you can think of an instance when X is not P, then you would deny the truth value of the proposition because it would not be universal. A proposition is universal if it is true universally or in every case.

On the other hand, a particular truth claim is true in particular cases. For instance, the proposition "all humans sin" is a universal truth claim. The word "all" is an easy way to spot a universal truth claim. However, the Bible teaches that Jesus was fully human yet without sin (Heb 4:15). So there is one human who did not sin. This one counterexample proves the claim "all humans sin" to be false. You would need to change the claim to something like "Every human except Jesus sins" or "Every *mere* human sins."

The ninth commandment prohibits lying. We tend to think of a lie as something that is entirely made up. However, a lie can also be an exaggeration. The concept of universal and particular truth claims helps us be honest about the claims we make. When we use words like "always" or "never," we should ask ourselves the question, "Am I telling the truth?"

In an argument, you open yourself up to easy criticism if you overstate your case. On the other hand, you strengthen your argument if you use words that accurately communicate the truth. For instance, 2 Tim 3:16 says "All Scripture is inspired by God and is profitable for teaching, for rebuking, for correcting, for training in righteousness." The apostle Paul wants us to know that all Scripture is inspired. This is a universal proposition about Scripture. God wants us to know that every word in the entire Bible is inspired, good, and true.

In the Apostles' Creed, Christians confess, "I believe in God the Father, the Almighty, maker of heaven and earth." This is another example of a carefully worded statement; God is maker of heaven and earth. While not explicit, the implication is universal: *All* of heaven and *all* of earth are created by God. There is nothing created in heaven or on earth that is not created by God or derived from that which God created. The words of the Apostles' Creed have been a blessing to the church over the centuries because they precisely state what we believe as Christians.

Question 4.14

Reproduce the Square of Opposition, labeling which arguments are universal or particular, and which are affirmative or negative.

_____

_____

Question 4.15

Locate the following arguments on the Square of Opposition.
  a) All giraffes are mammals.
  b) Some Americans are not from Europe.
  c) No reptiles live in Antarctica.
  d) Some penguins live in Africa.

Occam's Razor

William of Ockham—also spelled *Occam*—was a fourteenth-century English philosopher. He is one of the most important philosophers of the medieval era. One of Ockham's most important books is called *Summa of Logic*. In *Summa of Logic*, Ockham argued for a reductive approach to philosophy. A reductive approach is one in which concepts are whittled down to only that which is absolutely necessary to explain things. Anything beyond what is needed is unnecessary.

Earlier in this chapter we looked at universal and particular truth claims. In logic and rhetoric, universal truth claims apply all times and places where particular truth claims are more limited or contextual. There is another use of the terms *universal* and *particular*. In regard to metaphysics, a universal is the essence of a thing in the abstract, while a particular is a specific instance of thing. To illustrate the difference, consider the word *car*.

If I were to ask you, "Do you like cars?" you would think about their essence. Cars move people from one place to another. Cars generally have wheels, a body, and some kind of engine. Over the years, cars have had different styles, shapes, and colors. However, when considering cars as a universal concept, or in the abstract, you tend to think about cars in general.

However, if I were to ask you, "Do you like my car?" I would have to take you to the parking lot and show you my particular car. You would have to judge its color, shape, and technological features to determine whether you like my car. You might even want to drive it or at least sit in the seats to determine its level of comfort.

Cars as a universal concept refers to the idea of cars in the abstract. Cars as a particular refers to specific cars. To investigate the universal idea of cars, you need only think about what makes something a car. To investigate a particular car you need to go out and kick the tires, so to speak.

William of Ockham was a nominalist. A nominalist is someone who does not believe in universals. Ockham believed the world could be explained by pointing to particulars without the need to imagine some world of ideas like Plato had believed. This view of explaining the world as simply as possible has become known as *Occam's Razor*.

Occam's Razor says that, all things being equal, the simplest explanation should be preferred. The point is not that the simplest explanation is always right or best. The point is that explanations should not be needlessly complex. Complexity is only a good thing when it is necessary. When simple explanations will do, simple explanations are preferred, according to Occam's Razor.

It is important to remember the qualification "all things being equal." If two or more explanations explain the facts with precisely the same degree of success, then all things are equal. In this case, Occam's Razor rightly says that one should prefer the simpler explanation. Why? Because the complex explanation has excess baggage that does no explanatory work. The simpler explanation does just as good a job without the excess complexity of its rival. But keep in mind that Occam's Razor is a tie breaker. It should be applied only after the competing explanations have been evaluated and judged equally successful. It should not be applied at the beginning of evaluation to rule out a more complicated theory. After all, that theory may be better than the simpler theory at explaining the facts. In this case, Occam's Razor does not apply since the "all things being equal" condition is not satisfied.

Occam's Razor has great practical application. In medicine, for instance, doctors are trained to look for the simplest and obvious explanation before considering more complex explanations.

It may be that any set of symptoms are ultimately caused by an exotic and rare disease, but first, doctors are going to rule out the most obvious and simple explanations.

Occam's Razor also helps people avoid needless conspiracies. When a mysterious circle appears in a field or crops, for instance, some people automatically assume the circle was caused by aliens. The more immediate and probable explanation is that humans made the circle. Humans are known to do things for publicity or to dupe or prank others into believing something that is not true. Before you imagine intelligent beings from light-years away coming to earth to make circles in cornfields, you should probably consider someone in a small town using existing and available technology to make the circle in order to draw attention.

The cartoon *Scooby-Doo* is another example of the wisdom of Occam's Razor, and of the danger or allowing yourself to believe conspiracies rather than simple explanations. In the original version, every episode of *Scooby-Doo* followed a similar pattern that unfolded in the same way. First, the kids (Fred, Velma, Shaggy, Daphne, and Scooby) would find themselves in the presence of some unexplained monster. Second, Shaggy and Scooby would be convinced that the monster was real. Third, Fred, Daphne, and Velma would reveal that the monster was really just a bad person trying to scare people.

Occam's Razor is a helpful tool to process possible explanations. Before you become convinced of aliens and monsters, look seriously at more likely explanations. Imagination is often worse than reality, and Occam's Razor will help keep you from being carried away by conspiracy theories that often play to emotions.

There is one more distinction that should be made about Ockham's Razor: it is an epistemological principle that focuses on the simplicity or complexity of explanations. This stands in contrast with another simplicity principle we shall call *ontological parsimony*. Ontological parsimony is a metaphysical principle about what reality should be like: reality is (or should be) simple. Thus, the number of kinds of entities we discover in the world should be few and not many. The laws of nature should be simple, not complex.

But why should reality be like this? We often find that we need many different kinds of entities to grasp adequately the real world (e.g., particular things, events, properties, relations, numbers). And we often find that the laws that accurately capture reality are complex. Occam's Razor is correct, but ontological parsimony is quite controversial and, in our view, wrong because of the good reasons to believe that God has created a world for his glory that is full of rich diversity with billions of stars and unseen wonders.

Question 4.16

Describe the difference between particulars and universals.

_____

_____

Question 4.17

True or false: William of Ockham would be considered a realist, while Plato would be considered a nominalist.

Question 4.18

What is Occam's Razor?

_____

_____

Question 4.19

Apply Occam's Razor to select the best explanation for the following:
  a) Your professor informs you that he never received your final essay. Either . . .
      1. your professor intends to make your life difficult by destroying any trace of work he receives from you, or
      2. you forgot to turn in the paper.
  b) Strange drawings begin appearing on the campus sidewalks. Either . . .
      1. some of the art students are working on an art project, or
      2. a group of aliens posing as students are communicating with the mother ship.
  c) Your roommates have left their laundry in the washer again. Either . . .
      1. your roommates are planning ways to bother you so that you decide not to room with them again, or
      2. at least one of your roommates is absent-minded and forgot to get his or her laundry before going to class.

Rules of Inference

One of the most basic concepts in logic is that of inference. Inference refers to the process of reasoning, which leads to a conclusion. Inference can involve evidence, experience, and definitions. The expression "drawing inferences" illustrates that complex and personal process of reaching conclusions.

This chapter has provided a sample of tools to help you argue more effectively. However, keep in mind that no one can be forced into truly agreeing with the perspective of others. One of the ways you show respect in an argument is by helping people reach their own conclusions and not resorting to bullying tactics such as intimidation, threat, or mockery.

The rules of inference can be complicated, but in this final section, we will outline a few basic rules of inference so that you can help others reach conclusions on their own by showing them how you infer your conclusions. Like a math problem, seeing someone else's work helps you see how they arrived at their conclusion. The following rules have fancy names, but the concepts are simple and will help you lead others to reach proper conclusions.

The first rule of inference is called *modus ponens*, often symbolized like so:

$$\begin{array}{l} A \longrightarrow B \\ \underline{A \qquad\qquad} \\ \therefore \quad \mathbf{B} \end{array}$$

In this equation, A and B can stand for any propositions that are believed to be related (e.g., [A] "If my parents win the lottery then [B] I will get a new car"). For modus ponens, the first proposition is phrased as a condition (i.e., "if/then"). The second premise (A) then sets up the conclusions (B).

Next time you hear someone reason this way, you will recognize the use of modus ponens. Another example would be the following: "Mom and Dad, you said that if I get an A in philosophy, you would buy me a new phone. Well, I got an A in philosophy, so [modus ponens] when are we going shopping for that new phone?"

The second rule of inference is called *modus tollens*:

$$\begin{array}{l} A \longrightarrow B \\ \underline{-B \qquad\qquad} \\ \therefore \quad \mathbf{-A} \end{array}$$

Modus tollens is the opposite of modus ponens. The subtraction symbol (–) before a letter in logic (as in math) symbolizes its negation (i.e., not A). So the above could stand for: (A) if it rains then (B) the sidewalk is wet. Since the sidewalk is not wet (–B) then it did not rain (–A). The conclusion (it did not rain) is inferred from the sidewalk not being wet. You can see from modus ponens and from modus tollens that conclusions are inferred from what is and what is not the case. If your friend claims that her parents won the lottery, and you see your friend driving a new car, you may infer the truthfulness of her claim (i.e., "my parents won the lottery") from what is the case. If someone says "it rained last night" but the streets are dry, you may reject the truthfulness of his claim (i.e., "it rained last night"). The terms *modus tollens* and *modus ponens* may be new to you, but the process of reasoning that these rules represent are already familiar.

Question 4.20

Provide one example each for a modus ponens and modus tollens argument.

_____

_____

Chapter Review

Question 4.21

For each of the following scenarios, identify the fallacy. Then, provide a sound argument for the same position, remembering to argue with grace and love.

a) In an attempt to dissuade your friend from going to the kind of party that carries a bad reputation, you argue: "Todd, don't go to the party. If you go to the party, you'll get drunk. If you get drunk, you'll wake up with a hangover. If you wake up with a hangover, you'll miss your classes tomorrow. If you miss your classes tomorrow, you'll never pass. And if you never pass, you'll end up flipping burgers at a fast-food restaurant the rest of your life."

b) You are discussing a political candidate with your family. Your parents like him because he is a Republican. You agree with this politician in some matters, but also think that he agrees with his liberal New York colleagues on gun control, liberal voting laws, and free access to abortion. You argue, "He's no Republican. He's from New York City!"

c) Your older sister asks you if you like her dog, which is cute but sheds a lot and smells like the outdoors. You reply: "No. I hate the way dogs always smell and leave hair everywhere."

d) Imagine you are back in high school, with a 10:00 curfew. You want your parents to extend the curfew to 11:00 so that you can go see a movie with your friends. When your dad pushes back, you reply, "But you used to stay out after your curfew all the time when you were a teenager!"

Question 4.22

Restructure your arguments from question 4.21 as clear modus ponens or modus tollens arguments. You may need to alter your original argument to accomplish this.

_____

_____

5

Living the Good Life

If you are reading these words, then you possess the precious gift of life. This is not to say that life is easy. Life is not easy, but it is precious. To say that something is precious means that it is of great value. Precious things, like life, should not be wasted or taken for granted.

Despite all the challenges and hardships we face, life is a gift from God. It is filled with beauty and ugliness, comedy and tragedy, revelation and mystery. Your life, at this very moment, is evidence of God's love and grace.

Part of what makes life precious is its brevity. As the mischievous and charismatic protagonist Ferris said in the '80s classic film *Ferris Bueller's Day Off*, "Life moves pretty fast."[1] The New Testament writer James compared life to a vapor: here one moment and gone the next (James 4:14). The brevity of life should motivate courage and intentionality. In the words of African-American poet and activist Langston Hughes, "life is for the living."[2]

Living with intentionality requires direction, and direction requires aim. Whether or not you like it, or if you even know it, you are aiming your life in a direction. The question is, Are you aiming your life in the right direction?

---

[1] John Hughes, dir., *Ferris Bueller's Day Off* (June 15, 1986; Paramount Pictures), motion picture.
[2] *The Collected Poems of Langston Hughes*, ed. Arnold Rampersad (New York: Vintage, 1995), 200.

There is an urgency to this question. In the 2021 film *Old*, director M. Night Shyamalan makes the point about the precious nature of life. A group of people find themselves under mysterious circumstances on a beach where people age roughly two years every hour. As people realize how fast their life is passing, they begin spending their time enjoying the things and people they previously took for granted.

Ferris Bueller, James, Hughes, and Shyamalan invite us to consider what it means to make the most of life or to *carpe diem* (i.e., "seize the day"). Living a good life is more than checking items off a bucket list. It is greater than the YOLO (i.e., "you only live once") ethos that often commodifies adventure. Making the most of life in a philosophical sense is more than empty platitudes or religious slogans.

The brevity of life can lead you down a couple of different paths. The first path is one of fear and anxiety. Worry about things like death is common and can be paralyzing. The wrong kind of fear will keep you from living the good life. Another path is one of indulgence. The reality of mortality can lead some down the avenue of dulling the senses with food and drink and other indulgences of the flesh: "Let's eat and drink for tomorrow we die" (Isa 22:13). These indulgences lead to a life of shame, addiction, and regret; hardly a description of the good life.

Question 5.1

Living with intentionality requires direction, and direction requires _____.

Clarification of the Good Life: Four Crucial Points

What, then, does it mean to live the good life? The definite article (*the*) before the phrase *good life* emphasizes that there are competing and contradictory versions of the good life. Given the law of non-contradiction, you will have to decide what it means to live the good life. Ultimately, you must aim your life in a direction. The direction in which you aim your life reveals what you consider to be the good life.

In addition, *the good life* communicates two important things. First, living the good life is objective, not subjective. In other words, humans are free in many ways, but we are not free to define goodness. For instance, a person who finds joy and meaning in polluting the environment is not living the good life. However one might feel, needless pollution is simply not good.

Second, the phrase *the good life* implies that there is something other than the good life in the same way that saying "that is a good movie" implies that not all movies are good movies. Not all lives (or even most lives) capture what it means to live the good life. The phrase itself is aspirational. The very idea of the good life is an invitation to something greater.

Third, failing to live the good life has negative consequences for you and others. Societies in which people are confused about what it means to live the good life, or in which people fail to make sincere efforts at living the good life, tend to be unstable, unhappy, and unjust. Ignorance and apathy about the good life are socially destabilizing. On the other hand, citizens committed to living the good life are positioned to experience stability, happiness, and justice.

Fourth, the idea of the good life is not just about you as an individual but about society as a whole. Everyone benefits when people pursue the good life in community. If you want to love your neighbor, make it your goal to live the good life. If you want to live in a just society, strive to be a just individual. This is Plato's point about justice in *The Republic*.

Once you understand that the good life reflects a standard to which humans should aspire, then you are positioned to begin a serious pursuit of the good life. What is in it for you? In a word, happiness. Remember that the word *eudaimonia* means "happiness of soul" that comes from living a certain kind of life: the good life. Happiness of soul endures when other forms of happiness (popularity, health, wealth, etc.) go away. You should pursue the good life because it will lead to enduring (i.e., eternal) happiness.

Life is short and precious. The good life is worth pursuing, but it must be defined and understood in order to be properly pursued. This task is made more difficult by rival versions of the good life that distract many people from the true path to happiness and life.

Question 5.2

Why is it important that we talk about *the* good life, and not just *a* good life?

_____

_____

Four Approaches to the Good Life

To live the good life, we must first arrive at a definition of the term. The words *good* and *life* must be properly understood to have a correct understanding of the good life. The challenge to consider is this: not everyone defines the good life the same way. Consequently, there are different and competing approaches to the good life. Unless you are careful, you may find yourself pursuing the wrong idea of the good life.

Contemporary American philosopher Susan Wolf refers to "the meaningful life" and offers guidance on what this entails and why it matters:

> A meaningful life is, first of all, one that within it has the basis of an affirmative answer to the needs or longings that are characteristically described as needs for meaning. I have in mind, for example, the sort of questions people ask on their deathbed, or simply in contemplation of their eventual deaths, about whether their lives have been (or are) worth living, whether they have had any point, and the sort of questions one asks when considering suicide and wondering whether one has any reason to go on.[3]

These are helpful questions as we consider what it means to live the good life. What kinds of things will matter to you on your deathbed? What makes life worth living? What are the things that give life meaning?

In what follows, we will outline several popular theories of the good life before offering a definition that is consistent with the Christian faith. Keep in mind that these are general categories. While there is some overlap, each of these approaches to the good life is distinct, with an overriding concern such that it can be differentiated from other approaches.

The first approach to the good life is hedonism. Hedonism is a theory of the good life that prioritizes pleasure. As introduced in chapter 1, the basic idea of hedonism is that pleasure is happiness. A hedonist considers a life filled with pleasure to be a good life. In other words, the good life is the pleasurable life.

Pleasure comes in different forms. It can be a feeling or an attitude.[4] One way that a hedonist might pursue the good life is by seeking physical pleasure and avoiding physical pain. Another way that a hedonist might pursue the good life is by pursuing enjoyable feelings and attitudes.

Hedonism is reflected in popular culture by a rejection of anything that is perceived to be negative. People who offer a critique or criticism are dismissed as "haters" in the modern hedonistic milieu. Posting on social media about popular topics in order to get a good feeling

---

[3] Susan World, "The Meaning of Life" in *Exploring Philosophy*, 6th edition, ed. Steven M. Cahn (New York: Oxford University Press, 2018), 687–88.

[4] See Fred Feldman, "The Good Life: A Defense of Attitudinal Hedonism" in *Philosophy and Phenomenological Research* 65, no. 3, November 2002, 605.

based upon the perception that you are a good person (i.e., virtue signaling) has been called "alternative hedonism."[5]

The second approach to the good life is wealth. Materialism is a theory of the good life that prioritizes the accumulation of wealth. Pop singer Ariana Grande illustrates materialism in her song "7 Rings," in which she brags that her newest addiction is "retail therapy."[6]

In his book *The High Price of Materialism*, author Tim Kasser argues that people who pursue wealth as the good life experience great levels of unhappiness, anxiety, depression, and low self-esteem. His research shows that this is true regardless of age, income, or nationality.[7] It turns out that the old saying is true: money can't buy happiness.

Nevertheless, there are some who see the accumulation of wealth as the definition of the good life. Aristotle taught that money is a means to an end, and warned that making money an end in itself is a form of perversion.[8] The Bible puts it this way: "The love of money is a root of all kinds of evil, and by craving it, some have wandered away from the faith and pierced themselves with many griefs" (1 Tim 6:10).

The third approach to the good life is egoism. In ethics, egoism points to the idea that moral decisions should be made based solely upon self-interest. As a theory of the good life, egoism says that self-promotion and self-interests are the keys to soul happiness (i.e., *eudaimonia*).

Egoism existed long before social media, but social media seems to have intensified egoistic practices. Social media combines age-old egoism with new-age technology. The result is a new form of addiction centered around the self. According to *Psychology Today*, social media addiction is linked to narcissism: "Social media applications may serve as ideal social arenas for individuals who appreciate and are attracted to engaging in ego-enhancing activities, as they enable individuals to bolster their egos on the basis of instant feedback from potentially large numbers of other individuals."[9]

---

[5] Robert Caruana, Sarah Glozer, and Giana Eckhardt, "'Alternative Hedonism': Exploring the Role of Pleasure in Moral Markets" in *Journal of Business Ethics*, 166:143–58 (2020).

[6] Ariana Grande, vocalist, "7 Rings," by Ariana Grande et al., released on February 8, 2019, track 10 on *thank u, next*, Republic Records.

[7] See Tim Kasser, *The High Price of Materialism* (Cambridge, MA: MIT Press, 2002).

[8] See Scott Meikle, "Aristotle on Money" in *Phronesis*, Vol. 39, No. 1 (1994), 26–44.

[9] Jennifer Golbeck, "Social Media Addicts Need to Feed Their Egos," *Psychology Today*, September 26, 2017, https://www.psychologytoday.com/us/blog/your-online-secrets/201709/social-media-addicts-need-feed-their-egos.

In her book *Generation Me: Why Today's Young Americans Are More Confident, Assertive, Entitled, and More Miserable Than Ever Before*, psychologist Dr. Jean Twenge argues that "the ethos of self-belief" permeates popular culture with a message that what matters most in life is *you*.[10]

The self, like pleasure and wealth, is not bad in itself. However, such things are not ultimate or ends in themselves. As ultimate pursuits, they fail to truthfully define or describe the good life. Another theory is needed. Perhaps the greatest need of the moment is for Christians to understand competing theories of the good life and clearly articulate an alternative theory that is biblically faithful.

A fourth approach to the good life is virtue. The virtue approach focuses on goodness itself rather than pleasure, wealth, or ego. This approach insists that without virtue you cannot be truly happy in any circumstances, but with virtue, you can be happy in any circumstance.[11]

The hedonistic, materialistic, and egoistic approaches to the good life are incompatible with Christianity. While there is eternal pleasure in the next life, the Bible says that earthly life is short and filled with hardships (Job 14:1; Mark 9:35; 1 Cor 15:31). Jesus warned that a person cannot serve God and money and that being a part of the kingdom means dying to self and putting others first (Matt 6:24).

The virtue approach, on the other hand, emphasizes the centrality of God. God is the source of all virtue, and humans are created as image bearers to reflect the character of God. As we will argue in chapter 7, the content of character matters most. The only way to know what virtue truly is and to become virtuous is to know God by trusting in Jesus and to become transformed by God's Spirit.

Since God is the source of virtue, and since the power of God is the means by which we become virtuous, then happiness is not ultimately about pleasure, wealth, or fame but rather *seeking God*. In the words of the prophet Isaiah, "Seek the Lord while he may be found; call to him while he is near. Let the wicked one abandon his way and the sinful one his thoughts; let him return to the Lord, so he may have compassion on him, and to our God, for he will freely forgive" (Isa 55:6–7).

In summary, the four basic approaches to the good life are hedonism, materialism, egoism, and virtue. The virtue approach to the good life is compatible with the biblical command to love God and others (Matt 22:36–40). The emphasis of the virtue approach can be on God as the source of goodness and not on the human self or on material gain.

---

[10] Jean Twenge, *Generation Me: Why Today's Young Americans Are More Confident, Assertive, Entitled, and More Miserable Than Ever Before* (New York: Simon & Schuster Inc., 2014), 26–27.

[11] See Paul Bloomfield, *The Virtues of Happiness: A Theory of the Good Life* (Oxford: Oxford University Press, 2014), 6.

Question 5.3

What does Susan Wolf consider to be at the basis of a good life?
a) An attitude that bears all things with a stiff upper lip
b) An affirmative answer to life's deeper questions
c) Adherence to a major religion
d) A self-made philosophy

Question 5.4

Complete the chart with the four views presented in this section:

Approach to Life	Explanation	Possible Errors

Question 5.5

Which of the life views relates most directly to the prevalence of social media today?

_____

_____

Question 5.6

What do the first three approaches (hedonism, materialism, egoistic) have in common, which opposes them to Christianity?

_____

_____

Nietzsche's Fatalistic Alternative to the Good Life

The modern emphasis on self, wealth, and ego is downstream from Nietzsche. As we said in chapter 2, Nietzsche famously declared the death of God. Nietzsche believed that God was no longer needed for modern humans to find meaning and purpose. The good life, for Nietzsche, was in freely asserting one's will and passion with excellence. The good life is all about power, especially power over others.

This involves what Nietzsche called *amor fati* in *The Gay Science*. *Amor fati* means love of one's fate. The idea is of accepting the entirety of one's life, the good and the bad, without regret and with resoluteness and enthusiasm. He wrote in *Ecce Homo*: "My formula for greatness in man is! [*sic*] *amor fati*: the fact that a man wishes nothing to be different, either in front of him or behind him, or for all eternity. Not only must the necessary be borne, and on no account concealed,—all idealism is falsehood in the face of necessity,—but it must also be loved."[12]

Fatalism is the denial of human freedom. It is the view that life is shaped by random and purposeless forces outside one's control. Nietzsche thinks that the only "freedom" one possesses is in accepting one's powerlessness and by embracing whatever comes: *amor fati*.

The roots of Nietzsche's fatalism are evident in his first book, *The Birth of Tragedy*. In it, Nietzsche argued that there are two powers in philosophy. He coined the terms *Dionysian* and *Apollonian* in reference to impulses in art and philosophy. Both Dionysus and Apollo were Greek gods and sons of Zeus. For Nietzsche, Dionysus and Apollo are mythic symbols of two rival approaches to the good life.

The Dionysian impulse refers to chaos, suffering, loss, passion, and lust. The Apollonian impulse refers to order, victory, creation, reason, and beauty. Dionysus is the god of darkness and mystery while Apollo is the god of light and revelation. Nietzsche referred to the Dionysian impulse as a "tragic disposition."

Nietzsche believed that Greek culture died when the Dionysian was overshadowed by the Apollonian, and that modern culture was empty because it lacked tragic disposition; which is to say, room for tragedy, suffering, and uncertainty. The search for certainty in modern philosophy had ignored the mystery and tragedy of life and Nietzsche's hope was in the rediscovery of the Dionysian: "There is only one hope and one guarantee for the future of that which is human; it lies in this, that the tragic disposition will not perish."[13]

---

[12] Friedrich Nietzsche, *Ecce Homo* (Nietzsche's Biography), trans. Anthony M. Ludovici, https://www.gutenberg.org/files/52190/52190-h/52190-h.htm, 54.

[13] Nietzsche, "Richard Wagner in Bayreuth" in *Untimely Meditations*, in *Complete Works*, 4:131.

In his book *Twilight of the Idols*, Nietzsche referred to himself as "the last disciple of the philosopher Dionysus." Why is that? Because Nietzsche wished to affirm all of life without judgment. Reason only gets in the way of the will. As a nihilist, Nietzsche did not believe that good and bad exist; only life. Nietzsche did not mind reason, so long as it did not reach any conclusions that he was unprepared to accept.

The Nietzschean alternative to the good life seems quite popular today. Rather than seeking to define what is good and aim one's life in the direction of goodness, the Nietzschean alternative is simply to accept or choose to interpret all of oneself and one's life as good. The result is that your life *just is* the good life. The modern obsession with self easily falls prey to Nietzsche's narcissistic reinterpretation of the good life.

If Nietzsche is right, then there is no need to struggle or aspire. There is no need for forgiveness, repentance, or redemption. There is no guilt or shame for what one has, or has not, achieved. On the face of it, Nietzsche's alternative seems to be an opportunity for liberation and acceptance. No wonder Nietzsche is popular among self-love and self-acceptance advocates.[14] In the words of the Who in their classic song "Baba O'Riley," "I don't need to be forgiven."[15]

Nietzsche's position, however, is self-defeating and inconsistent. It is self-defeating because if there is no objective truth about right or wrong, as Nietzsche asserts, then there is no reason why self-acceptance is better than self-criticism. There is no reason why loving one's fate is preferable to hating one's fate. Nietzsche dismissed the existence of God, yet he nevertheless seems inclined to maintain the categories of right and wrong as if God still existed.

Nietzsche's position is also strikingly inconsistent. Having criticized the tendencies of Apollonian philosophers for insisting on order and reason, the self-ascribed Dionysian philosopher rejects the chaos he claims to embrace by establishing his own moral order. He even goes so far as to conceive of a theory of time called *eternal recurrence* whereby the rightness or wrongness of an action is determined by whether it is worthy of eternity.

This is but one example of Nietzsche's inconsistency. He refers to Socrates as "the lowest of the low" in *Twilight of the Idols* (in a section called "The Problem with Socrates") only to seemingly betray his own principles and construct a positive alternative version of the good life but without any belief in the reality of goodness itself.

---

[14] See David Owen, "Autonomy, Self-Respect, and Self-Love; Nietzsche on Ethical Agency," in *Nietzsche on Freedom and Autonomy*, ed. Simon May (New York: Oxford University Press, 2011).

[15] "Baba O'Riley," track 1, in The Who, *Who's Next*, Polydor, 1971.

Here is the point. Nietzsche serves as a cautionary tale. God has designed humans with an innate desire for and pursuit of transcendent realities such as goodness, truth, and beauty. Putting God at the center makes sense of these desires and of this noble pursuit. Removing God from the equation causes the calculation to fail. The truth is that we are all made in God's image, even Nietzsche. Consequently, we all have buried within us an inescapable need and hunger for real, objective meaning, purpose, and eudaimonia in life. We can try to act as if we can disregard this hunger, but it will always bubble up in our lives because that's the way we were made to function.

Question 5.7

When Nietzsche claims that "God is dead," he means:
   a)   Jesus never rose from the dead.
   b)   Like Tinker Bell, God stops existing once we stop believing in him.
   c)   God must have been really old.
   d)   Humans no longer need the idea of God to find meaning.

Question 5.8

Nietzsche's *amor fati* is translated how? How does this idea contribute to his notion of the good life?

_____

_____

Question 5.9

True or false: Nietzsche prefers reason over will.

Question 5.10

Did Nietzsche live consistently with his philosophy?

_____

_____

A Christian Approach to the Good Life

Christianity points to relationship with God as the essence of the good life. If God is the source of goodness and life, then living the good life means having God at the center. The good life is not ultimately about what you possess or how you feel, but who you know.

The Christian understanding of the good life is therefore centered on relationship with God through faith or trust in the person and work of Jesus. Jesus is the ultimate revelation of God because Jesus is God in the flesh. Jesus was a real historical person whose existence and death on a cross are well-established historical facts. Extrabiblical sources agree with the Gospels (Matthew, Mark, Luke, and John) that Jesus really existed; these include the Roman historian Tacitus, the Babylonian Talmud, the Roman senator Pliny the Younger, and the Jewish historian Josephus. While these (and any other) historical documents can be scrutinized, they help to establish that Jesus was a real historical person who claimed to be a Savior, died on a cross, and was believed to have risen from the dead.

As explained in chapter 1, God's story in the Bible unfolds in four acts: creation, the fall, redemption, and restoration. Each of these acts helps us to understand the good life. Creation reminds us that God is personal and created humans to have a relationship with him and with one another. The fall reminds us that sin is the source of suffering and broken relationship with God and that God is not the author or source of sin. Redemption reminds us that God promised to defeat sin and death for humans and that Jesus fulfilled that promise on the cross. Restoration reminds us that our ultimate hope is not from anything on earth but from Jesus who reigns in heaven and will return to right every wrong.

Many people misunderstand the Christian approach to the good life and therefore reject a straw man (i.e., a misrepresentation or caricature of a view that is easy to dismiss). The Christian approach to the good life is not about self-improvement, getting rich, being healthy, or enjoying earthly success. People who anticipate these things are inevitably disappointed and often end up rejecting Christianity. In reality, God never promised these things in this life. While there are practical benefits of obedience, and while the blood of Christ provides for perfect health in resurrected bodies in the life to come, the Christian good life is not about health, wealth, or prosperity in this life.

So, what is the Christian approach to the good life? It starts with God: God is life. Theologians call this the doctrine of aseity. The word *aseity* is Latin. The prefix *a* means "from" and *se* means "self." The word *aseity* means that the Triune God (Father, Son, and Spirit) has life from himself.

All life, including human life, is from God. God created humans for life. God's desire for human life is reflected in the following Scripture where God speaks to his people: "Tell them, 'As I live—this is the declaration of the Lord GOD—I take no pleasure in the death of the wicked, but rather that the wicked person should turn from his way and live. Repent, repent of your evil ways! Why will you die, house of Israel?'" (Ezekiel 33:11).

God delights in the act of imparting life (1 John 5:11–12). The life God delights in imparting is referred to in the Bible as eternal life. A person receives eternal life the moment they put their faith (or trust) in Jesus. Consider Rom 6:23, which says: "For the wages of sin is death, but the gift of God is eternal life in Christ Jesus our Lord."

Eternal life refers not only to duration but to quality. In John 10:10, Jesus referred to God's life as abundant life: "A thief comes only to steal and kill and destroy. I have come so that they may have life and have it in abundance."

The word "abundance" (*perissos*) in John 10:10 can be translated as "greater." Relationship with God is not just the good life; it is *the great life*; it is abundant life and eternal life. Relationship with God through faith in Jesus is greater than anything apart from Jesus.

Even philosophers who do not believe in God, such as British philosopher Bertrand Russell who wrote an essay titled "Why I Am Not a Christian," longed to live the good life and believed that the good life was possible. In his book *What I Believe*, Russell said that love and knowledge are essential to the good life: "The good life is one inspired by love and guided by knowledge. . . . Neither love without knowledge, nor knowledge without love can produce a good life."[16]

Russell is right that love and knowledge are important components of the good life. Unfortunately, as far as we know, Russell never came to realize that God is the source of life, goodness, love, and truth. Relationship with God is the good life.

Question 5.11

The Christian view of the good life is centered on _____ _____ _____.

Question 5.12

What is the doctrine of aseity? What does it mean for the good life?

---

[16] Bertrand Russell, *What I Believe* (London: Routledge Classics, 2004), 10.

Human Flourishing

Philosophers have tended to connect the good life with human flourishing. Basically, the good life should produce true happiness (i.e, a deep sense of well-being, human flourishing) and virtue. Relationship with God through faith in Jesus results in the indwelling presence of the Holy Spirit in a believer. The Holy Spirit cultivates virtue and moral transformation through human effort according to God's grace. According to William of Saint-Thierry, a twelfth-century theologian: "You first loved us so that we might love you—not because you needed Our love, but because we could not be what you created us to be, except by loving you."[17]

Relationship with God (i.e., "loving You") is the means by which humans become what God intends; this is what it means to flourish. To flourish is to know God and to become more like God through spiritual discipline. When this happens, we properly experience soul happiness (eudaimonia).

Unlike the hedonistic, materialistic, or egoistic conceptions of the good life, the Christian approach sees self-centeredness not as the primary means to the good life but as the primary hindrance to the good life. American writer Flannery O'Connor, author of *A Good Man Is Hard to Find*, eloquently summarized pride and ego as barriers to the good life in her prayer journal:

> Dear God. I cannot love Thee the way I want to. You are the slim crescent of a moon that I see and my self is the earth's shadow that keeps me from seeing all the moon. The crescent is very beautiful and perhaps that is all one like I am should or could see; but what I am afraid of, dear God, is that my self shadow will grow so large that it blocks the whole moon, and that I will judge myself by the shadow that is nothing.
>
> I do not know You God because I am in the way. Please help me push myself aside.[18]

The self-shadow of sin keeps us from living the good life and experiencing human flourishing. In her writing, O'Connor creates characters who are described as freaks and misfits, hardly deserving of God's love and life. Nevertheless, her writing shows how the grace of God reaches the

---

[17] William of Saint-Thierry, "He Loved Us First," in *The Liturgy of the Hours According to the Roman Rite*, vol. I, *Advent & Christmas Seasons* (n.p.: Catholic Book Publishing, 1975), 271–72.

[18] Flannery O'Connor, *A Prayer Journal* (New York: Farrar, Straus and Giroux, 2013), 3.

most unlikely souls. In fact, O'Connor's final short story is called "Revelation," which she wrote while she was dying at the young age of thirty-nine. In it, O'Connor describes a character's vision of heaven being filled with different people who had found life in God: ". . . battalions of freaks and lunatics shouting and clapping and leaping like frogs."[19]

Human flourishing is not about perfection but moral transformation. The reformation theologians referred to the state of the redeemed in this life as *simul justus et peccator*, which means "at the same time justified and sinner." That is the state of the redeemed in this life, sinners in need of ongoing confession, repentance, and forgiveness (which is promised by the merit of Christ).

Part of moral transformation is the realization of one's sinfulness and need for God's grace. This perspective is embodied in the Gospel of Luke and the story of the Pharisee and the tax collector. Pharisees were regarded as good in Jesus's day, while tax collectors were regarded as bad. The twist of the story is that God rejects people who think that self-exaltation is the means to the good life or to happiness. On the other hand, as illustrated by the tax collector, God exalts the humble: "But the tax collector, standing far off, would not even raise his eyes to heaven but kept striking his chest and saying, 'God, have mercy on me, a sinner!' I tell you, this one went down to his house justified rather than the other, because everyone who exalts himself will be humbled, but the one who humbles himself will be exalted" (Luke 18:13–14).

In summary, human flourishing can be understood as relationship with God through faith in Jesus that results in moral transformation by the power of the Holy Spirit dwelling within a believer. Happiness, as described by Jesus in the Sermon on the Mount, is the experience of receiving the love of God and being changed to reflect his love to others. Unlike material gain, pleasure, or ego, the Christian understanding of the good life and human flourishing is based upon something that cannot be earned, and that once received, cannot be lost.

In *The Consolation of Philosophy*, Boethius warned against what he called "the allurements of false happiness." By allurements, Boethius was referring to something that is enticing but false. In other words, unbiblical notions of happiness are attractive fiction that ultimately disappoint. Boethius further explained what he meant by false happiness, describing it as that which is "certain to depart."[20] In contrast, consider the following verses about a believer's confidence in eternal relationship with God through faith in Jesus:

---

[19] Flannery O'Connor, *Revelation*, in *Philosophy of Human Experience* (2004–5), https://www.ohio.k12.ky.us/userfiles/1153/Classes/7791/OConner%20Revelation.pdf, 34.

[20] Boethius, *The Consolation of Philosophy*, bk. II.1, Project Gutenberg ebook, https://www.gutenberg.org/files/14328/14328-h/14328-h.htm.

Keep your life free from the love of money. Be satisfied with what you have, for he himself has said, I will never leave you or abandon you. (Heb 13:5)

Who can separate us from the love of Christ? Can affliction or distress or persecution or famine or nakedness or danger or sword? . . . For I am persuaded that neither death nor life, nor angels nor rulers, nor things present nor things to come, nor powers, nor height nor depth, nor any other created thing will be able to separate us from the love of God that is in Christ Jesus our Lord. (Rom 8:35, 38–39)

I give them eternal life, and they will never perish. No one will snatch them out of my hand. (John 10:28)

These and many other verses point Christians to the certainty of God's love in Christ. The love of God grounds human reason and true happiness. Or, as summarized by Boethius in *The Consolidation of Philosophy*: "How happy is mankind, if the love that orders the stars above rules, too, in your hearts."[21]

Before we turn to the role of the local church on fostering human flourishing, we should summarize the ancient, particularly the Christian notion of happiness, and contrast it with the contemporary understanding. The former defines happiness as eudaimonia—a life of character, well-being, wisdom, flourishing by living the way God made us to function best and by being relationally connected to God. The latter defines happiness as pleasurable satisfaction, a feeling of gratification, or an adrenaline rush. This chart summarizes the difference:

Contemporary Happiness	Ancient and Biblical Happiness
Pleasurable satisfaction	Virtue and well-being
An intense feeling	A settled tone
Dependent on external circumstances	Springs from within
Transitory and fleeting	More permanent and stable
Addictive and enslaving	Empowering and liberating
Split off from rest of self, doesn't color rest of life, creates false/empty self	Integrated with entire personality, colors everything else, creates true self

---

[21] Anicius Manlius Severinus Boethius, *The Consolation of Philosophy*, trans. David R. Slavitt (Cambridge, MA: Harvard University Press, 2008), bk. 2, song 8, p. 58.

Achieved by self-absorbed narcissism; success produces a celebrity	Achieved by self-denying apprenticeship to Jesus; success produces a hero
God is irrelevant	God is central

Question 5.13

From a Christian perspective, what does it mean to flourish? What keeps us from flourishing?

_____

_____

Question 5.14

Simul justus et peccator means _____.

Question 5.15

What grounds human reason and true happiness?

_____

_____

Question 5.16

In each circumstance, does the person more likely adhere to a modern view of happiness or an ancient/biblical view of happiness?

    a) George's mother agrees to take him to the zoo on Saturday if he behaves today. He does not behave, but still gets angry with his mother for not letting him go to the zoo.

    b) John's girlfriend gets him a new chess set for his birthday. He is pretty sure he mentioned many times that he wanted a set of golf clubs. So, he breaks up with her for her carelessness. He regrets it the next week, when he sees her on a date with another guy.

    c) Sarah has an exam tomorrow morning, but she is really enjoying her favorite TV show and opts to finish the new season instead of studying and then getting enough sleep. In the moment, she is enjoying the TV show. The next day, she regrets the late night and fails the exam.

    d) Clara has been looking forward to a steak dinner all day. Her family made plans to go to her favorite steakhouse tonight for her brother CJ's birthday. An hour before dinner, her brother declares that he would rather go to McDonald's and, since it is his birthday, that is where they go. When her mother sympathizes, Clara is bright and cheery, assuring her, "It's okay, Mom! I'm glad that CJ is enjoying his birthday!"

Question 5.17

In the scenarios from 5.16, how would someone with the opposite view of happiness respond in the same situation?

_____

_____

The Role of the Local Church in Human Flourishing

In this section we will consider the importance of the church in terms of living the good life and flourishing. First, let us clarify what we mean by church. The church can refer to all believers across all times and places. This is called the universal church, and it is an important doctrine to describe what John Calvin called the "invisible church" of all believers since the beginning of time until the end of time.

Another way to refer to the church is the local church. In general, the local church (hereafter church) refers to a particular set of believers who are committed to regularly gather for worship. Their purpose in worship is to do the things Christ has commanded (taking communion, baptizing, preaching, praying, singing, etc.) as an expression of belief in the gospel and out of a shared desire to follow Jesus and to help one another follow him.

The church is essential to a believer's pursuit of the good life and to human flourishing. German theologian Dietrich Bonhoeffer wrote about the human institutions that God established for particular purposes. These institutions include the family, the church, the government, and labor. All of life is bound to these institutions, because all of life is bound to God. All of life is sacred as it is lived in the presence of God for his glory.[22]

Because of our sin, our human institutions are flawed. This fact does not excuse any injustice or abuse that takes place in any human institutions. It is not to minimize any experience of suffering to which God is opposed. It is only to say that these institutions remain God's ordained means of human flourishing. Despite our flaws, the institutions God established are worth preserving and improving.

What is the church? The church is the body of Christ (1 Cor 10:17; Eph 2:22). It is composed of believers who are connected to God and to one another by faith in Jesus. The metaphor of a body in describing the church is important for at least two reasons. First, it helps us see that Jesus is the leader of the church; he is the head of the body (i.e., church). Second, it helps us see our need for each other. Each believer is a member of the body of Christ (i.e., the church). In the same way that the health of your body parts requires that they be connected to your body, so, too, your spiritual health (i.e., flourishing) requires that you be connected to the body of Christ.

The church does not save a person. The robber on the cross next to Jesus was saved (Luke 23:40–43) but was not a part of a church nor was he baptized. We are saved by faith alone and not by works (Eph 2:8–10).

However, this (and other) examples should not be used to minimize the importance of the church in the life of a believer. Christ saves us into his church. In the same way that it is normal and right that babies are born into human families, a person is born again (i.e., saved) into the family of God. Family is another metaphor for the church (Eph 3:14–19). Ideally, a person grows and matures in the context of a loving family. Similarly, a person grows and matures spiritually in the context of God's love expressed and taught in the context of the local church as a spiritual family.

Why is the church important? The purpose of relationship with God, as we have seen, is not only salvation but moral transformation. Moral transformation is referred to as discipleship. Discipleship is the process of becoming a more faithful disciple of Jesus.

When a person comes to faith, Jesus becomes not only their Savior but also their Lord. In the words of A. W. Tozer, "A notable heresy has come into being throughout evangelical Christian circles—the widely-accepted concept that we humans can choose to accept Christ only because

---

[22] See Dietrich Bonhoeffer, *Ethics* (New York: MacMillan, 1959), 207.

we need him as Savior and that we have the right to postpone our obedience to him as Lord as long as we want to! . . . salvation apart from obedience is unknown in the sacred scriptures."[23]

American philosopher Dallas Willard has taught that without discipleship, a person is locked in moral defeat and without inward transformation of thought, feeling, and character.[24] Willard observes that duplicity (i.e., hypocrisy) comes naturally because of our fallen (i.e., sinful) nature. Discipleship is the business of the local church, heeding the command of Jesus to "follow me."

As Jesus was about to leave his disciples, he gave them directions that have become known as "The Great Commission": "Jesus came near and said to them, 'All authority has been given to me in heaven and on earth. Go, therefore, and make disciples of all nations, baptizing them in the name of the Father and of the Son and of the Holy Spirit, teaching them to observe everything I have commanded you. And remember, I am with you always, to the end of the age'" (Matt 28:18–20).

Christians are commanded not only to believe but also to faithful obedience. The local church is the primary place where Christians learn to obey. There are many ministries outside that also help people to follow Jesus, but these ministries should be understood to be supportive of and supplemental to the local church and not to replace the local church.

If relationship with God through faith in Jesus is the good life, and if flourishing means walking by the Spirit in obedience to God's Word, and if the local church is the primary place where we learn to know and put into practice what God has said, then the local church is essential to a believer's pursuit of the good life. In other words, a person cannot truly flourish apart from the local church or from the ministries that are born from local churches. The local church is God's plan for human flourishing.

Question 5.18

True or false: God only established the church; all other social institutions are given by man.

---

[23] A. W. Tozer, *I Call It Heresy* (Harrisburg, PA: Christian Publications, 1974), 5.

[24] See Dallas Willard, "Why Bother with Discipleship?" in *The Great Omission: Reclaiming Jesus's Essential Teaching* (San Francisco: HarperCollins, 2006), 13–17.

Question 5.19

What does it mean that the church is the body of Christ? Why is this significant for the good life?

_____

_____

Practical Steps to Living the Good Life

The good life is not about getting more stuff, becoming famous, or physical pleasure. The good life is experiencing a relationship with God through saving faith in Jesus and walking under the control of God's Spirit. In this final section, we offer some practical steps to living the good life.

First, put your faith in Jesus. Acknowledge your sin to God, confess that you are unable to save yourself, and trust in Jesus as God's perfect and final sacrifice for sin. The Bible puts it simply: "If you confess with your mouth, 'Jesus is Lord,' and believe in your heart that God raised him from the dead, you will be saved" (Rom 10:9).

Second, find and start attending a local church where they teach the Bible, affirm the Trinity, and believe that salvation is God's gift by faith alone. The local church is the place where you will learn from other believers what it looks like to follow Jesus. The local church is the place where you can be baptized as a public declaration of your belief in Jesus and your commitment to following him.

Third, take steps to *grow* in your faith. Spend time every day reading your Bible, talk to God in prayer, and endeavor to allow his Word to direct your thoughts, attitudes, beliefs, and emotions. This takes time and practice. When you stumble and fall, do not give up: be quick to confess and then get back to following Jesus.

Fourth, have a group of Christian friends who share your commitment to following Jesus. Thomas Aquinas wrote in *Summa Theologica* about friendship: "There is nothing on this earth more to be prized than true friendship . . . friendship is the source of the greatest pleasures, and without friends even the most agreeable pursuits become tedious."[25]

---

[25] Thomas Aquinas, *Summa Theologica*, II.II, Question 23, Article 1; Question 25, Article 1; Question 26, Article 3.

By "true friendship" Aquinas means friends who "preserve and promote" godliness.[26] He knew the power of friendship with others whom you share beliefs about God and the meaning of life. Of course, it can be meaningful and is not wrong to have friendships with people who do not agree on issues of faith. Indeed, Jesus did not limit himself to friendships with people who were serious about faith. However, it is wise for Christians (especially new Christians) to make, strengthen, and deepen Christ-centered friendships.

In the same way that the good life is about relationship with God, it also consists largely in relationships with others who follow Jesus. Our love for God results in love for others and our desire to serve others, especially those in God's family by faith (John 13:34–35; Gal 6:10). Learning to treasure faithful friends, and to be a faithful friend, is a practical way to experience (and encourage others to experience) the good life and to flourish in your walk with Jesus.

Chapter Review

Question 5.20

Matching:

A. Bertrand Russell	____ "My formula for greatness in man is! [*sic*] *amor fati*: the fact that a man wishes nothing to be different . . . for all eternity."
B. A. W. Tozer	____ "Life moves pretty fast."
C. Isaiah	____ "How happy is mankind, if the love that orders the stars above rules, too, in your hearts."
D. Boethius	____ "A meaningful life is, first of all, one that within it has the basis of an affirmative answer to the needs or longings that are characteristically described as needs for meaning."

---

[26] Thomas Aquinas, *On Kingship to the King of Cyprus*, https://wisdomhomeschooling.com/images/courses/humansociety/reading28deregnoonkingship.pdf.

E. Ferris Bueller   _____ Is addicted to "retail therapy."

F. Flannery O'Connor   _____ "Life is for the living."

G. Susan Wolf   _____ "There is nothing on this earth more to be prized than true friendship."

H. Ariana Grande   _____ "I do not know you God because I am in the way. Please help me push myself aside."

I. Friedrich Nietzsche   _____ "Seek the Lord while he may be found; call to him while he is near."

J. Langston Hughes   _____ "The good life is one inspired by love and guided by knowledge."

K. St. Thomas Aquinas   _____ "Salvation apart from obedience is unknown in the sacred scriptures."

Question 5.21

Why is the church necessary for the good life? Do you see your own local church as necessary to your flourishing and happiness? Are there other institutions (family, school, work, etc.) where you see the universal church working toward true happiness in their communities?

_____

_____

Question 5.22

What is your vision of the good life? Will it lead to true, lasting happiness?

_____

_____

Question 5.23

Pick one or two films. Evaluate the vision of happiness presented in these movies according to principles given in this chapter.

_____

_____

6

Fearfully and Wonderfully Made

In the Shakespeare play *King Lear*, the fictional title character asks the question, "Who is it that can tell me who I am?" to which another character responds, "You are King's Lear's shadow."[1] The implication is that King Lear had become an empty shell of his former self. Once great, King Lear had descended from his former glory.

Thousands of years before the writing of *King Lear*, Israel's King David asked a similar question:

When I observe your heavens,

the work of your fingers,

the moon and the stars,

which you set in place,

what is a human being that you remember him,

a son of man that you look after him? (Ps 8:3–4)

King Lear and King David were both seeking answers to questions that we all, royalty and commoner alike, have pondered: What does it mean to be human? What makes humans unique

---

[1] Shakespeare, *King Lear*, 1.4.230.1.

from other living creatures? Why is it that humans are capable of such goodness and such evil? What can explain our nobility and our depravity? Are humans special in the universe or just another random by-product of natural selection and random mutation? Are humans merely physical or do we have souls?

These are the questions addressed in this chapter. The good news is that there are answers. The Bible says that humans are "remarkably and wondrously made" (Ps 139:14). The King James version of the Bible translates it "fearfully and wonderfully made." The full text of this phrase from Psalm 139 is worthy of consideration:

> For it was you who created my inward parts;
> you knit me together in my mother's womb.
> I will praise you
> because I have been remarkably and wondrously made.
> Your works are wondrous,
> and I know this very well.
> My bones were not hidden from you
> when I was made in secret,
> when I was formed in the depths of the earth.
> Your eyes saw me when I was formless;
> all my days were written in your book and planned
> before a single one of them began. (vv. 13–16)

Humans are the special work of God. The psalmist used a number of different words to make this point, including "created," "made," and "knit." Elsewhere, God's relationship to humans is compared to that of a potter and clay. God's relationship to humanity is personal, direct, and intimate.

You might be wondering, *Are not humans "made" by their parents?* Of course. God uses and guides natural processes. In fact, the Bible says that God knit us together in our mothers' wombs (Ps 139:13).

But causation is complex. Aristotle wrote about four different types of causes in his books *Physics* and *Metaphysics*: material, efficient, formal, and final. Knowing that there are different types of causes is helpful to understanding our relationship to God.

The material cause is the physical stuff from which something is made. The efficient cause is the physical process that brings something into being. The formal cause is the design of the thing that is made. The final cause is the purpose for which a thing is made.

To illustrate these four types of causes previously mentioned, consider your smartphone. What explains the existence of your smartphone? Let's use Aristotle's understanding of causation to try and answer the question.

In terms of materials, smartphones are mostly plastic, metal, and glass. These things are the material cause of your smartphone. The efficient cause of your smartphone, on the other hand, may be the machines in factories that construct smartphones. Material and efficient causation refer to the physical components and construction of the object.

In terms of formal causation, your smartphone is caused by software and hardware engineers. These people plan out the look, shape, form, and function of the phone. The final cause of the phone is the purpose it serves every day: to connect you with other people, give you access to information and entertainment, and enable you to do daily tasks more efficiently.

Your phone's existence has multiple layers of explanation, so does your existence. Your material cause of your body is comprised of basic elements like oxygen and carbon. Your efficient cause is gestation (i.e., the nine months you spent in your mother's womb). Your formal cause is perhaps God's design of the human body as contained in your unique DNA code. Your final cause, or ultimate purpose, is to glorify God through faith in Jesus Christ. It makes sense that everything should glorify God, because directly or indirectly, He is the creator of everything.

Aristotle's four causes help in understanding that there are immediate and ultimate explanations for people and things. As a human person, your existence requires a greater explanation than just your biological parents and your physical components; you have a design and an ultimate purpose. And you have a spiritual, mental component that has yet to be explained.

God is the one who designs human persons and assigns our purpose. This assignment is not some arbitrary purpose that God gives to us. Rather, it is an assignment that is appropriate to the kind of thing a human person is by nature. Thus, our assigned purpose is the best way for human persons to flourish throughout their lives. By design, human persons each have a body and a soul. We do not share a soul or participate in a world soul, but rather, each of us possesses an individual soul. The creation account of humanity in Genesis makes this point: "Then the Lord God formed the man out of the dust from the ground and breathed the breath of life into his nostrils, and the man became a living being" (Gen 2:7).

The Bible uses terms in the Old Testament such as *nephesh* (frequently translated as "soul") and *ruach* (frequently translated as "spirit").[2] The soul in Scripture sometimes stands in for the

---

[2] See J. P. Moreland, *The Soul: How We Know Its Real and Why It Matters* (Chicago: Moody, 2014), 9.

whole person, as in Psa 103:1, which says, "My soul, bless the Lord, and all that is within me, bless his holy name."

Human beings are not *just* physical. The essence of a human person is a soul. A soul is nonphysical and cannot die. While your body (which is physical) is the product of natural processes, your essence (i.e., your soul) cannot be explained by natural processes. That which is natural does not produce that which is spiritual (i.e., nonphysical). Accordingly, some Old Testament texts use *nephesh* to refer to the soul as that which leaves the body at death. For example, speaking about Rachel: "With her last breath—for she was dying—she named him Ben-oni, but his father called him Benjamin" (Gen 35:18).

When the Bible says that humans are fearfully and wonderfully made, it connects a proper understanding of anthropology (i.e., the study of humans) to right living (ethics) in two ways. First, being fearfully made means that the richness of the human body and soul leaves a person in awe or wonder at the power of God. As we will see in chapter 7, the fear of the Lord is the starting point for living the good life.

Second, being wonderfully (*palah*) made speaks to how each person is distinct and distinguished. You are, quite literally, one of a kind. No two humans—even identical twins—are alike; not only because of physical features such as fingerprints and DNA, but because you are a unique soul.

Question 6.1

What are Aristotle's four causes, and how do they help us understand a Christian view of what it means to be human?

_____

_____

Question 6.2

Match the Hebrew words on the left with their corresponding English translation.

Ruach	Wonderfully
Palah	Soul
Nephesh	Spirit

Question 6.3

To say that humans are fearfully and wonderfully made connects a proper _____ with _____.

What Is a Soul?

Aristotle's classic book on the soul (*De Anima*) begins with words worth reading and considering:

> Holding as we do that, while knowledge of any kind is a thing to be honoured [*sic*] and prized, one kind of it may, either by reason of its greater exactness or of a higher dignity and greater wonderfulness in its objects, be more honourable (sic) and precious than another, on both accounts we should naturally be led to place in the front rank the study of the soul. The knowledge of the soul admittedly contributes greatly to the advance of truth in general, and, above all, to our understanding of Nature, for the soul is in some sense the principle of animal life. Our aim is to grasp and understand, first its essential nature, and secondly its properties; of these some are taught to be affections proper to the soul itself, while others are considered to attach to the animal owing to the presence within it of soul. To attain any assured knowledge about the soul is one of the most difficult things in the world.[3]

In the above quote, notice three things. First, Aristotle believed that souls exist. Second, the knowledge of souls is important. Third, a soul is a difficult concept to grasp. Aristotle went on to make it clear in *De Anima* that the soul is distinct from the physical body.

In terms of philosophical significance, the question of whether humans have souls is perhaps one of life's most important questions, second only to God's existence. Like the question of God's existence, answering the question of whether souls exist is a matter of inferential and deductive reasoning. Since God and souls are immaterial (i.e., nonphysical), there can be no direct empirical evidence for their existence.

What is a soul? Here is a simple definition: a soul is an immaterial substance that contains and unifies consciousness and animates/enlivens its body. To elaborate, a soul refers to the non-physical *self*. Other terms for the nonphysical self (i.e., soul) include *person* or *mind*. These three terms (person/mind/soul) can be used interchangeably to refer to the nonphysical self.

---

[3] Aristotle, *On the Soul*, http://classics.mit.edu/Aristotle/soul.mb.txt.

Another way to think about the human soul is as the essence of a human. The word *essence* comes from the Latin word *esse*, which mean "to be." To be human is to be a human soul. You have a body but you are a soul. While you can exist without your body, you cannot exist without your soul because you are identical with your soul. While we are souls, Christianity implies that we function best and were meant to be embodied. So the body is crucial for our functioning, but not necessary for our existence.

The soul is what has human consciousness. Further, the soul unifies all of our simultaneous conscious states in that they all belong to the same soul. Consciousness refers to a range of mental states: thoughts, sensations, beliefs, desires, and intentions. These states of consciousness may be associated with brain states, but they are not identical with brain states, as we will see in the next section. Feeling pain, seeing blue, believing in justice, wanting to finish college are states of consciousness that the soul best explains.

Other living things with consciousness may have souls too. This need not blur important distinctions between humans, animals, and other living things (trees, for instance). Animals may have animal souls and animal levels of consciousness, while humans have human souls and human levels of consciousness. The question of plant consciousness is interesting, and recent books such as *The Overstory* have brought new research to light regarding the communication of trees.[4] However, we follow the long historical tradition by noting that when we attribute a soul to a plant, we are not ascribing consciousness to that plant. Rather, we are using "soul" to be the unifying principle of life that accounts for why that plant is more than just a physical machine.

The concept of souls means that there is more to life than meets the eye. Like the castle of enchanted objects in the classic tale *Beauty and the Beast*, God's world is filled with mystery, wonder, and enchantment. Christians have unique reason for exploration and environmental preservation based upon the idea that consciousness and intelligence exists all around us.

There are many ways to describe a human, from hair color to personality, intelligence, height, or ethnicity. A human can be a human and have any hair color, or no hair at all. You can lose your hair and still be human. A person can be extremely intelligent or comatose and still be human. Humans are tall, short, and everything in between. You can be human and have a strong ethnic identity, multiple ethnic identifies, or no ethnic identity whatsoever.

Things like hair, personality, intelligence, height, and ethnicity are incidental to your existence: you could exist without them. They are properties of *you* but not the essence of *you*. Your

---

[4] See Richard Powers, *The Overstory* (New York: W. W. Norton, 2018).

essence is not physical. You are a soul. This means that your nonphysical self (i.e., the soul) is the most important thing about you. While the body is important as is attending to its health, the cultivation of a virtuous, spiritually mature soul is even more important.

You are aware of your*self* separate from your body. As a thought experiment, you can imagine yourself being taller or shorter, with different color hair or different color skin, with wings like a bird or with a tail like a mermaid. This kind of thought experiment goes to show that you are distinct from your body and that you are aware of yourself as a being that can exist separately from your body.

If you were just a body, then someone describing your body would be describing all there is to say about you. But describing you physically would not capture everything about you, let alone the most important things about you. This goes to show that you are more than a body. After all, if you want to get to know someone, you do not get very far by measuring their height, mass, shape, and various chemical, physical components of that person's body. Instead, you focus your attention on getting to know the person's soul and the inner life of emotions, beliefs, desires, and so on that characterize that person.

Most people believe that humans have a body and are a soul. This is called *dualism*. Dualism is the belief that human beings are a soul or mind (i.e., an immaterial self) that is distinct from the body they inhabit and the brain they use.[5] Sometimes called *substance dualism*, this common view holds that the soul and the body are different substances.

One of the reasons the soul makes sense is that it explains how a person endures over time and through physical change. Consider those embarrassing pictures your parents have of you as an infant. How are you the same person you were as an infant? After all, you look totally different. You are a different person physically; by now, all of your cells have been replaced several times. You have no memories of being an infant.

You are the same person you were when you were an infant because you are the same soul. Your soul is what endures throughout your lifetime of great physical change. Without the soul, it is impossible to say that you were once an infant, which of course, we all know is true.

The soul explains both the sameness of personhood over time and the animating power (i.e., life) of a body. When a person dies, there is sometimes a viewing of the body where loved ones gather to say goodbye. The lifeless body of the deceased lies in the casket. The body is present but the person is not. The soul can be thought of as either the life of the body or the person who

---

[5] See Moreland, *The Soul*, 9.

occupies the body. This is Plato's theory of the soul in *Phaedo*, in which he says that death is the parting of the body and the soul.[6]

A human person does not need a human body to exist. The apostle Paul said that it is preferable to be absent from the body and present (*endémeó*, meaning "to be at home") with the Lord (2 Cor 5:8). Paul clearly believed it is possible for a person to exist separated from their body.

During the crucifixion, Jesus said to one of the robbers hanging on a cross next to him, "Today you will be with me in paradise" (Luke 23:43). That same day, the robber to whom Jesus said these words died. His body was likely buried in an unmarked grave. How then could the robber be with Jesus in paradise (i.e., heaven) if it were not possible for a person to exist separately from their body?

Historically, philosophers have tended to agree with the Bible. Living beings have immaterial (i.e., nonphysical) souls. A soul is the seat of consciousness and personhood. A person can exist without a body but not without a soul.

While dualism understands the soul or mind to be an immaterial thing different and separate from the body, this does not mean your body has no value. Christian dualists, in particular, understand the value of the body and the soul; both are made by God and are important for the story of redemption. The goal of life is not to escape the physical body. Christians believe in the physical resurrection of Jesus and in a future physical eternal state. Heaven is not a place for disembodied souls to float on clouds. Heaven will be filled with redeemed souls joined to resurrected and glorified bodies fit for a new heaven and earth.

A person need not be a dualist to believe in the existence of an immaterial self or soul. Idealism is the metaphysical view that only minds and ideas exists. According to idealism, ideas are those thoughts pertaining to the senses (touch, taste, smell, sight, etc.). Idealists believe in the physical world in terms of the ideas we associate with the physical world, but not in the sense of material substance, which exists independent of mind. If physical objects do not exist separately from minds but only as ideas in minds, then what gives rise to our ideas about the physical world? Christian idealists, such as George Berkeley, believe that God communicates ideas directly to human minds.

---

[6] See Plato, *Phaedo*, http://classics.mit.edu/Plato/phaedo.html.

While Berkeley insists that his view is that of common sense, most people are not idealists. Nevertheless, substance dualists (like Descartes) and idealists (like Berkeley) agree an immaterial soul/mind/self exists. Idealists believe in minds but do not have the trouble of having to explain what is called the mind-body problem.

The mind-body problem refers to the question of how the soul, which is a nonphysical substance, directs and interacts with the body, which is a physical substance. The properties of the body are physical (i.e., size, weight, color, texture, odor, etc.). The properties of the soul are nonphysical (reason, desire, belief, etc.). How is it that the immaterial you (i.e., the soul) moves and directs the physical you (i.e., the body)?

To understand the mind-body problem, consider how you cannot move physical objects without exerting physical force. If you were lying on your bed on one side of the room and wanted a bag of chips on the other side of the room, you could not will, desire, or wish the bag of chips into your hands. Unlike Luke Skywalker of *Star Wars*, who uses "the force" to cause objects to fly across the room into his hands, those of us who are not Jedi masters must get up and walk across the room to physically take possession of chips if we want them.

And yet, every day your soul directs and moves your physical body. Your body somehow responds to your mental states. You will or desire to get out of bed, walk across the room, retrieve the chips, and then get back into bed and your body responds. These kinds of physical activities are initiated by conscious states or the agent himself or herself, which are nonphysical. Mental states are translated to the brain, and through the brain to other parts of the body by the central nervous system.

René Descartes is a philosopher who raises the issue of the mind-body problem. In the course of his writings, there are various versions of the problem, the first few of which are in his book *Meditations on First Philosophy*, and then later in his final book *The Passions of the Soul*.

On the one hand I have a clear and distinct idea of myself, in so far as I am simply a thinking, non-extended thing [that is, a mind], and on the other hand I have a distinct idea of body, in so far as this is simply an extended, non-thinking thing. And accordingly, it is certain that I am really distinct from my body, and can exist without it.[7]

---

[7] René Descartes, *The Philosophical Writings of Descartes*, vol. 2, trans. John Cottingham et al. (Cambridge: Cambridge University Press, 1984–1991), 54.

These questions presuppose amongst other things an explanation of the union between the soul and the body, which I have not yet dealt with at all. But I will say, for your benefit at least, that the whole problem contained in such questions arises simply from a supposition that is false and cannot in any way be proved, namely that, if the soul and the body are two substances whose nature is different, this prevents them from being able to act on each other.[8]

Question 6.4

True or false: Whether humans have souls is a theological concern, not a philosophical one.

Question 6.5

What is a soul? What is consciousness?

_____

_____

Question 6.6

Which of the following, philosophically speaking, can have a soul?

   a) The snapdragons in your garden
   b) Your pet dog
   c) Your next-door neighbor
   d) The jellyfish that stung you last week
   e) All of the above

Question 6.7

Explain what the author means by the claim that you are a soul.

_____

_____

---

[8] Descartes, 275.

Question 6.8

Describe the following viewpoints in relation to the soul, and provide a proponent of each (look ahead for *physicalism*):

Viewpoint	Description	Proponent
Dualism		
Idealism		
Occasionalism		
Physicalism		

Question 6.9

What is the mind-body problem?

_____

_____

Minds and Bodies

Contrary to dualism, standard physicalism is the view that everything that exists is physical. Physicalism denies the existence of the soul or mind. On this view, humans are merely physical beings comprised of physical parts. If physicalism is true, then brains and minds are identical, and there is nothing about human persons that is nonphysical.

Physicalism is incompatible with theism, and therefore, with Christian theism. God is a nonphysical being. If physicalism is true and only physical objects exist, then God does not exist.[9] Physicalism is not true. God does exist and soul/mind are distinct from body/brain.

---

[9] See J. P. Moreland, *Scaling the Secular City* (Grand Rapids: Baker Books, 1987), chap. 3.

It is a common mistake to confuse brain with mind. A brain is physical and a mind is non-physical. You are a mind and you have a brain, but your mind and brain are different. Your mind uses your brain like a driver uses a car but is different from the car, or a piano player uses a piano but is different from the piano.

In his book *Discourse on Metaphysics*, philosopher Wilhelm Leibniz presented the law of identity, according to which, if two things (X and Y) are identical, then everything true or possibly true of one thing (X) is also true or possibly true of the other thing (Y).

In order to prove that minds are not identical to brain, there need only be one thing that is true of a mind that is not true of a brain. What follows are four things true of minds that are not true of brains. If sufficient reason is given to show that minds are different than brains, then you should be convinced that you are more than just a physical body with a physical brain; you are a soul.

First, physical objects (e.g., the brain or body) are wholes with parts that can be gained or lost. Half of a person's brain could be removed and a person could exist and function with the remaining half. However, it makes no sense to say that someone living in such a condition is only half a person. A person may lose some percentage of their cognitive functioning, but they are no less a person. Persons are all or nothing things.

Second, as noted above, we remain quite literally the same human person over time but our bodies do not remain the same. Our bodies are aggregates of atomic parts and cells that are constantly changing. The existence of your soul accounts for your ability to endure as the same person while your body is constantly in a state of flux.

Third, even if there is no such thing as disembodied life after death, virtually everyone agrees that disembodied life is possible. When skeptics watch an episode of *Dateline* that presents the evidence for and against the truth of near-death experiences, they might be skeptical and remain unconvinced of their veracity. But they are willing to let the evidence settle the matter and are curious about the evidence.

No one seeks evidence for something that is logically or metaphysically impossible. If *Dateline* presented an episode claiming that archeologists had found square circles in a cave in Montana, no one would watch. We would know ahead of time that such a discovery is *impossible*. That people are willing to hear the evidence for near-death experiences does not in itself prove that there is life after death; rather, it shows that people know that life after death is possible.

What does this mean about you? It means that you have the property of being possibly disembodied. It is possible that you could exist separately from your brain and your body. If the self can exist apart from the body, but the body cannot exist apart from the brain, then the self must be something possibly separate from the body. The most plausible explanation is that you are a soul.

Fourth, you are a free agent. When you act, it is up to you as to whether you raise your hand to vote or choose to refrain. Things influence your choices, but they do not determine your choices against your will. To be free means that nothing determines your choices apart from human will and desire.

There is no law of nature that determines your actions. However, if you were simply a brain or a body, you would not be a responsible free agent because your body movements (e.g., raising your hand) would be determined by things outside of your control (e.g., the laws of physics and chemistry). Since you know that you sometimes act freely by simply being aware of your own exercise of intentional power, you cannot be any material object. The most plausible alternative is that you are a soul.

For these and other reasons, we conclude that we are souls that possess consciousness. Yet, as Aristotle was quoted earlier, "To attain any assured knowledge about the soul is one of the most difficult things in the world." Some have rejected the idea of an immaterial self as separate from the body.

David Hume, for instance, argued that a person is merely a bundle of perceptions:

For my part, when I enter most intimately into what I call myself, I always stumble on some particular perception or other, of heat or cold, light or shade, love or hatred, pain or pleasure. I never can catch myself at any time without a perception, and never can observe any thing but the perception. When my perceptions are removed for any time, as by sound sleep; so long am I insensible of myself, and may truly be said not to exist. And were all my perceptions removed by death, and could I neither think, nor feel, nor see, nor love, nor hate after the dissolution of my body, I should be entirely annihilated, nor do I conceive what is farther requisite to make me a perfect non-entity. If any one, upon serious and unprejudiced reflection thinks he has a different notion of himself, I must confess I call reason no longer with him. All I can allow him is, that he may be in the right as well as I, and that we are essentially different in this particular. He may, perhaps, perceive something simple and continued, which he calls himself; though I am certain there is no such principle in me.[10]

---

[10] David Hume, "Of Personal Identity" in *A Treatise of Human Nature*, https://www.gutenberg.org/files/4705/4705–h/4705–h.htm).

Hume's bundle-theory position is famous in the history of philosophy. As an empiricist, Hume demands physical sensation of the soul in order to have knowledge of the soul's existence. Since the soul is immaterial and no such direct empirical evidence can be produced, Hume concludes that the immaterial self is like Santa Claus—a helpful fiction.

But Hume should know that there are things like laws of logic that exist but have no physical properties and therefore cannot be experienced by the senses. Reducing reality to the concepts and categories to which one is familiar and comfortable is the wrong way to do philosophy. As Thomas Nagel said in his famous essay on consciousness, "What Is It Like to Be a Bat?": "Philosophers share the general human weakness for explanations of what is incomprehensible in terms suited for what is familiar and well understood, though entirely different."[11]

Nagel's point in the essay is that there is something about human consciousness that cannot be reduced to the body (i.e., physicalism or materialism). Others, such as Australian philosopher Frank Jackson, have made the same point. In Frank Jackson's article "What Mary Didn't Know" he argues, like Nagel, that distinctions between physical and nonphysical aspects of human existence are logically necessary, nonphysical facts about humans are true, and physicalism is therefore wrong.[12]

Question 6.10

True or false: Physicalism is compatible with theism.

Question 6.11

What is Leibniz's law of identity? How does the author use this law to disprove physicalism?

_____

_____

---

[11] Thomas Nagel, "What Is It Like to Be a Bat?" *Philosophical Review* 83 (October 1974): 435.
[12] See Frank Jackson, "What Mary Didn't Know," *Journal of Philosophy* 83 (May 1986): 291–95.

Question 6.12

By arguing that a person is merely a bundle of perceptions, David Hume means:
   a)   To be is to be perceived.
   b)   The human body is really a bag of feelings, and we do not have any organs.
   c)   There is no proof of human essence beyond what we perceive.
   d)   Humans do not exist at all.

Ethics, the Soul, and Eternity

In this section we will explore some of the significant ethical issues associated with the soul. The main point of this section is that knowledge of the soul is important to various ethical issues. Knowledge of the soul has practical application in regard to morality.

First, as previously mentioned, the soul explains the durability or sameness of personhood over time. You are the same person you were a decade ago because you have a soul. The durability of personhood is required to justify imprisonment. It would be wrong to imprison someone for a crime they did not commit. If you went to prison for a crime somebody else committed, that would be unjust.

If not for the soul, how can a person be imprisoned at age fifty for a crime they committed at age thirty? Are they not a different person? Do we not sometimes say, "I am a different person"? But even that statement begs the question: What is the "I" if not the soul? While your behavior may change and your outlook or thinking may change, you are the same person over time because you have a soul.

In September 2021, a ninety-six-year-old former Nazi soldier was arrested in New York. Irmgard Furchner escaped to America after World War II but was arrested and charged with over 11,000 counts of accessory to murder. During the war, Ms. Furchner was a secretary at a concentration camp when she was eighteen years old. The so-called Secretary of Death was arrested and is awaiting trial.

How can a ninety-six-year-old be charged with crimes committed when she was eighteen? The soul maintains personhood over time and across continents. If she were only a body, Ms. Furchner could perhaps argue that she is a different person. However, because she is a soul, and because our criminal justice system is based upon the durability of personhood, she has been charged and will face justice.

Second, the soul has significance on bioethical issues such as abortion and active euthanasia (intentional killing). When an unborn baby is killed (i.e., abortion), a *person* is killed. You were once an unborn baby, and you are a person because you have a soul. In the same way, an unborn baby is a person with a soul. To kill the unborn baby is murder in the same way that to kill you or any other person is murder.

Murder is often justified by the claim that the people being murdered are less than human. It is psychologically difficult to kill someone you view as fully human. Mass murder usually requires a process of dehumanization. The Nazis dehumanized the Jews, European settlers dehumanized Native Americans, and slave owners often dehumanized slaves.

To justify the murder of abortion, unborn babies are dehumanized. Rather than call them humans, we call them fetuses. In fact, they are *human* fetuses. Fetus simply refers to a developmental state, just as there are human children, human teenagers, human adults, and elderly humans. At every stage, a human has a soul and to kill a human unjustly is murder.

This same consideration applies to the question of active euthanasia. Allowing someone who is dying to die is humane, i.e., it honors the human life by allowing for pain management during natural death and by not extending life artificially. On the other hand, active euthanasia rushes or expedites the process of death unnaturally. Solomon, the wisest man in the Bible (other than Jesus) said that there is a time to be born and a time to die (Eccl 3:2). Wisdom requires preparation for death but also the patience to let it happen according to God's timing.

Active euthanasia makes some sense if humans are only physical beings. We regularly disregard physical objects that are no longer useful. Broken-down computers, cars, and appliances are destroyed because they no longer function. Humans, however, are fundamentally different; they are not merely physical beings. Human life has value even when the body is broken because humans have souls and are made in the image of God.

Finally, the soul has significance for ethics in regard to the afterlife. One of the primary motivations for living virtuously is the promise of reward (heaven) and the threat of punishment (hell). This moral calculus makes no sense if humans are only physical bodies. If physicalism is true, then once the body ceases to function and bodily life is over then a person ceases to exist. If physicalism is true, then there is no reward or punishment beyond the consequences of this earthly life.

In reality, there is a future beyond death for every human person. Because Jesus was raised from the dead, and because humans possess souls that are made in God's image and are fit for eternity, we can be assured that there is an afterlife. Near-death experiences provide evidence of conscious life after death.

According to the Bible, there are only two places where humans will spend their conscious eternity—heaven or hell. Heaven is a wonderful place for those who have received Jesus Christ by faith: "But to all who did receive him, he gave them the right to be children of God, to those who believe in his name" (John 1:12). In order to go to heaven, a person must receive Jesus by faith in this life. There is no post-mortem (i.e., after death) opportunity to trust in Jesus and be saved (Heb 9:27).

Hell is a place of eternal and conscious punishment. Jesus warned about hell more than anyone else in the New Testament. He said, "Don't fear those who kill the body but are not able to kill the soul; rather, fear him who is able to destroy both soul and body in hell" (Matt 10:28).

The Bible warns that hell is real and that it is avoidable. The only way to avoid hell is to turn from sin and believe in Jesus. *Universalism* is the myth that everyone will go to heaven. Jesus specifically warns that not everyone will go to heaven: "'Not everyone who says to me, 'Lord, Lord,' will enter the kingdom of heaven, but only the one who does the will of my Father in heaven'" (Matt 7:21).

Annihilationism is the view that people in hell will simply cease to exist at some point. Annihilationism is wrong for at least two reasons. First, hell is eternal because humans can never atone for their sins against an infinite God. While Jesus could say "it is finished" on the cross, a sinful person in hell lacks the holiness to pay the penalty for their own sin. Consequently, unsaved people in hell eternally bear the weight of God's judgment, but can never atone for their sin nor can they redeem themselves. All the more reason to turn from sin and trust in Jesus in this life.

Second, human souls are made for eternity. When Jesus spoke of fearing him who is able to destroy the soul and body in hell, he was speaking about the conditions under which people will spend eternity. The word for "destruction" (*apollumi*) that Jesus used refers to the permanent condition of violence and perishing. Hell is an eternal state of perishing for those who sin against God and do not receive forgiveness through faith in Jesus.

Question 6.13

Historically, mass murder requires a process of _____.

Question 6.14

True or false: Physicalism provides a compelling case for ethical values.

Question 6.15

The myth that all souls go to heaven is _____. The myth that souls in hell eventually cease to be is _____.

Heart and Soul

A final word about the soul has to do with love. Love is something that cannot be fully explained by natural processes, brain states, or body chemistry. The Bible speaks about love in mysterious ways. A husband and wife are said to be joined together and to become one flesh. This refers not only to sexual intimacy but to the mysterious union of two people who journey through life together in a covenant relationship.

In the garden of Eden, God institutes marriage saying, "This is why a man leaves his father and mother and bonds with his wife, and they become one flesh" (Gen 2:24). The Bible reiterates this command in the books of Matthew, Mark, and Ephesians. The idea of "one flesh" clearly does not mean that two physical bodies become one physical body in marriage. While sexual intimacy is a part of marriage (as evidenced by the next verse that says that Adam and Eve were naked and unashamed), the idea of "one flesh" refers to more than sexual (i.e., physical) intimacy.

In his *Letter to Laymen*, the fourth-century church father Ambrose called the idea of "one flesh" a great mystery about Christ and the church.[13] The apostle Paul made this same connection in the New Testament book of Ephesians. When speaking about marriage, Paul said, "This mystery is profound, but I am talking about Christ and the church" (Eph 5:32). The covenant of marriage (a sacrament or means of grace, according to Augustine) between a man and a woman involves sexual intimacy that results in a mysterious union.

This union is more than physical. It involves spiritual, emotional, and relational intimacy. Love, sex, and romance in marriage (as God intended) involves all of the states of consciousness listed above. The mystery of sexual intimacy involves bodies *and souls*. John Calvin made this same point in his commentary on Genesis: "Something was taken from Adam, in order that he might embrace, with greater benevolence, a part of himself. . . . He now saw himself, who had before been only half complete, rendered whole in his wife."[14]

---

[13] Ambrose, *Letter to Laymen*, 85. Quoted in *Ancient Christian Commentary On Scripture*, vol. 1., ed. Thomas Oden (InterVarsity Press, 2001), 71.

[14] John Calvin, *Commentary on Genesis* (2:21), http://btsfreeccm.org/pluginfile.php/22760/mod_resource/content/6/Commentary%20Genesis.pdf, 58–59.

It is safe to say we live in a culture where there is a lot of confusion about marriage, love, sex, and romance. At the heart of this confusion, in many cases, is the absence of biblical anthropology (i.e., a biblical understanding of what it means to be human). As we have said, one fundamental mistake is the idea that humans are merely physical beings.

The practical result of this mistake leads to confusion and regret. People who think that sex is just about the body may think it is okay to practice casual sex. Casual sex is based upon the idea that humans are simply bodies, sex is only physical, and that once sex is over there are no strings attached (so long as things are consensual and agreed upon). According to the American Psychological Association, between 72 and 78 percent of men and women report a history of regret after uncommitted sex.[15] People regret casual sex because humans are bodies and souls and because sex is physical and spiritual.

This idea is not only in the Bible but also in philosophical literature. Descartes wrote extensively about the union of a man and woman in his book *The Passions of the Soul*. The term *de volonté* refers to the voluntary joining of two souls in a relationship where they are two parts of one whole: "Love is a commotion [i.e., sensation] of the soul caused by a movement of the spirits, a commotion [i.e., sensation] that impels the soul to join itself *de volonté* to objects that appear to be agreeable to it."[16]

Descartes's entire definition and understanding of love involves the soul and not merely the body. Understanding the place of the soul in love, romance, and sex is important for many reasons. Loving a person is not simply about being attracted to their body. The body changes over time, but the soul endures. Love that is rooted in the soul is therefore capable of enduring, but love that is confined to the body alone is bound to change as the body changes.

Question 6.16

Much of the contemporary confusion about sex, love, and romance has to do with a lack of biblical _____.

---

[15] "Sexual Hookup Culture: A Review," *Review of General Psychology* 16, no. 2 (2012): 161–76; https://www.apa.org/monitor/2013/02/sexual-hookup-culture.pdf.

[16] René Descartes, *The Passions of the Soul*, Early Modern Texts ed., §79, p. 22, https://www.earlymoderntexts.com/assets/pdfs/descartes1649.pdf.

Question 6.17

Why is belief in the soul necessary for stable marriages?

_____

_____

Soul Care

Most people understand the importance of caring for their body. You probably brush your teeth, wash your body, and make sure to eat food. These are basic things you do to care for yourself physically.

Few people understand the importance of caring for their soul. You may wonder what that even means, or the basic things you can do to care for yourself spiritually. Plato's theory of the soul in *Republic* compared the body with the soul, and soul care with body care. A helpful analogy for self-care is: If you are a soul and have a body, then self-care involves caring for your body and your soul.

In Plato's day, as in our own, caring for your body meant going to the gymnasium for exercise and to the physician for treatments. Body care involved preventing and treating disease. In *Timaeus*, Plato wrote about "diseases of the soul" and the need to care for the soul as you do the body.

Understanding what Plato meant by diseases of the soul clarifies what soul care might entail. In both *Republic* and *Timaeus*, there is an analogy between vice and disease. In the same way that illness is a defect of the body, vice is a defect of the soul. In general, Plato believed that the best way to promote soul health and practice soul care is to commit yourself to virtue. "Virtue seems, then, to be a kind of health, fine condition, and well-being of the soul, while vice is disease, shameful condition, and weakness."[17]

The cultivation of character and virtue reflects the health of the soul like temperature and blood pressure reflect the health of the body. American philosopher Dallas Willard has written extensively on soul care. He emphasizes the virtue of love as the starting point, or as Jesus calls it, the Great Commandment: "Love the Lord your God with all your heart, with all your soul, with all your strength, and with all your mind," and "your neighbor as yourself" (Luke 10:27).

---

[17] Plato, *Republic*, translated by G. M. A. Grube (Indianapolis: Hackett , 1992), 121.

The point is not that we are called to merely *act* like we love God and others, but to *actually* love God and others. For Willard, the health of the soul expressed in love (and the other fruit of the Spirit) is the by-product of dwelling in the presence of God. Called "practicing the presence of God" by Catholic Brother Lawrence or "*Coram Deo*" by such reformers as Martin Luther, the idea is expressed by the English Puritan pastor and author Thomas Watson:

> The first fruit of love is *the musing of the mind upon God*. He who is in love, his thoughts are ever upon the object. He who loves God is ravished and transported with the contemplation of God. *"When I awake, I am still with thee"* (Ps. 139:18). The thoughts are as travelers in the mind. David's thoughts kept heaven-road. *"I am still with Thee."* God is the treasure, and where the treasure is, there is the heart. By this we may test our love to God. What are our thoughts most upon? Can we say we are ravished with delight when we think on God? Have our thoughts got wings? Are they fled aloft? Do we contemplate Christ and glory? . . . A sinner crowds God out of his thoughts. He never thinks of God, unless with horror, as the prisoner thinks of the judge.[18]

American pragmatist philosopher William James spoke of his "general philosophical reflection on the healthy-minded way of taking life."[19] This way of "taking life" is built upon repentance (or getting away from sin, as James puts it) goodness, and redemption. The sick-soul way of living, on the other hand, is the misery of unwholesomeness instead of living in the light.[20]

Can you imagine what a sick soul might look like?

Conclusion

You are a soul. God made you with a body, and your body matters to God. Our culture spends a lot of time caring about the body, but has forgotten about the soul. In order to think rightly about life, you must have a biblical anthropology. Understanding that humans have souls makes sense of human experience, ethics, and the most intimate relationships. Caring for your body but neglecting your soul is a recipe for misery.

---

[18] Thomas Watson, *All Things for Good* (Carlisle, PA: Banner of Truth Trust, 1986), 74.
[19] Williams James, "The Sick Soul" in *The Varieties of Religious Exeperience: A Study in Human Nature*, https://www.religion-online.org/book-chapter/lectures-6-and-7-the-sick-soul/.
[20] See James, "The Sick Soul."

Chapter Review

Question 6.18

Match the philosopher with the corresponding quote/idea:

A. David Hume

B. John Calvin

C. Aristotle

D. Thomas Watson

E. King David

F. René Descartes

G. Jesus

H. Nicolas Malebranche

I. Thomas Nagel

J. St. Paul

K. Wilhelm Leibniz

L. Solomon

M. George Berkeley

_____ God communicates ideas directly to the human mind.

_____ "What is a human being that you are mindful of him?"

_____ "The first fruit of love is the musing of the mind upon God.

_____ If two things are identical, everything true of one is true of the other.

_____ "And were all my perceptions removed by death . . . I should be entirely annihilated."

_____ It is preferable to be absent in the body and present with God.

_____ There is a time to be born and a time to die.

_____ "It is certain that I am really distinct from the body, and can exist without it."

_____ "To attain any assured knowledge of the soul is one of the most difficult things in the world."

_____ "Something was taken from Adam, in order that he might embrace, with greater benevolence, a part of himself."

_____ "What is it like to be a bat?"

_____ Only God has causal powers.

_____ "Fear him who is able to destroy both soul and body in hell."

Question 6.19

How does a proper view of the soul explain the following three areas:
   a)   Human experience
   b)   Ethics
   c)   Romantic intimacy

Question 6.20

What do the Scriptures say about the soul? Find some examples and bring them into discussion with the ideas from this chapter.

_____

_____

7

The Content of Character

In August 1963, civil rights activist Martin Luther King Jr. gave a speech from the steps of the Lincoln Monument in Washington, DC, as part of an event called the March on Washington for Jobs and Freedom. In the speech, which has become known as the "I Have a Dream" speech, King expressed his deep longing for a day when the defining characteristic of a person is his or her character and not his or her color.

The topic of character was not a new theme for King. While he was only thirty-four when he delivered the "I Have a Dream Speech," as a Baptist minister, King had been thinking about the importance of character since he was a young man. In fact, at the age of eighteen, King even published an article titled "The Purpose of Education" at Morehouse College (where he was a freshman) in which he argued for the importance of character, even stating that the goal of education is the cultivation of character.[1]

What is character? *Character* is a word that summarizes the kind of person you are on the inside. More specifically, one's (good) character is the sum total of that person's (good) habits,

---

[1] See Gerald Robinson, "The Content of Their Character: King's Theme Throughout the Years," American Enterprise Institute, January 17, 2020, https://www.aei.org/articles/the-content-of-their-character-kings-theme-across-the-years/.

ingrained tendencies to think, feel, or act in virtuous ways without thinking about it. *Character* is another word for virtue, which is a word we will look at more closely later in this chapter. You can tell a person's character by his or her actions, but the character of a person is what explains his or her actions. The content of character, King said, is what society should judge about a person.

In the years since King spoke about the importance of character, it has seemed to many that character has been in decline. In fact, some have argued more forcefully about the decline of character. In his book *The Death of Character: Moral Education in an Age Without Good or Evil*, author James Davidson Hunter writes, "Character is dead. Attempts to revive it will yield little. Its time has passed."[2]

Hunter is not saying that character is totally absent in modern society or that no one has character. Rather, he is arguing based upon empirical study that moral education and moral formation come from somewhere. Character corresponds to moral standards. Modern societies have tended to dismiss moral standards, thereby causing confusion about what character is and how to develop character (i.e., the death of character as a coherent concept).

Others have similarly argued that modern society has killed character by dismissing the religious beliefs that were the foundation and source of moral education and character formation. The result has been societies with unprecedented wealth, opportunity, and moral decay. Will Herberg was a Jewish immigrant who came to America to escape Tsarist Russia during the same time frame, and under the same circumstances, depicted in the movie *Fiddler on the Roof*. Herbert coined the term "cut flower culture" to describe the spiritual rootlessness of America and Europe.

Think for a moment about a vase of flowers. The flowers grew to be beautiful in rich soil with deep roots. Having been cut, they retain their beauty and fragrance, but only for a time. Once cut, the flowers are dying. Unless they are replanted, the flowers will die completely.

The rich soil of character formation for centuries was comprised of awareness that God existed, respect for his moral standards, and anticipation that each person would give an account to God for his or her decisions and actions while on earth. These things cultivated what the Bible refers to as the fear of the Lord. The fear of the Lord is not the kind of fear you have at a scary movie or on a roller coaster. The fear of the Lord can be summarized as belief *in* God and love and respect *for* God expressed in joyful obedience *to* God.[3]

---

[2] James Davidson Hunter, *The Death of Character: Moral Education in an Age Without Good or Evil* (New York: Basic Books, 2001), xiii.

[3] See Michael Reeves, *Rejoice and Tremble: The Surprising Good News of the Fear of the Lord* (Wheaton, IL: Crossway, 2021), 53, 66, 69.

The fear of the Lord is the rich soil from which the flowers of character have been cut and to which they must return if there is to be a revival of moral formation and character development. The Bible makes the connection between the fear of the Lord and moral formation quite clear in the opening section of Proverbs, which is a book in the Bible about relationship to God as the only path to moral life:[4] "The fear of the LORD is the beginning of knowledge; fools despise wisdom and discipline" (Prov 1:7).

Think of moral formation and character development as a journey. Without the fear of the Lord, you never even leave your front door! The fear of the Lord is the beginning of knowing God and being conformed (i.e., changed from the inside out) to the content of his character.

This chapter deals with ethics. As we said in the first chapter, ethics is the branch of philosophy that explains morality and goodness. It is traditionally divided into three sections: metaethics, normative ethics, and applied ethics. Each of these three sections will be explained and considered in the course of this chapter.

We use the word *good* to describe something that is right (i.e., as it should be). If you order a hamburger and it is cooked right and has all the right toppings, then you say it is good. Goodness in the context of ethics means right living: living life as it should be lived.

Question 7.1

Martin Luther King Jr. argued that education's goal is:
    a)   Money and power
    b)   The ability to succeed in life
    c)   Happiness and knowledge
    d)   Intelligence and character

Question 7.2

The author claims that good character is rooted in a fear of the Lord expressed through obedience. Give a practical example of this principle.

_____

_____

---

[4] See Tremper Longman, *The Fear of the Lord is Wisdom* (Grand Rapids: Baker Academic, 2017).

Question 7.3

Goodness in the context of ethics means _____ _____.

Ethics as Worship

The branch of moral philosophy that deals with the source or foundation of morality is called metaethics. Metaethics asks the big questions such as, "What is the source of morality?" and "Is morality objective or subjective?" The idea that morality is objective goes by the name *moral realism*. In ethics, realism is the view that moral facts such as "murder is wrong" has the same truth value as biological facts such as "all living things are made up of cells." Just as the statement about cells corresponds to the real world, so too the statement about murder.

Naturalism is the view that moral statements (i.e., "murder is wrong") do not appeal to moral principles or facts separate from the world itself; rather, they are merely ways of stating observations about the world in which we live. In the same way that "George Washington is the first president of the United States of America," statements such as "murder is wrong" may also be reduced or equated with other statements, such as "I don't like murder" or "our society disapproves of murder." Both of these statements may be true, but in naturalism, moral facts are reduced to such things as empirical statements or personal or societal preference.[5]

Christian ethics is a form of realism. Goodness (i.e., morality) is grounded in God's character. The reason why morality does not change from time to time or from culture to culture is that God does not change: "Because I, the LORD, have not changed, you descendants of Jacob have not been destroyed" (Mal 3:6). The Bible goes on to say that God "does not change" and that he is "the same yesterday, today, and forever" (Jas 1:17; Heb 13:8).

Naturalistic approaches to ethics are subjective. In such systems, morality is usually something that humans invent.[6] Christian ethics understands morality to be objective, grounded in God's character, and revealed. God reveals morality in his Word and in his world. The revelation

---

[5] Most naturalists are correctly characterized by our descriptions in these paragraphs. But there is a minority of naturalists who embrace moral realism without God by claiming that when matter reaches a certain level of complexity (for example, when sophisticated brains appear), then objective, intrinsic value emerges and this grounds objective goodness and rightness. Unfortunately, the view seems to be a case of getting something (emergent value) from nothing (pure matter with no inherent potential for intrinsic value). We will continue to characterize naturalism as the proper way to describe the majority view.

[6] See Evan Lenow and Mark Liederbach, *Ethics as Worship* (Pittsburgh: P&R, 2021), xix.

of objective morality in God's world is sometimes called the Natural Moral Law: the existence and knowability of objective moral laws rooted and revealed in creation.

Ethics is more than just following rules or commands. It is more than behavior modification or habituation. Morality, properly understood, is about entering into an eternal relationship with the living God (the source of goodness) through faith in Jesus, by faith. Once a person trusts in Jesus, they are saved from the wrath to come (1 Thess 1:10). In this sense, salvation (forgiveness and pardon) is immediate.

In another sense, Christians are being saved. In his famous passage on the resurrection, the apostle Paul wrote to the church in Corinth, "Now I want to make clear for you, brothers and sisters, the gospel I preached to you, which you received, on which you have taken your stand and by which you are being saved, if you hold to the message I preached to you—unless you believed in vain" (1 Cor 15:1–2).

We are saved and we are being saved. By holding fast to the gospel, Christians are being made into the image of Jesus: "Do not be conformed to this age, but be transformed by the renewing of your mind, so that you may discern what is the good, pleasing, and perfect will of God" (Rom 12:2).

Moral transformation is therefore ongoing and requires faith, reason (i.e., the mind), and discernment. The Bible makes it clear that God supplies the power for ongoing faith and moral transformation through the Holy Spirit. Such transformation is intended to take place in the community of the local church. Finally, moral transformation in this life is not immediate or perfect, but ongoing and bumpy.

A helpful analogy for spiritual transformation and the processes of "being saved" (i.e., transformed) is the process called metamorphosis by which a caterpillar becomes a butterfly. While Christians will emerge from the resurrection in glorified bodies in a sinless eternal state (i.e., butterflies), we live our lives in a sort of spiritual cocoon: we are not what we were, but we are not yet what we will become. The notion of transformation provides an important insight about moral growth: moral growth is an essential component of human flourishing. We were made to function best when we develop the character that underwrites a solid moral life.

Because morality is about relationship and inside-out transformation (i.e., metamorphosis), it is perhaps best to understand ethics as worship. Worship is a word that refers to what happens in us when we behold God by faith in Jesus Christ by the power of the Holy Spirit. This can happen when we are at church singing and hearing a sermon, but it can also happen walking to class or driving to work. In fact, the Bible says, "And whatever you do, in word or in deed, do everything in the name of the Lord Jesus, giving thanks to God the Father through him" (Col 3:17).

Worship is life and life is worship: *Whatever you do, in word or in deed . . . everything*. Morality is therefore not limited to only those specific issues the Bible addresses, but to the character, attitude, and perspective you have in everything you do. Morality includes the things you do (commission) and the things you fail to do (omission).

From the passage above, for instance, failing to live with gratitude is a moral failure. Whether you choose the cobb salad or the chicken sandwich, are you grateful?

The result of this perspective is twofold. If ethics is worship, and if the moral life is about doing everything in a way that reflects the character of God and our hope in Christ, then most of us are probably less moral than we tend to think. Understanding ethics as worship is humbling, because while we may avoid some of the "big sins," we all fall short of doing *everything in the name of the name of the Lord Jesus* with gratitude.

The bar is higher than we tend to think. Jesus said that looking upon another person with lust is adultery, and hating another person is murder (Matt 5:21–45). He reminded the religious leaders that anyone who did not honor their father or mother under the old covenant would have been put to death (Exod 21:17; Mark 7:10).

When you understand God's holiness, the commands to love God and love others selflessly, and the way that God deserves both outward obedience and inward affection, you cannot help but agree with Jesus when he said to the rich young ruler, "No one is good except God, alone" (Mark 10:18). Only God is perfectly good. Humans have all sinned and fallen short of God's moral perfection (Rom 3:23).

The second result of ethics as worship, related to the first, is that this understanding of ethics lends itself toward a greater sense of moment-by-moment dependence on God's grace to live morally. While other religious ethical systems leave a person feeling empowered, Christian ethics should leave a person feeling dependent—dependent on Jesus to forgive and cleanse, dependent on the Holy Spirit to empower transformation, dependent on God's Word for direction, and dependent on the community of God's people for encouragement and accountability. Paradoxically, the greater a Christian's sense of dependence upon God, the more empowered that person feels.

Question 7.4

Identify each statement as descriptive of moral naturalism or moral realism.

Statement	Moral Naturalism	Moral Realism
Morality is objective.		
Moral claims have the same truth value as biological facts.		
Moral principles arise from observations about the world.		
Christian ethics most resembles this view.		
Allows morality to adapt to social and personal norms and convictions.		

Question 7.5

Explain how ethics and worship are connected in a Christian worldview.

_____

_____

Jesus as Moral Exemplar

Normative ethics is the branch of ethics that seeks to establish criteria for right and wrong, as well as a general system of ethics that best captures the nature of moral rules and actions. Virtue ethics and moral relativism are two examples of such systems. Of course, there is not agreement about the best criteria for thinking about morality and how best to determine what is good. The three general approaches to normative ethics are virtue, deontology, and consequentialism. Virtue ethics focuses on character, deontology focuses on rules and one's duty to obey rules, and consequentialism focuses on consequences.

Since God's character is the source of all morality, and since the commands of Scripture are boiled down to loving God and loving others, many Christians (especially during the medieval era) understood the emphasis of Christian ethics to be on virtue. While actions and consequences are important, they flow from virtues like faith, hope, and love (the theological virtues). From faith, hope, and love come things like courage, wisdom, justice, and moderation (the cardinal virtues). In Latin, the word *cardo* means hinge. All the other virtues hinge on courage, wisdom, justice, and moderation.

In his book *The Screwtape Letters*, C. S. Lewis muses that in order to defeat virtue, Satan would first want to destroy courage among humankind ("to make a deep wound to his charity, you should therefore first defeat his courage.") The reason for this is then explained, from the perspective of Satan: "Courage is not simply one of the virtues, but the form of every virtue at the testing point, which means, at the point of highest reality. A chastity or honesty, or mercy, which yields to danger will be chaste or honest or merciful only on conditions. Pilate was merciful till it became risky."[7]

A person can feel kindness or compassion toward someone in danger and do nothing. Courage moves a person from intention to intervention.

Before considering a few of the advantages of the virtue approach to ethics, let's first consider what many consider to be its chief weakness. Virtue ethics does not provide a list of do's and don'ts: This can leave some feeling as though virtue ethics is vague and unspecific. Rather than telling a person they can or cannot drink alcohol, for instance, virtue ethics asks, "What is the wise thing to do?" and "Can it be done in moderation?" While the Bible does offer instruction about virtue, most notably for love in 1 Corinthians 13 (i.e., "love is patient, love is kind . . . it does not envy . . ."), those looking for concrete directives can tend to be disappointed.

That said, there are significant advantages to a virtue approach to ethics. First, it helps make connections between those aspects of God's character of which we partake as believers. Sometimes called the communicable attributes of God, these are the attributes of God that believers can also practice. While humans are not able to be all-knowing (omniscient), all-present (omnipresent), or all-powerful (omnipotent) like God, we can and should partake in and practice his holiness, love, justice, mercy, kindness, and so forth. It seems like a strength of the virtue approach to have immediate and clear lines between the source of morality and what it means to live morally.

Another advantage of the virtue approach is that it keeps us from making the mistake of confusing right behavior with morality. While right behavior is important, it is only part of the equation. Jesus had strong and confrontational words for those who thought they were good just because they acted good. He made it clear that morality is about what is inside, not just about how we act on the outside. From an ethical perspective, right actions that flow from and accurately reveal a good heart and character are actions that count the most.

---

[7] C. S. Lewis, *The Screwtape Letters* (New York: HarperCollins, 2001), 161–62.

For instance, it is hypocrisy to hate someone on the inside but smile at them on the outside. Hypocrisy is not a good way to live because it does not reflect God. Humans are created in God's image (*imago Dei*), which includes the capacity for moral behavior. Since God is not a hypocrite, humans do not reflect his glory when there is a disconnect between one's inner life (private) and outer life (public). God is not fooled, and eventually, all hypocrisy will be revealed.

God desires integrity. Integrity means there is alignment between the good on the inside and the good on the outside. It also means that the person you are in private is consistent with the person you are in public in regard to your character and habits.

In the history of humanity, Jesus is the only sinless human. He is perfect in character and in obedience to God's commands. He possesses absolute integrity between what he says and what he does. While on earth, Jesus lived a perfect life and was able to be a sinless sacrifice (i.e., "the Lamb of God who takes away the sin of the world" [John 1:29]). Now risen, Jesus continues his faithful ministry while reigning in heaven.

Christian morality is more than defining virtues and abstract concepts. Christian morality is about looking to Jesus. He is God incarnate (i.e., in the flesh) and embodies all virtue (John 1:14; Titus 2:11; 1 John 4:9). No wonder the author of Hebrews described the Christian life thus: "Therefore, since we also have such a large cloud of witnesses surrounding us, let us lay aside every hindrance and the sin that so easily ensnares us. Let us run with endurance the race that lies before us, keeping our eyes on Jesus, the pioneer and perfecter of our faith. For the joy that lay before him, he endured the cross, despising the shame, and sat down at the right hand of the throne of God" (Heb 12:1–2).

Keeping our eyes on Jesus is a good way to summarize Christian ethics. He is the moral exemplar, which means that he is the ultimate model of moral excellence. While he is more than a good teacher or moral example (he is God, after all!), we cannot forget that he is also the only perfect human.

Reading biographies is a good way to learn leadership principles. If you read biographies of presidents or other major leaders, you see an inevitable mixture of strengths and weaknesses, victories and failures. It is common to learn from the mistakes of others and to try to avoid those mistakes ourselves.

Yet, when looking to Jesus, there are no moral weaknesses and no moral failures. Jesus "has been tempted in every way as we are, yet without sin" (Heb 4:15). Jesus faced all the external temptations that we face—all the things in the world that are thrown at us that can cause us to stumble or fall into sin. Yet, unlike us, Jesus did not possess a sin nature. He did not have internal temptations that came from doubt or sinful desires (lust, greed, etc.).

What does it mean to look to Jesus in order to live morally? After all, we cannot physically see Jesus. What we can do is look to Scripture to see how Jesus embodies and fulfills all that God has promised, all that God is, and all that God wants us to be. However, this does not mean that we only pay attention to the "red letters" of Scripture (i.e., those specific words of Jesus).

There are many things Jesus did not talk about simply because they were not controversial issues in his day, such as child abuse or bestiality (human sex with non-human animals). Just because there are no red letters about child abuse or bestiality does not mean that those things are not wrong. It shows us the wisdom of Jesus in addressing the actual sins and moral struggles of his audience and the courage of Jesus to confront the pet sins of his age. Jesus did not engage in moral grandstanding on issues about which everyone at the time agreed.

Returning to the three main approaches of normative ethics (virtue, commands, and consequences), Jesus embodies the virtues to which Christians aspire, and to which virtue ethics draws our attention. However, Jesus did not discount the commands of Scripture or the consequences of actions.

While rules and outcomes do not determine morality, God uses them in important ways. Our attitude toward God's commands reveals our relationship with God (i.e., Jesus said, "If you love me, you will keep my commands" [John 14:15]). The Bible is filled with references to consequences to motivate moral behavior (blessings and curses, heaven and hell, reward and punishment, etc.). Even Jesus, "for the joy that lay before him," endured the cross (Heb 12:2). In many ways, Christian ethics is inseparably connected to the consequences of God's glory and human happiness through relationship with God.

Looking to Jesus is not just about learning from him and following him; it is also about finding happiness and identity in him. Immoral behavior is often motivated by a misguided search for happiness. In contrast, finding happiness in Jesus enables you to say no to things that are immoral and only generate temporary happiness. A person who finds his identity in Jesus shifts his understanding of self (and the behavior that follows) away from misguided and harmful categories that are according to the flesh and onto Christ and his kingdom.

One way to think of this phenomenon is that behavior follows belonging. Many sociologists and criminologists have studied what draws young people into gang activity. It turns out, the primary motivation is not money (few people actually make significant money in gang activity). The primary motivation for gang activity, whether it be street gangs or biker gangs, is a sense of belonging. People will go to extreme (and often dangerous lengths) to gain a sense of belonging. Looking to Jesus for moral direction avoids the pitfalls of fruitless searches for belonging. Knowing that you were created by God and belong to God makes clear whose directions in life you should be following.

Question 7.6

The three general approaches to normative ethics are _____, _____ and _____.

Question 7.7

Of the three approaches, medieval Christians most adhered to:

    a) Virtue
    b) Deontology
    c) Consequentialism
    d) None of the above

Question 7.8

Discuss the advantages and disadvantages of virtue ethics.

Question 7.9

In your own words, define *integrity*.

Question 7.10

How does a Christian approach to ethics go beyond mere virtue ethics and avoid the pitfall of being too abstract?

Question 7.11

How do rules fit into a Christian vision of ethics?

Morality and Human Flourishing

In the first chapter, the concept of eudaimonia (soul happiness or human flourishing) was introduced. Morality is about not only personal fulfillment but also societal improvement. Oftentimes, people feel discouraged from being good because there are times when society rewards the wicked. This is nothing new. Over 2,700 years ago, the Jewish psalmist Asaph wrote, "I envied the arrogant; I saw the prosperity of the wicked" (Ps 73:3). Understanding the concept of human flourishing motivates personal morality and helps us to understand how our actions affect others.

As noted earlier, an individual who is practicing the virtues and living morality experiences soul happiness (eudaimonia). On the other hand, Plato observed that a person who does what they know to be wrong feels unhappy.[8] Modern society seems to have lost this important connection between morality and true happiness.

Aristotle defined happiness in Book One of *Nicomachean Ethics* as "living well and doing well." He had in mind not a single act of good or one day of living well, but a life of dedication to virtue: "For one swallow does not make a summer, nor does one day; and so too one day, or a short time, does not make a man blessed and happy."[9] In order to be truly happy, a person must remain dedicated to a lifetime of virtue.

A person who wants to get in shape will not see results after only one day at the gym. In the same way that doing sit-ups for a day does not give you a "six-pack," neither will living virtuously one day suddenly make you virtuous.

It takes time to see the *results* of virtue.

There is something equitable about this understanding of happiness. In many societies, happiness is about wealth, leisure, health, education, or "me time." All of these things cost money.

---

[8] See A. W. Price, *Virtue and Reason in Plato and Aristotle* (Oxford: Oxford University Press, 2011).

[9] Aristotle, *Nicomachean Ethics*, 3.7, http://classics.mit.edu/Aristotle/nicomachaen.1.i.html.

No wonder people tend to connect the pursuit of happiness with the accumulation of money. Countries that are more affluent tend to rank higher on various happiness scales or indexes.

Morality, on the other hand, is equally available to everyone. Anyone can be just, loving, kind, and so on. Your ability to experience the happiness that comes from living virtuously does not depend on where you are from, how much money you have (or do not have), or how many degrees you are able to complete.

Jesus talked about morality during his famous Sermon on the Mount. He repeatedly used the word "blessed" to describe a life of virtue. Another way to translate the word "blessed" is "happy." Jesus was saying that living in a way that glorifies God (i.e., virtue) is a means of personal happiness.

Keep in mind that the kind of happiness that relates to virtue, of which Plato, Aristotle, and Jesus were alluding, is not the same thing as levity, giddiness, or lightheartedness. At the end of C. S. Lewis's book *The Last Battle*, there is a scene where Peter, Lucy, Lord Digory, and Eustace realize that the old world is over and a new one is beginning. This realization brings them a sense of solemnness: "Very quickly they all became grave again: for, as you know, there is a kind of happiness and wonder that makes you serious. It is too good to waste on jokes."[10]

Virtue leads to a sense of happiness that may be subdued and internal (i.e., more on the inside than on the outside). Soul happiness can be less evident to friends who may be more used to recognizing "happiness" by laughter or think of "happiness" as fun. While there is nothing wrong with laughter and fun, these things are not the same as true happiness.

Confusing fun with happiness is personally unfulfilling and bad for society. The result is depicted in F. Scott Fitzgerald's classic modern novel *The Great Gatsby*. In it, the character Daisy Buchanan personifies the emptiness of confusing fun for happiness. The following quote from the book illustrates Daisy's pursuit of fun and how it left her feeling sad rather than happy (i.e., gay): "Her face was sad . . . but there was an excitement in her voice . . . a singing compulsion, a whispered 'Listen,' a promise that she had done gay, exciting things just a while since and that there were gay, exciting things hovering in the next hour."[11]

---

[10] C. S. Lewis, *The Last Battle*, The Chronicles of Narnia, holiday 2005 ed. (New York: HarperCollins, 2005), 212.

[11] F. Scott Fitzgerald, *The Great Gatsby*, https://www.planetebook.com/free-ebooks/the-great-gatsby .pdf, 12.

Daisy illustrates the ethos of those who believe in this life alone. She represents those who think of happiness in terms of the flesh without regard for the soul. As the apostle Paul said, "If the dead are not raised, 'Let us eat and drink, for tomorrow we die'" (1 Cor 15:32).

The Great Gatsby is ultimately about a notion of happiness and of the good life that is bad for the individual and negatively impacts society. The main characters such as Daisy, Gatsby, Nick, and Tom are profoundly unhappy. Eventually, the music stops and the party ends. This inevitability is the underlying sadness in the lives of those, such as Daisy, who live their life in an endless pursuit of "exciting things" and of gayety (i.e., lightheartedness or cheerfulness).

The Great Gatsby captures the end of America's "Roaring Twenties" and the transition from glitz and glamour to the poverty and destitution of the Great Depression (1929–1939). This is a fitting metaphor for the eventual collapse and depression that befalls any society that disregards virtues such as moderation and defines happiness merely as the pursuits of pleasure and material gain (i.e., materialism).

Question 7.12

Aristotle used the word _____ to describe happiness. A similar word used by Jesus in the Sermon on the Mount is _____.

Question 7.13

Provide a few examples from literature or television that highlight the difference between "happy" and "fun."

_____

_____

Practical Questions for Moral Decisions

This final section offers practical questions for making moral decisions. The branch of moral philosophy that deals with the practical application of morality is called *applied ethics*. As the name suggests, applied ethics seeks to apply the insights of metaethics and normative ethics to specific situations where you are faced with difficult choices that are moral in nature.

Not all choices are moral in nature. For instance, the choice of what to order off of a restaurant menu is usually not moral in nature. Unless you are a vegetarian for moral reasons, choosing between a chicken sandwich or cobb salad is a decision, but it is a decision about taste and preference, not morality. There are probably not any moral facts about chicken sandwiches or cobb salads that cause you to wonder which of the two you would order.

On the other hand, whether or not you watch pornography is a moral decision. Moral decisions include particular social issues like the environment, war, abortion, suicide, end of life or reproductive decisions, racism, and the death penalty. Moral decisions also include personal and relational issues related to sex, honesty, keeping promises, dependability, and doing your own work to the best of your ability. Moral decisions also involve the attitudes and motivation behind actions, which as we will see, adds a moral dimension to everything.

Moral decisions usually refer to those decisions that pertain to moral facts, involve one's sense of moral duty or obligation, or call into question one's character or virtue. On the one hand, it is wrong to mistake decisions about taste (i.e., chicken sandwich versus cobb salad) with moral decisions. On the other hand, it is wrong to think that all decisions are merely about taste or preference. Just as there are mathematical facts and historical facts, so too there are moral facts. Decisions in life that involve moral facts are moral decisions.

Practical steps help, whether you are constructing a new piece of furniture or playing a new board game. Just as there are practical steps to constructing furniture or playing board games, there are also practical steps for moral decisions. What follows are five steps to making moral decisions. The order of the steps is intentional and reflects the weight and priority of each question. For any issue, one or two of the questions below may settle the matter. More complex issues may require a careful consideration of all five questions to bring clarity.

First, find out what the Bible has to say. This opening question in the decision-making matrix is often not as easy as it appears. Before looking at some of the complexities involved in turning to Scripture, let us first appreciate some of the reasons for caring about what Scripture has to say.

The Bible is God's Word (i.e., literally breathed out by God) (2 Tim 3:15–16). Just as God cannot lie, so too his Word is truth without error (Ps 19:7–9; John 17:17; Heb 6:18). The Bible, through which we have saving knowledge of God, is sufficient for life and godliness and is able to make a person "complete, equipped for every good work" (2 Tim 3:16–17; see also 2 Pet 1:3). In regard to faith and morality, the Bible is a sufficient and ultimate guide to faith and morality (Ps 119:105).

The Bible is compared to a sword (Heb 4:12). That is a helpful metaphor in regard to moral decisions. The Bible enables us to cut through the issues, to discern our intentions, and to weigh the options in a moral dilemma. The Bible is also compared to a light, another helpful metaphor. It brings light, clarity, and direction in times of moral confusion. However, the Bible is also compared to a fire and a hammer (Jer 23:29). It has ultimate authority in regard to morality and is the power of God in the life of the believer. The relationship between God, his Word, and morality is summarized by Benjamin Warfield: "The trustworthiness of the Scriptures lies at the foundation of trust in the Christian system of doctrine, and is therefore fundamental to the Christian hope and life."[12]

The challenge is knowing how to apply the Bible to the Christian life. In what follows, we lay out some qualifying principles to aid in the rightful and wise application of Scripture to moral decisions.

In applying God's Word to moral decisions, consider what the Bible says as a whole. Probably the best advice in regard to interpreting Scripture is that Scripture interprets Scripture. While one verse may appear to settle the matter, a study of all that Scripture has to say often opens up a range of possible moral choices. While we all want clear and easy direction, life is messy. The Bible usually has nuance to account for the complexity of moral dilemmas.

Take divorce, for instance. The Bible says that God hates divorce (Mal 2:16). That one verse may appear to imply that there is no room for a Christian to get divorced. However, in the Sermon on the Mount, Jesus added, "I tell you, everyone who divorces his wife, except in a case of sexual immorality, causes her to commit adultery. And whoever marries a divorced woman commits adultery" (Matt 5:32).

Jesus's words are believed by many to give room for divorce in cases of sexual immorality. His words also raise new concerns about the possibility of remarriage. Later in the New Testament, Paul seems to teach that abandonment is another instance where divorce is not prohibited. So, while God hates divorce and it is not a part of his intended plan for marriage (Matt 19:6), there are also gracious provisions for divorce in certain circumstances, according to Scripture. Scripture is not contradictory; it is nuanced.

While there is debate among Christians about moral issues like divorce and remarriage, we agree that our position on such moral issues should have biblical support. There may be a range of acceptable Christian positions on such issues, but not caring about what the Bible says is not an acceptable position for a Christian to hold in regard to morality.

---

[12] Benjamin Warfield, "A lecture" in *Bibliotheca Sacra*," v. 51 (1894), 614–40.

Some moral issues are clearly addressed in Scripture and more straightforward than divorce. Racism, for instance, is not a moral option for Christians because humans are created equally in God's image and humans are not to judge each other according to human categories (Gen 1:27; 2 Cor 5:16). The Bible clearly teaches that God created humans male and female, so transgenderism does not lead to human flourishing. While the Bible says there is "a time to kill" (Eccl 3:3), such as in cases of just war, murder (i.e., unjust killing) is prohibited in the sixth commandment (Exod 20:2–17).

When making moral decisions, one must take into consideration all that the Bible teaches as a whole, and not only in parts. The danger is that we all tend to select the parts we like, and avoid the parts we do not like. Taking the Scripture as a whole mitigates against the sinful tendency to confirmation bias (i.e., only seeing what you *want* to see).

Not only should Scripture be interpreted in light of Scripture, but Scripture should always be interpreted in context. Some parts of Scripture make use of literary devices such as metaphor or are poetic in nature. While the point of such passages is true, the language is not literal. For instance, Jesus told the following parable: "The kingdom of heaven is like a mustard seed that a man took and sowed in his field. It is the smallest of all the seeds, but when grown, it is taller than the garden plants and becomes a tree, so that the birds of the sky come and nest in its branches" (Matt 13:31–32).

The Bible is clear that Jesus was telling a parable, a fictitious story illustrating a spiritual truth. The spiritual truth in the above parable is about the kingdom of heaven. The kingdom will start small but will grow.

Some have read this parable and claimed that Jesus is wrong, since there are other smaller seeds than a mustard seed. Jesus is talking to people for whom the mustard seed was likely the smallest of seeds they knew. This is an example of God contextualizing truth in order to aid in learning; something that teachers and other communicators regularly do. However, there is always a danger when such rhetorical devices (e.g., parables, metaphors, and analogies) are taken too far or too literally.

In regard to ethics and morality, metaphors help us understand passages like 2 Cor 5:17, which says: "Therefore, if anyone is in Christ, he is a new creation; the old has passed away, and see, the new has come!" Could a person use this passage to avoid the consequences of their actions? Could someone convicted of kidnapping argue that since they are a new person in Christ that they are not the same person who was convicted of the crime and therefore deserve to be let out of prison early?

These arguments misunderstand the metaphor. New creation does not imply a different person but a changed person. In the same way that over the course of your life you physically develop from an infant into an adult yet remain the same person, so, too, believers are saved and spiritually develop (i.e., sanctification) but remain the same person. The experience of moral transformation is a glimpse of the ultimate transformation believers will experience at the resurrection ("Listen, I am telling you a mystery: We will not all fall asleep, but we will all be changed" [1 Cor 15:51]). It would be wrong to argue that the metaphor of "new creation" absolves a person of criminal activity.

Looking to Scripture with an understanding of the story of redemption and with respect to context and genre is the first step in making moral decisions. When tempted by Satan, Jesus quoted Scripture. In order to follow Jesus in regard to morality, you must highly value Scripture as an authority for all life.

Second, try to anticipate whether your decision will lead to guilt or regret. In the same way that modern homes are built with smoke and carbon monoxide detectors, God has built humans with conscience. The capacity for moral decisions, rather than merely instinctual decisions, is one thing that makes humans distinct from other animals. The word *conscience* literally means "with knowledge." Even if you never read Scripture, there are certain things humans come into the world knowing internally and naturally (i.e., what theologians call Natural Law).[13]

When you violate or go against your conscience, you feel a sense of guilt or shame. Similar to how a smoke detector sounds an alarm if there is fire, the conscience initiates guilt or shame if there is immorality. Only a fool would turn off a fire alarm and go back to sleep without first looking around to make sure there was not a fire. In the same way, only a fool would ignore their conscience by doing things that led to guilt and regret without first investigating the reason for those feelings.

Of course, it is possible for a fire alarm to go off when there is not a fire. Similiarly, guilt and shame are not infallible in regard to morality. Our consciences can be dulled or disconnected by our passions and influences. If you ignore your conscience enough, eventually you become morally dull and find it easier and easier to do things you know are wrong.

---

[13] Theologians call those things known by reason "Natural Law." In Luke 11:11 Jesus said, "What father among you, if his son asks for a fish, will give him a snake instead of a fish?" Here, Jesus was appealing to a moral principle that any reasonable person should know; it's wrong for a father to deprive his child of food.

Guilt and shame can be calibrated to the wrong things. Sometimes our feelings of guilt and shame have to do with people's standards rather than God's standards. Jesus makes a strong distinction between the Word of God and the traditions of man (Mark 7:1–13).

Guilt and shame are also not helpful in the life of a believer in regard to past sins that have been confessed and forgiven. The Bible says that once a person is forgiven, their sins are forgiven "as far as the east is from the west" and that God "forgives their wrongdoing" and "never again remembers their sins" (Ps 103:12; Heb 8:12).

Despite the ways in which guilt and shame can be negative, they also have great power to help in moral formation. Nuclear fission can be used to power cities and protect nations, but it can also be used to kill and destroy. Guilt and shame, like nuclear fission, can be either good or bad depending upon its purpose.

The apostle Paul contrasted good and bad uses of guilt. He referred to the right use of guilt as "godly grief," and the wrong use of guilt as "worldly grief": "I now rejoice, not because you were grieved, but because your grief led to repentance. For you were grieved as God willed, so that you did not experience any loss from us. For godly grief produces a repentance that leads to salvation without regret, but worldly grief produces death" (2 Cor 7:9–10).

In your quest to live a good life, God has equipped you with a conscience that notifies you when something is not right. When you are living contrary to God's plan as revealed in Scripture, you should experience sorrow. If your sorrow leads you to change your mind and actions about what is right and wrong (i.e., repentance), then it is a cause for rejoicing and will lead to life. Like a fire alarm that notifies you of a small fire, which is then extinguished before it burns down the house, if you pay attention to your conscience and allow it to be guided by Scripture, it will keep you from great harm.

So the second step in making moral decisions is to respect the power and purpose of the conscience. When making decisions, ask yourself, "Will I regret this?," "Will this lead to guilt or shame?," or "Will I be sorry that I did this?"

Third, be honest about whether you are making your decisions freely or out of compulsion. Many philosophers, including Immanuel Kant, have emphasized the relationship between freedom and morality. For Kant, freedom and reason are the essential component of morality. In fact, Kant said that "no misfortune can be more terrifying" than compulsion, slavery, and the lack of freedom.[14]

---

[14] Immanuel Kant, *Observations on the Feeling of the Beautiful and Sublime*, quoted by Edward Demenchonok in "Learning from Kant" in *Revista Portuguesa de Filosofia* 75 (2019): 191–230; https://www.jstor.org/stable/26625467?seq=1#metadata_info_tab_contents, 191–92.

Those who follow Jesus are set free: "So if the Son sets you free, you really will be free" (John 8:36). When faced with moral decisions, ask yourself whether you are acting *freely* in obedience to Jesus or out of *compulsion*. Compulsive behavior includes acting in ways that you feel others expect you to act.

Sometimes called "peer pressure," compulsive behavior lacks freedom because it leads to decisions out of fear of losing friends, relationships, or social standing. The bottom line is this: It is never right to do something you know is wrong because you feel obligated. As Prov 29:25 says, "The fear of mankind is a snare, but the one who trusts in the Lord is protected."

Compulsive behavior can also involve addiction. Addiction is compulsive behavior with harmful consequences. Addiction can involve things like nicotine, alcohol, overeating, sex, pornography, or other drugs.

Moral decisions require freedom. When faced with choices, ask yourself whether your behavior is free or compulsive. If you are engaged in compulsive behavior, seek counseling. There is hope for freedom from addiction and compulsive behavior.

Fourth, pay attention to what other serious Christians think about the issue involved in your moral decision. In the garden of Eden, before sin entered the world, God said, "It is not good for the man to be alone" (Gen 2:18). This passage is usually quoted in reference to marriage, because God's solution to man's loneliness was to create "a helper corresponding to him," which was Eve, his wife. However, the bigger picture is that humans are created to live in relationship with other humans (i.e., community) who know each other intimately (i.e., beyond superficiality). Marriage and family is one very important communal institution, but there are others, such as the church.

Moral decisions need not be and should not be made in isolation. Consider the following verses about seeking wise counsel:

The fear of the Lord is the beginning of knowledge; fools despise wisdom and discipline. (Prov 1:7)

A fool's way is right in his own eyes, but whoever listens to counsel is wise. (Prov 12:15)

Listen to counsel and receive instruction so that you may be wise later in life. (Prov 19:20)

The key word is *wise* counsel. Listening to fools has the opposite effect of listening to wise counselors: "The tongue of the wise makes knowledge attractive, but the mouth of fools blurts out foolishness" (Prov 15:2). Everyone should aspire to have *good* friends and be a *good* friend.

Christian ethics emphasizes the importance of learning from the wisdom and experiences of others. In his book *A Community of Character*, Stanley Hauerwas argues that for Christians, the most important social task is hearing the story of God in Scripture and then living as a community in a manner that is "faithful to that story."[15] The church's primary impact on society is that it is the only community that "pledges to live its life by that truth."[16]

In the same way that a person develops life skills in community, humans develop moral skills in community as well. The word *virtue* literally means skilled living or living with excellence. There are communities of people committed to the certain skills such as sports (teams), education (colleges), and special interests (clubs). The church is a community dedicated to the story of the gospel and to living skillfully (i.e., virtuously) in faithfulness to the truth of the gospel.[17]

A person who wants to get good at a sport probably finds a coach. The coach (in most cases) has experience playing the sport they are teaching and is further along in their skillset. The church is filled with Christians who are further along in their walk with God and who help each other navigate life decisions and develop the skill of living out the Christian faith.

The best way to learn is to observe. Aristotle argued in *Poetics* that art has the ability to portray virtue in a way that can be imitated. While Plato had looked down upon art as a kind of imitation of nature, Aristotle saw imitation (*mimesis*, from which we get the word *mimic*) as a powerful way to learn virtue. Imagine watching a movie like *Captain America* and learning virtues like loyalty or honor.

In *Nicomachean Ethics*, Aristotle argued that the best way to learn virtue is to watch others who are virtuous, imitate their virtue, and eventually your imitation of virtue will be internalized and become second nature (i.e., habit). Just like people can develop bad habits, so too it is possible to develop good habits.

Christian ethics is inherently *hopeful*. The gospel (i.e., good news) is that having paid for sins by his blood on the cross, Jesus is risen from the dead and is eternally victorious over sin and death. Through faith we participate in his victory and experience moral transformation in this life. While other ethical systems argue that behavior is determined by biology or upbringing, Christianity teaches that by God's grace people *who want to change* can experience change and

---

[15] Stanley Hauerwas, *A Community of Character* (South Bend, IN: University of Notre Dame Press, 1982), 1.

[16] Hauerwas, 1.

[17] See Stanley Hauerwas, "Learning to See Red Wheelbarrows: On Vision and Relativism," *Journal of the American Academy of Religion* 45, no. 2 (June 1977): 225.

freedom from harmful behavior: "Let the thief no longer steal. Instead, he is to do honest work with his own hands, so that he has something to share with anyone in need" (Eph 4:28).

Christians would disagree that morality is simply about habit formation. True virtue flows from faith, hope, and love. These virtues are instilled and cultivated by the Holy Spirit (i.e., the fruit of the Spirit). However, Christians can agree with Aristotle that humans tend to learn by watching others and cultivating habit through spiritual disciplines.

Learning from others is the normal course of human development. Children learn by watching their parents. Learning from others is also the normal course of human *moral* development. Jesus's disciples learned by watching him for three years. Today, all Christians can observe virtue in the lives of other Christians and learn what it looks like to put faith into practice (i.e., discipleship) (Titus 2:1–14). Titus 2 shows the compatibility of learning from others and being transformed by the Holy Spirit.

When making moral decisions, learn from others who have dealt with the same kinds of issues. The Bible assures us that "there is nothing new under the sun" and that "no temptation has come upon you except what is common to humanity" (Eccl 1:9; 1 Cor 10:13). Others in the church have gone through what you are going through, and through them, God will generously give you wisdom (Jas 1:5).

Fifth, consider the likely consequences of your actions. In psychology, this is called foresight: the ability to predict future outcomes. Proverbs 22:3 says, "A sensible person sees danger and takes cover, but the inexperienced keep going and are punished." God designed the world so that many likely outcomes are often easy to anticipate.

Consider the following examples. If you drink too much alcohol, you will probably experience a hangover. If you do not save your money, you will likely need to borrow from others when your car breaks down. If you date someone you know has been unfaithful to others, they will probably be unfaithful to you. When likely outcomes transpire, it is foolish to act surprised.

"What were you thinking?" This is a question parents often ask their kids when they make childish (or foolish) decisions. Usually, the child responds by saying, "I wasn't thinking!" As children mature into adults, they begin to think about their decisions and choices. Similarly, moral maturity means acting virtuously (i.e., according to principles) with foresight and being controlled less and less by impulse.

Does this emphasis on considering the consequences of actions imply that a Christian view of morality includes the normative system known as utilitarianism? Properly understood, the answer is "not at all." According to the various versions of utilitarianism, the sole factor that makes a moral rule or a particular moral action right is the total amount of good versus bad consequences compared to alternative rules or actions. No moral rule or act is intrinsically right or wrong.

Utilitarianism is clearly inconsistent with a Christian ethic, which is a combination of virtue and deontological ethics. On this view, two things make a rule or action morally right: One, the rule/act is intrinsically right or wrong depending on whether it is grounded in and follows from the character of a good, virtuous God. Two, the rule/act is an accurate reflection of the good character of the moral agent.

Does this mean that Christians do not take into account the consequences of the rules they embrace or the acts they perform? No, and here's why. Christians reject the utilitarian idea that consequences are what make a moral rule/act correct. But Christians also recognize that there are inherently correct moral rules/acts that reflect God's and the agent's good character that imply an assessment of consequences as a guide for the best way to honor the intrinsically correct rule. Here, consequences do not make the rule/act right; rather, they provide guidance as to the best way to follow the rule that is intrinsically right. Consequences matter! They are one way that God has designed the world to encourage wisdom and virtue.

An example may help. In bioethics, the following is an intrinsically correct moral rule that is part of a virtue and deontological ethical perspective: Benefit your patient and do not harm the patient. However, different treatments may benefit or harm the patient to a greater or lesser degree. So, a doctor who is attempting to follow this rule will need to assess the likely consequences of alternate treatments to decide which treatment will best obey the moral rule. In this case, consequences are relevant to assessing the best way to obey an intrinsically valuable rule; consequences are not what make the rule correct.

Question 7.14

Moral decisions are both _____ and _____.

Question 7.15

When making moral decisions, how is the Bible like a sword? How is it like a light?

_____

_____

Question 7.16

True or false: Applying God's law to any given situation means finding a verse that is the most like your situation and following that verse.

Question 7.17

When it comes to making moral decisions, our "smoke detector" is our _____.

Question 7.18

When are guilt and shame helpful for Christians, and when are they unhelpful?

_____

_____

Question 7.19

Moral decisions require _____ rather than compulsion.

Question 7.20

True or false: Cultivating virtue is really a personal project.

Question 7.21

Because of the cross, Christian ethics are marked by:

    a)   Punishment
    b)   Being fair
    c)   Hope
    d)   Rules

The Hidden Things Belong to God

In his book *Moral Choices: An Introduction to Ethics*, author Scott B. Rae offers seven practical steps to making moral decisions.[18] The last step in Rae's decision-making matrix is important but often overlooked: *make a decision.*

You cannot deliberate (i.e., think about options) forever; at some point you have to decide. It is foolish to make decisions too quickly (without thinking), but it is also foolish to equate wisdom with indecision. Living life means making decisions.

This sentiment—that life is to be lived with intent and deliberation—is reflected in Henry Thoreau's famous book *Walden; or, Life in the Woods* in a section titled "Where I Lived, and What I Lived For." Here Thoreau writes: "I went to the woods because I wished to live deliberately, to front only the essential facts of life, and see if I could not learn what it had to teach, and not, when I came to die, discover that I had not lived."[19]

Rae's point echoes Thoreau: one cannot be paralyzed in endless deliberation. The paralysis of overanalysis must give way to the movement of decision and of action. The book of Proverbs calls the person who makes decisions hastily or without understanding a fool (18:13; 19:2). On the other hand, Prov 14:23 also warns that "endless talk leads only to poverty." The talk and deliberation of moral contemplation must lead to action.

Some issues are black and white, given the criteria above. Racism, for instance, is clearly wrong. Personal prejudice and unjust laws are clearly immoral. Other issues, however, are more complex and less clear. Neither black or white, moral decisions can sometimes be gray.

For instance, end-of-life decisions are complex. Even if a person has clear end-of-life directives, loved ones often have to interpret those decisions. A person who does not want to be kept on life support may say something like, "I do not wish to be kept on artificial life support unless it is temporarily." Well, how do you define *temporarily*? Honoring someone's end-of-life wishes is an example of how moral choices are often fraught with complexity. In such cases, all possible choices have corresponding pros and cons and the potential for regret. And yet, decisions have to be made.

Making complex moral choices requires a sense of God's sovereignty. Moses wrote, "The hidden things belong to the LORD our God, but the revealed things belong to us and our children forever, so that we may follow all the words of this law" (Deut 29:29).

---

[18] See Scott B. Rae, *Making Moral Choices: An Introduction to Ethics* (Grand Rapids: Zondervan, 2009), 111.

[19] Henry David Thoreau, *Walden; or Life in the Woods* (Boston: Ticknor and Fields, 1854), 143.

Consider variables, unknown outcomes, competing interests, conflicting facts, and contradictory advice as hidden things. Those things belong to the Lord. We do not know many things, but we know what his Word says. Moral decisions in gray areas often require disciplined focus on what is revealed and the ability to trust in God's sovereignty with what is unknown.

God's sovereignty and love will guide you through decisions in the gray areas of life. Consider Paul's words to Christians navigating the messiness of life:

> What, then, are we to say about these things? If God is for us, who is against us? He did not even spare his own Son but gave him up for us all. How will he not also with him grant us everything? Who can bring an accusation against God's elect? God is the one who justifies. Who is the one who condemns? Christ Jesus is the one who died, but even more, has been raised; he also is at the right hand of God and intercedes for us. Who can separate us from the love of Christ? Can affliction or distress or persecution or famine or nakedness or danger or sword? . . . No, in all these things we are more than conquerors through him who loved us. For I am persuaded that neither death nor life, nor angels nor rulers, nor things present nor things to come, nor powers, nor height nor depth, nor any other created thing will be able to separate us from the love of God that is in Christ Jesus our Lord. (Rom 8:31–35, 37–39)

When difficult moral choices need to be made, Christians are comforted knowing that God is in control and that God is on their side (i.e., for them) in Christ. This allows believers to act with boldness and courage and then to trust boldly and courageously in the inseparable and eternal love of God.

Question 7.22

The last step of a moral decision is _____ _____ _____.

Chapter Review

Question 7.23

For each of the following scenarios, imagine a process of thoughts or actions that you would take to resolve the moral dilemma. Incorporate the themes from this chapter, especially the five steps for practical decisions.

a) You and your friend find a purse in a train station behind a bench. There is no one else in the train station. The purse has $700 in cash, as well as several personal items. The only clue to the person's identity is a sheet of paper with a phone number and address, although it is unclear whether this refers to the purse's owner or someone else. The condition of the purse suggests that it has been sitting behind the bench for a long time, perhaps even weeks. Your friend suggests you take the money and leave the rest, since whoever owns the purse likely would have come back for it at this point. What do you do with the purse?

b) You and your sisters are out Christmas shopping. You make a small purchase at a hobby shop, before you all walk down the street to a department store. You find the perfect gift for your parents, and each check your wallets/purses to see if you have enough to pay for it. You do, but there's one problem . . . you realize that the clerk from the hobby store mistakenly gave you a hundred-dollar bill in change instead of a ten! Your older sister advises you to keep the money as a "gift," while your younger sister says she is worried that the clerk may lose her job. What do you do?

c) You accidentally cut off a driver while merging onto the highway. He honks his horns multiple times and offers a rude gesture while passing you. A few minutes later you enter a fast-food restaurant . . . only to notice the same gentleman ahead of you in line. When he completes his order, he abashedly notices that his wallet is in his car. How do you respond? In this response, do you ever reveal your identity to this man?

Question 7.24

Discuss how faith, hope, and love provide the foundation for a Christian vision of virtue and ethics.

8

Let's Get Political

Politics is one of those topics people tend to avoid. No one likes to be around a bunch of people arguing about what they read on Facebook or Twitter, what they heard on NPR, or what they watched on CNN, MSNBC, or Fox News. Just the word *politics* is enough to give some people a headache.

Mostly what people hate is partisan politics. The word *partisan* refers to someone who belongs to a particular political party or adheres (passionately) to a particular political faction. Partisan politics is about political parties, red versus blue, donkeys and elephants. Most people's impression (and experience) of partisan politics can rightly be described as inflexible, dogmatic, dismissive, and condescending.

This chapter is not so much about partisan politics as it is about politics in general. Of course, in most countries, being involved in politics requires partisanship (or membership and activism in a particular political party). Many people naturally feel an affinity for one party over another. The goal is not to disparage partisanship, but rather to give you a larger perspective on politics and to make you aware that philosophy and politics go together. Far too often, people select a party or vote for an issue without having a political philosophy—a careful, reflective view of what the purpose and limits of the state should be. In this chapter, we provide tools for starting to develop such a philosophy.

The word *politics* comes from the Greek word *polis*, meaning city or state. Plato was one of the first to write about politics in his book *Republic*. As mentioned in earlier chapters, Plato's *Republic* deals primarily with the question of justice. What is justice, and what is a just society?

Plato's *Republic* centers on the city, or what we might call society. What is good for society? What is a *good* society as opposed to a *bad* society? What kinds of laws are good for society? Who should guard a society, and who should rule a society?

The word *city* brings to mind the word *citizenship*, another theme of *Republic*. What does it mean to be a good citizen? What are the responsibilities of a society to its citizens, and what are the responsibilities of citizens to their society?

These fundamental questions transcend political parties, but they also relate to current political issues such as immigration and Second Amendment rights. While our society does not have masters and slaves like Greek society in Plato's day, the issues he raised pertain to modern debates ranging from equality and social justice to health care and gerrymandering (i.e., the practice of drawing electoral boundaries to favor one political party).

Political philosophy seeks to understand these concepts and answer these questions in a way that transcends (i.e., goes beyond) any particular country or political party. The idea in political philosophy is to establish principles or values that would apply in any society. In a sense, political philosophy aims to establish a rational, true depiction of an ideal society. Partisan politics then seek to translate those ideals into strategies and policies that implement those ideas. People from different political parties often agree on the ideal (safety, prosperity, freedom, etc.) but disagree on the best policies to practically achieve those ideals.

Common words like *democracy* and *tyranny* come to us from over 2,500 years ago when Greek thinkers like Herodotus explored the relationship between freedom, justice, and rule. During Herodotus's lifetime and for hundreds of years, Greek city-states practiced limited self-government.[1] Countries around the world today aspire to achieve the ideal of democracy that was born and practiced, however imperfectly, in ancient Greece. Unlike in other parts of the world, Greek city-states were ruled by citizens. Greek citizens were not slaves of the king but had rights and could effect change. For all its shortcomings and failures, democracy offered the hope of

---

[1] See Alan Ryan, *On Politics: A History of Political Thought from Herodotus to the Present* (New York: Liveright, 2012), 5.

change without violence. As Malcolm X once said, "It'll be ballots, or it'll be bullets."[2] Herodotus, Plato, and Malcolm X are all asking the same question: In what kind of society do you want to live? Or more accurately, in what kind of society should you want to live?

Question 8.1

The word *partisan* refers to:
- a) A person whose politics are governed by news sources
- b) Politics that come from Plato's *Republic*
- c) Politics that are based on free votes
- d) A person who adheres to a specific political party

Question 8.2

How is Plato's *Republic*, written thousands of years ago, still relevant to contemporary politics?

_____

_____

Why Do We Need Government?

In the book *Lord of the Flies*, author William Golding writes about a fictitious group of boys stranded on a desert island. Initially, they maintain moral order. Over time, however, this tentative order breaks down and the group devolves into tyranny, as one group of boys rules (brutally) over all the others by force. In the words of Alexander Hamilton: "If men were angels, no government would be necessary."[3]

Government exists for several reasons, one of which is to protect citizens. In a perfect world, people would not steal from each other. In a world where there is evil (such as theft), governments are needed to ensure the well-being of citizens. Thomas Hobbes argued in his book *Leviathan* that governments exist because people want to survive. In a state of nature (i.e., individuals on their

---

[2] From *Malcolm X Speaks*, ed. George Breitman (New York: Grove Press, 1965) quoted in Manuel Velasquez, *Philosophy: A Text with Reading*, 7th ed. (Belmont, CA: Wadsworth, 1999), 662.

[3] Alexander Hamilton, Federalist Paper No. 51, 1788, https://guides.loc.gov/federalist-papers/text -51-60.

own without any government for protection), according to Hobbes, "life of man is solitary, nasty, brutish, and short."[4]

Hobbes and Hamilton seem to echo the apostle Paul, who said the following about the purpose of government:

> Let everyone submit to the governing authorities, since there is no authority except from God, and the authorities that exist are instituted by God. So then, the one who resists the authority is opposing God's command, and those who oppose it will bring judgment on themselves. For rulers are not a terror to good conduct, but to bad. Do you want to be unafraid of the one in authority? Do what is good, and you will have its approval. For it is God's servant for your good. But if you do wrong, be afraid, because it does not carry the sword for no reason. For it is God's servant, an avenger that brings wrath on the one who does wrong. Therefore, you must submit, not only because of wrath but also because of your conscience. And for this reason you pay taxes, since the authorities are God's servants, continually attending to these tasks. Pay your obligations to everyone: taxes to those you owe taxes, tolls to those you owe tolls, respect to those you owe respect, and honor to those you owe honor. (Rom 13:1–7)

This passage makes it clear that governments are instituted by God. This does not mean that all governments are good or that God approves of everything done by governments. It means that God established governments for a good purpose. Governing authorities are to do good (i.e., "God's servant for your good"). One way that the governments do good is by bringing punishment on the "one who does wrong." The government bears a sword (v. 4), which implies that governments possess the power to protect, defend, enforce, and punish.

Does this mean that citizens always must obey? This question is often debated in political philosophy. Irish philosopher George Berkeley argued in his book *Passive Obedience* that citizens should always obey or willingly accept the punishment for refusing to comply with an unjust law, but never rebel or engage in revolution against governing authorities. According to Berkeley, resisting the government is the same as resisting God.

There are at least two ways one can argue against Berkeley. First, Berkeley talks about the "Supreme Authority," but is not clear who exactly is the "Supreme Authority" in government. For instance, in America, one could argue that the Supreme Court is the highest authority to which a person must give ultimate allegiance. Others may argue that the supreme authority

---

[4] Thomas Hobbes, *Leviathan* (1651), https://www.gutenberg.org/files/3207/3207-h/3207-h.htm.

in America is the Constitution. Since Berkeley is not clear, it is difficult to put his principles into practice.

Second, Berkeley's argument does not make sense of passages in Scripture where Christians disobey the "Supreme Authority" (i.e., government). For instance, in the Old Testament Daniel is thrown into the lions' den for his refusal to obey a government decree against praying to anyone except the human king, Darius (Dan 6:1–22). Other examples of what we might call righteous disobedience are found in Acts 5 where the apostles refuse to obey a government directive against preaching about Jesus:

> After they brought them in, they had them stand before the Sanhedrin, and the high priest asked, "Didn't we strictly order you not to teach in this name? Look, you have filled Jerusalem with your teaching and are determined to make us guilty of this man's blood." Peter and the apostles replied, "We must obey God rather than people. The God of our ancestors raised up Jesus, whom you had murdered by hanging him on a tree. God exalted this man to his right hand as ruler and Savior, to give repentance to Israel and forgiveness of sins. We are witnesses of these things, and so is the Holy Spirit whom God has given to those who obey him." (vv. 27–32)

In the case of Daniel and the apostles, obedience to God is the highest obligation. Whenever a person faces a choice between obeying God or some human rule that contradicts God's clear commands in Scripture, a person is justified in disobeying a government or human ruler in order to obey God. Civil disobedience should never be undertaken lightly or invoked for mere personal disagreement with government, but instead should always be a last resort when clear biblical commands are at stake.

While Berkeley believed in near-absolute obedience to government, others have disagreed. Jean-Jacques Rousseau was a French philosopher whose ideas influenced the Declaration of Independence and the American Revolution. Rousseau believed in the consent of the governed; that there exists a social contract between those governed and those governing.

In *Of the Social Contract*, Rousseau argued that an oppressive and unjust government essentially violates the social contract with its citizens, who are therefore free to form a new government.[5] For example, the American Revolution was just because King George III had violated

---

[5] See Jean-Jacques Roussseau, *Of the Social Contract*, ed. Jonathan Bennet (2017), https://www.earlymoderntexts.com/assets/pdfs/rousseau1762.pdf, 45.

the social contract with excessive and burdensome taxation, leaving the colonists free to form a new government.

Scottish philosopher David Hume argued against the social contract theory. Hume's empiricism led him to reject social contract theory because it is an abstract theory and not something observable. Hume argued that in most places, one observes governments that are based upon conquest, not contract: "Almost all the governments, which exist at present, or of which there remains any record in history, have been founded originally either on usurpation or conquest or both, without any pretense of a fair consent or voluntary subjection of the people."[6]

Is Hume right? Can you reject social contract theory by observing that consent of the governed is rare and therefore does not truly exist? If Hume were alive today, he could not make that argument. He would see that democracy, whether full or flawed, is either a reality, an aspiration, or a pretense for the majority of governments.[7]

Another response to Hume about social contract is that just because something is rare does not mean it does not exist. The ideas of social contract, that citizens should be self-governed and that government power is not absolute, may be true whether or not these ideas are being put into practice.

In rejecting social contract in favor of strength to rule, Hume is echoing Plato and anticipating Friedrich Nietzsche. In Book One of Plato's *Republic*, a character called Thrasymachus says, "Justice is nothing else than the interest of the stronger." This idea that "might makes right" is picked up by Nietzsche. What is known of Nietzsche's political philosophy from writings such as *The Antichrist* and *Ecco Homo* can be summarized as follows: the few who are strong should rule the many who are weak. Plato, Hume, and Nietzsche believed that social contract is fiction and that societies should be ruled by some form of aristocracy.

Whether governments are legitimate because of the consent of the governed (i.e., social contract theory), because rulers are strong and able to maintain their rule (i.e., might makes right), or because God ordains the ruler and the people submit to the ruler as a form of submission to God (i.e., divine right of kings), most people believe that we need government and it is better to focus our energy on improving government rather than abolishing it.

There are some who believe in the dissolution of government. Anarchists believe that governments are oppressive and should be dissolved through violence, if necessary. They take the

---

[6] David Hume, "Of the Original Contract," in *Essays and Treatises on Several Subjects*, vol. 1 (Oxford: Oxford University, 1822), 437–38.

[7] See Drew Desilver, "Despite Global Concerns about Democracy, More Than Half of Countries Are Democratic," Pew Research Center, May 14, 2019, https://www.pewresearch.org/fact-tank/2019/05/14/more-than-half-of-countries-are-democratic/.

writing of Rousseau and see man in a state of nature as equal, and governments as the source of inequality.

Do they have a point? One can make a strong argument that in human history, governments have been responsible for more death than any other single cause. In the twentieth century alone, more than 169 million people were killed by the Soviet, Chinese, North Korean, Nazi, Cambodia, and other murderous regimes.[8] Lord Acton wrote in his letter to Bishop Creighton: "Power tends to corrupt; absolute power corrupts absolutely."[9] Or, as R. J. Rummel summarizes it in his book *Death by Government*: "Power tends to kill, and absolute power kills absolutely."[10]

One of the strongest proponents against anarchism in the twentieth century was British author and journalist G. K. Chesterton. In his book *The Man Who Was Thursday: A Nightmare*, he argues that anarchy betrays the interests of the poor:

> You've got that eternal idiotic idea that if anarchy came it would come from the poor. Why should it? The poor have been rebels, but they have never been anarchists; they have more interest than anyone else in there being some decent government. The poor man really has a stake in the country. The rich man hasn't; he can go away to New Guinea in a yacht. The poor have sometimes objected to being governed badly; the rich have always objected to being governed at all. Aristocrats were always anarchists.[11]

Chesterton, a committed Christian, is essentially saying that if you love the poor and the downtrodden, you will be committed to improving government because the poor are more likely to thrive under good government policy than in the absence of government. This echoes the words of the apostle Paul in Romans 13: "It [the government] is God's servant for your good" (v. 4).

In fact, democratic ideals are based upon a certain understanding of authority. What kind of understanding of authority sustains democracy and compels its improvement and advance? We will now turn our attention to the question of authority as a foundation of democracy. Before we do, however, it may be helpful to learn a simple distinction between authority and power. Authority is a normative notion according to which something with (genuine) authority has the right to

---

[8] See R. J. Rummel, *Death by Government* (London: Routledge, 1994).

[9] Rummel, 1.

[10] Rummel, 1.

[11] G. K. Chesterton, *The Man Who Was Thursday: A Nightmare*, https://www.gutenberg.org/files/1695/1695-h/1695-h.htm, chap. 11, "The Criminals Chase the Police."

command compliance. Power is a descriptive notion according to which something with power has the ability to force compliance. Something can have authority and not power, and conversely.

Question 8.3

True or false: Because God establishes all governments, they are all inherently good.

Question 8.4

George Berkeley argued that any resistance to the state is resistance to God. How would you argue against this position?

_____

_____

Question 8.5

Matching:

A. Friedrich Nietzsche

B. David Hume

C. Jean-Jacques Rousseau

D. George Berkeley

____ There exists a social contract between those governed and the governor(s).

____ The few who are strong should rule the weak.

____ Governments are based not on contract but on conquest.

____ Christians should never rebel against governing authorities.

Question 8.6

What is the appeal of anarchism? What are its flaws?

_____

_____

Question 8.7

Distinguish between *authority* and *power*.

_____

_____

One Nation under God: The Question of Authority in Political Philosophy

The Declaration of Independence begins with words chosen carefully by the authors: "We hold these truths to be self-evident, that all men are created equal, that they are endowed by their Creator with certain unalienable Rights, that among these are Life, Liberty and the pursuit of Happiness."

Implicit in this statement is the social contract theory of government: the job of government is to respect the equality of citizens (i.e., rule of law) and to promote and protect the rights of citizens (i.e., life, liberty, and the pursuit of happiness). Notice, however, the source of the equality and rights of citizens: "endowed by their Creator."

The Declaration of Independence sparked a revolution in two senses. First, it began a literal revolution fought between the colonists who wanted political independence from Great Britain. This revolution concluded on September 3, 1783, when the combatants (America and Great Britain) signed the Treaty of Paris, which ended what we now call the Revolutionary War. Those who claim that ideas do not matter need to reflect on this fact.

Second, the words of the Declaration of Independence began a social revolution that spread around the world and continues to be realized to this day in America. The social revolution is fought in courts and with legislation, such as the Civil Rights Act of 1964, which prohibited discrimination on the basis of race, color, religion, sex, or national origin. Unlike the war fought between the American colonists and Great Britain, the social revolution for life, liberty, and happiness continues to take shape and be a source of vigorous debate within the realm of partisan politics.

What must not be lost is the source of authority explicit in the Declaration of Independence. God, the Creator, is the ultimate authority over government. The colonists appealed to God in their decision to declare independence from King George. Appealing to God only makes sense if God is over King George and every other human leader.

This echoes many verses in Scripture, such as Rev 1:4–5: "John: To the seven churches in Asia. Grace and peace to you from the one who is, who was, and who is to come, and from the seven spirits before his throne, and from Jesus Christ, the faithful witness, the firstborn from the dead and the ruler of the kings of the earth."

This observation does not imply that the proper form of government is a theocracy. Most Christians would agree that we should seek a just, good government and not a theocracy. But how does one do that while retaining the belief that God is the ultimate authority over government? The answer to this question is important. God has revealed the nature of his moral and political authority in Scripture and in the Natural Moral Law available to everyone independently of the Bible. Christians who reject the idea that we should establish a theocracy hold that the state answers to God's authority (whether they know it or not, e.g., atheists) as revealed in the Natural Moral Law and not as revealed in Scripture, though the two will be consistent, having come from God.

Why does it matter if there is an authority *over* the kings, rulers, and government of the earth? First, human rights are recognized by governments but do not come from governments. Governments have no authority to take away or redefine the things God has established and defined. Certain things go back to creation, as recognized by the writers of the Declaration of Independence, and are the foundation of government: things such as marriage, family, gender, work (i.e., free markets and private property), and sexuality. These things are unalienable (i.e., they cannot be taken away or redefined by government).

Second, if God rules over the kings and governments of the earth, then human authorities are not absolute. Human rule is only legitimate *if it aligns with the legitimate purposes of government* (i.e., to be a servant for good). A human ruler can claim to have absolute authority. Human rule is always under divine rule and human laws are always subject to divine laws.

The murderous regimes of history, from Tito in Yugoslavia to Stalin in the former Soviet Union, featured rulers who pretended as if their rule was absolute. Such governments are often called authoritarian, totalitarian, or tyrannical. These words have slight nuance but in each case there is a disregard or complete denial of God's authority over human rulers and of God as the Creator and source of irrevocable human rights.

Authoritarian governments demand obedience and limit or deny individual freedom. They have power but not genuine authority. For instance, an authoritarian ruler might illegalize criticizing the leader or critiquing government policies. Authoritarian leaders see loyalty as the highest virtue. In authoritarian countries, freedom of speech, freedom of press, and freedom of religion are almost always limited or restricted. In such societies, the government is *the* authority.

Totalitarian governments are even more controlling (i.e., total control). In such countries, every aspect of life falls under the control of the government. In North Korea, for instance, the government rules over every aspect of life. The "Supreme Leader" controls where you can live, what kind of haircut you can get, where you can travel, how (and who) you can worship, and what you can say. There is no individual freedom in a totalitarian state.

Both authoritarian and totalitarian governments are tyrannical in nature. The word *tyranny* comes from the Latin root word *tyrannus*, referring to someone with absolute rule. A tyrannical government or ruler sees itself as the final and ultimate authority with little or no room for individual freedom, minority rights, or God. Such rulers have one set of rules for the people and another for the rulers. In other words, there is no rule of law.

Tyrannical governments lack checks and balances. Checks and balances are ways that a government ensures that no one person, party, or institution has absolute power. For instance, in America, the Constitution is the governing document, interpreted by the courts, which in theory guarantees God-given rights the government cannot take away.

If Congress passes a bill that is then signed into law by the president, a lawsuit can be filed and ultimately the Supreme Court can rule that the law is unconstitutional, thus nullifying the law. State laws can also be found unconstitutional and nullified. For instance, in 2012, the Supreme Court struck down state laws in Alabama and Arkansas in *Miller v. Alabama* requiring mandatory life imprisonment without the possibility of parole for juvenile offenders convicted of homicide.[12]

The idea of checks and balances reflects a belief in the doctrine of human depravity. Humans were created good and in God's image, but sin has entered the world and humans are corrupt (Genesis 3; Mark 10:18; Rom 3:9–20; Eph 2:1–10). While humans still bear God's image and are not as bad as possible because of God's restraining grace, societies need checks and balances to ensure that human sinfulness and the human tendency toward corruption are curtailed.

Question 8.8

The Declaration of Independence assumes a _____ _____ theory of government.

---

[12] See *Miller v. Alabama*, 567 U.S. _, No. 10–9646, slip op. (2012), https://law.justia.com/constitution/us/state-laws-held-unconstitutional.html.

Question 8.9

How is God's complete authority compatible with man's authority?

_____

_____

Question 8.10

Identify as authoritarian, totalitarian, or tyrannical (some may apply to more than one):

	Authoritarian	Totalitarian	Tyrannical
Absolute power invested in the government			
Tyrannical in nature			
Absolute power invested in one person			
Lacks any checks and balances in government			
Allow some, albeit little, freedom for individuals			

Question 8.11

Checks and balances assume the Christian doctrine of _____ _____.

Who Should Rule: The One, the Few, or the Many?

Once you accept the legitimacy of government as an agent for good and the need for checks and balances to protect against the corruption of absolute power that Lord Acton warned against, you must now decide what form of government is best. In other words, who should rule: the one, the few, or the many?

Earlier in the book we discussed Plato's taxonomy of the soul. You can imagine a human body with a brain, a heart, and a stomach. Like the body, Plato divided the soul into three parts, each with a corresponding virtue. The virtue of the brain is reason. The virtue of the heart is spirit or courage. The virtue of the stomach or appetite is self-control.

Like the body and the soul, society divides into three parts. Like the mind guides the body, so too society should be guided by a small group of people who possess intellect, reason, and wisdom. These are the philosopher kings.

Under the philosopher kings is a larger group of soldiers to enforce the rules of the philosopher kings. A soldier needs courage and must be spirited. The heart of society is, therefore, the soldier class, according to Plato.

Finally, the largest group in society is the working class. In *Republic*, Plato argued that the masses should possess self-control. Plato thought the rulers may need to tell the people a "noble lie" in order to keep them in check: "How then may we devise one of those needful falsehoods of which we lately spoke—just one noble lie which may deceive the rulers, if that be possible, and at any rate the rest of the city?"[13]

Plato assigns metals to indicate what he considered the purity and value of each level of society. The rulers or guardians are gold. The soldier class is silver. Finally, the worker class (i.e., the masses) is bronze. In essence, Plato is saying you do not want the masses to rule themselves because they lack wisdom and should be kept in check with stories designed to keep them from rising up and demanding power. For Plato, the most dangerous thing is mob rule.

Socrates and Plato opposed democracy because they did not trust the masses to make wise decisions based upon reason. In fact, as described by Plato in the dialogue *Apology*, Socrates is forced to commit suicide by drinking poison because he goes against Athenian democracy in favor of what we would call aristocracy (i.e., the rule of the few).

In book 6 of *Republic*, Plato warned against what he considered to be the danger of democracy (i.e., the rule of the many). There were teachers in the days of Socrates and Plato called *Sophists* who were paid money to make whatever argument the people wanted to hear. They did not care about truth, but only about hearing what they liked to hear. They were the ancient equivalent of those today who watch their favorite cable news channel so they hear endless agreement with their own views and are never challenged to question their political positions.

---

[13] Plato, *The Republic*, trans. Benjamin Jowett (n.p.: Wildside Press, 2018) 271, ebook, https://www.google.com/books/edition/The_Republic_The_Republic_of_Plato/MLFhDwAAQBAJ?hl=en&gbpv=0.

Plato uses a metaphor in which the masses are like a wild beast. Imagine having something wild as a pet, like a wolf or a bear. You may teach the animal some tricks, but it would never be truly tamed; it would always be wild, unpredictable, and dangerous. Plato was warning that the masses are wild, unpredictable, and dangerous:

> I might compare them (the masses) to a man who should study the tempers and desires of a mighty strong beast who is fed by him—he would learn how to approach and handle him, also at what times and from what causes he is dangerous or the reverse, and what is the meaning of his several cries, and by what sounds, when another utters them, he is soothed or infuriated; and you may suppose further, that when, by continually attending upon him, he has become perfect in all this, he calls his knowledge wisdom, and makes of it a system or art, which he proceeds to teach, although he has no real notion of what he means by the principles or passions of which he is speaking, but calls this honorable and that dishonorable, or good or evil, or just or unjust, all in accordance with the tastes and tempers of the great brute. Good he pronounces to be that in which the beast delights and evil to be that which he dislikes; and he can give no other account of them except that the just and noble are the necessary, having never himself seen, and having no power of explaining to others the nature of either, or the difference between them, which is immense.[14]

Public opinion is untrustworthy. It changes and cannot (by itself) determine what is true. Just because everyone thinks that something is right does not make it right. Plato was exposing the lie of what we might call subjective truth or pragmatism—that truth is just what the masses believe or what works for the most people (i.e., utility). Socrates literally died for his beliefs that went against public opinion.

Most of us believe that democracy (in some form) is a better form of government than any viable alternative. However, it is worth considering Plato's warnings to understand the downside of the rule of the many. When the masses rule (as in direct democracy), the rights of individuals and minorities tend to be trampled underfoot. The danger of the rule of the many is mob rule.

What about aristocracy (the rule of the few), which was the preferred method of government for Socrates, Plato, and Aristotle? The danger of Aristocracy was pointed out by French philosopher and economist Alexis de Tocqueville in his book *Democracy in America*. Tocqueville warned

---

[14] Plato, *Republic*, Book Six, https://www.gutenberg.org/files/1497/1497-h/1497-h.htm#link2H_4 _0009.

that democracy in America will devolve through industry into a rule of the rich. Eventually, he feared, a small number of wealthy persons will essentially control American politics.

The fear of aristocracy is that the people (i.e., the masses) would end up with a government that did not understand their struggles, did not look out for their interests, did not handle money in a way that was responsible, or used power in self-interested ways rather than in ways that promoted the public good. Do these concerns resonate with you? Are these the kinds of complaints that people have about government today? Do you think de Tocqueville was right?

Aristocracy may provide a stability that democracy lacks, but it often lacks responsiveness and accountability to the people paying the taxes. In the same way that the colonists threw over a million dollars of tea (in modern value) into Boston Harbor in protest to King George's oppressive taxes, the aristocracy often enrich themselves by policies that impoverish citizens.

Lastly, there is the rule of the one. In most cases, this is a monarchy. A king or queen rules by claiming that God established their rule (i.e., the divine right of kings). A monarchy can be a good form of government if the monarch is good. However, if the monarch is bad, then it is probably a miserable experience for those living under their rule.

In the Old Testament, we see this dynamic in the books of 1 and 2 Kings. One good king is followed by a bad king. There is blessing and then curse, as the people (usually following the example of the king) fail to live consistently in step with God's commands. The point of those books is to show that God's people need a faithful King who will always be in step with God's commands and whose eternal reign will correspond to eternal life and eternal blessing. Jesus is the long-awaited King who now reigns in heaven and will one day reign on a new earth, where everything wrong has been made right.

The danger of monarchy, given the inevitable inconsistency of even the best king or queen and the sinfulness of all human rulers, is dictatorship. Single rulers tend to forget that they are responsible for the good of the people, that God is the absolute ruler, that the purpose of power is to be God's servant for good.

Which, then, is the best form of government: the rule of the one, the rule of the few, or the rule of the many? To answer that question, consider the American experiment. While not perfect (as no human institution is perfect), America is an historic experiment in combining the strengths of these three forms of rule and minimizing each of their weaknesses. In America, the one, the few, and many rule together under "we the people."

Consider for a moment that America has one president. According to the United States Constitution, the president of the United States shall be the commander in chief. There is only one leader of the executive branch, one person who can sign or veto bills, one person who can convene or adjourn Congress, one person who can reprieve and pardon. These powers belong to the president alone.[15] The president represents the rule of the one.

The US Senate represents the rule of the few. Two senators are elected from each of the fifty states for an unlimited number of six-year terms. Longer than the terms of either the president or members of the House of Representatives, senators have the luxury of time. They move more slowly and deliberately than the House. The Senate tends to be more bipartisan and collegial than the House. It has historically been the closest thing America has to a formal aristocracy.

Lastly, there is the House of Representatives. While there are only 100 senators, there are 435 members of Congress. Due to the number of congressional legislators and the short two-year terms they serve, the Congress tends to be more fast-paced, dynamic, unpredictable, and volatile. While each state gets two senators, the number of congressmen allocated is based on a state's population. Congress represents the rule of the many.

Keeping all three in check is the Supreme Court, which enforces the governing document of "We the People," the United States Constitution. Article 3, section 2 of the Constitution says, "The judicial Power of the United States, shall be vested in one supreme Court, and in such inferior Courts as the Congress may from time to time ordain and establish." The Supreme Court ensures the constitutionality of laws, the rights of citizens, and the rule of law. While in other nations the ruler gets to do whatever they want (i.e., rex is lex, or the king is the law), in America, the law is the rule (i.e., lex is rex, or law is king).

For all its flaws, America is a brilliant experiment. The founders took into account the concerns of ancient philosophers, the warnings of Thomas Hobbes about man in a state of nature, the Bible's teaching about the role of government under God, and pieced together a compromise to celebrate the inherent nobility (i.e., made in the image of God) and corruption (i.e., sinfulness) of humanity.

Question 8.12

Draw a diagram of Plato's outline of man, and draw a parallel diagram of Plato's outline of government.

_____

_____

[15] See "Keeping the Balance: What a President Can and Can't Do," Truman Library, accessed July 7, 2022, https://www.trumanlibrary.gov/education/three-branches/what-president-can-do-cannot-do.

Question 8.13

On what basis does Plato reject democracy?

_____

_____

Question 8.14

Complete the following chart:

	Description	Strengths	Weaknesses
Democracy			
Monarchy			
Aristocracy			

How to Develop a Biblically Based View of Government

The previous section has put us in position to raise a couple of questions: (1) How does one develop a biblical view of government? (2) What is a biblical view of government? Unfortunately, Christians of goodwill do not agree on the answers to these questions. That said, we shall develop brief answers to them that we think are worth considering.

Let's begin with question number one. According to the approach we are presenting, it is risky to develop a view of what a non-theocratic government ought to be by focusing on the government of biblical Israel. Why? Clearly, Israel was a theocracy and it is more closely analogous with the current people of God—the church—than with the government. Of course, universal moral principles (e.g., Do not murder) given to Israel apply to all governments, but many Old Testament commands were specifically directed at the unique theocracy of Israel (e.g., tithe laws).

The best way to proceed is to derive a biblical view of government from two types of texts—Old Testament passages where Israel's prophets and wisdom literature are directed toward the responsibilities of pagan rulers (e.g., Amos 1 and 2), and four New Testament texts that speak about the general purpose of governments outside Israel (Matt 22:21; Rom 13:1–7; 1 Tim 2:1–2; and 1 Pet 2:13–14).

Further, an important distinction between positive and negative rights will help us understand these passages more accurately. A positive right is a right to have something given to the right holder. If Smith has a positive right to X, say to health care, then, limiting our focus on the government's duties regarding rights, the government has an obligation to give X to Smith. In general, if someone has a positive right to something, then a duty is placed on others—in our case, the government—to provide that right to that person (or class of persons). Thus, the government has the moral right to impose on citizens the duty to provide that right to the right holder.

A negative right to X is a right to be protected from harm while one seeks to get X on one's own. It is a right not to be subjected to some action or state of affairs that would harm or unfairly discriminate against a citizen. If Smith has a negative right to X—again, within our limited focus—the government has an obligation to protect Smith from discrimination and unfair treatment in his attempt to get X on his own.

Space forbids us to examine the relevant texts, but when one does, a surprising and important understanding arises: the purpose of the government is to protect the negative rights of its citizens, and not to provide them with positive rights. Thus, according to the view under examination, a biblical view of government is a limited one. This is the answer to question number two. We invite you to look at the texts yourself and reflect on the rationality of this view of government and the implications that follow from it.

While this view is offered as the biblical view of government, one need not believe in God or the Bible to accept it. A Christian who holds this position does, indeed, derive it from Scripture. But, subsequently, that believer will look for arguments (e.g., from Natural Moral Law) that are independent of the Bible but which, nevertheless, support the biblically derived position.

Question 8.15

Israel's theocracy most resembles:
   a)   The church
   b)   The state

Question 8.16

Label each as upholding a *positive* or *negative* right:

	Positive Right	Negative Right
Each citizen has the duty to go to school until age eighteen.		
No citizen may trespass upon another's land.		
Each citizen has the right to an attorney if taken to court.		
No citizen may murder another citizen.		
The state will not interfere in any private religious practice.		

Question 8.17

A biblical view of government authorizes the state to enforce:
 a) Positive rights
 b) Negative rights
 c) Both
 d) Neither

What Is My Job? The Role of Citizens in Society

Everyone wants to live in a good society. Patriotism, in the best sense, is wanting what is good for the country in which you are a citizen. The Old Testament prophet Jeremiah spoke to God's people while they were living in captivity, saying, "Pursue the well-being of the city I have deported you to. Pray to the LORD on its behalf, for when it thrives, you will thrive" (Jer 29:7).

Christian patriotism is praying and working for the good of the country where God has you living. Babylon, the "city" where God had deported Israel, was not what we would call a free and virtuous society. There was no representative democracy, no Bill of Rights, no due process, and no religious freedom; yet God's people were commanded to work for the good of society.

This same principle is true today. Christians are called to live at peace with all men, as much as it is possible (Rom 12:18). Christians are permitted, like the apostle Paul, to assert their rights as citizens in the country of their citizenship (Acts 22:22–25). Christians are dual citizens, and their eternal citizenship is in heaven, and their ultimate allegiance is to Jesus as Lord (Phil 3:20).

While on earth, though, Christians are called to be good citizens. Each of us has a job to do, and that job goes all the way back to the garden of Eden. In the garden, God did not say, "Relax, enjoy yourself, and take it easy!" No, God told Adam and Eve to "work . . . and watch over" the garden (Gen 2:15). These words refer to working, caring for, and preserving the place where God has put you to live.

This same mandate applies to humans on earth today. Just as God continues to bless marriage, procreation, and work, he continues to bless those who cultivate and work to preserve and defend the places where God has put them to live. In a biblical sense, conservatism is working to God's glory to protect and defend what is good in God's eyes about the place and the ways of wherever God has established your earthly citizenship. Working to change what is wrong in God's eyes and to preserve what is good in God's eyes summarizes the job of every Christian in every society, since the dawn of time until Christ's return.

The Christian hope is not that by our effort we will turn the fallen world back into the garden of Eden. The Christian hope is that God is glorified when we honor him by following his Word and that he will establish his kingdom. The Christian hope is that our labors for what is good are used by God as a testimony to the resurrection and reign of our Lord Jesus. The Christian hope is that one day Jesus will establish a new heaven and a new earth in which there will be an end to sin and death for all who believe.

Aristotle wrote in the *Nicomachean Ethics* that good politicians promote public virtue, and good citizens act virtuously. However, in order to be truly virtuous, citizens must deliberate and be free.[16] A person must consider the best course of actions and then freely choose the best course of action in order to be virtuous.

John Locke made a similar argument in his *Second Treatise on Government*. Locke argued that the first human (Adam) was guided by the laws of reason and freedom, and that these laws "govern all his posterity."[17] Locke saw the problems of society as stemming from how humans do

---

[16] See Aristotle, *Nicomachean Ethics*, Book Three, http://classics.mit.edu/Aristotle/nicomachaen.3.iii.html.

[17] John Locke, *Second Treatise on Government*, chap. 6, sec. 57, https://www.gutenberg.org/files/7370/7370-h/7370-h.htm.

not operate from reason and do not govern themselves (i.e., self-control). Government, then, is needed to act as parents who must increase the rules over the children because the children are out of control.

One reason why Christian citizens stand up for freedom is because they desire virtuous societies, and in order to have a virtuous society, citizens must be given freedom to act virtuously. In this sense, there is no inherent conflict between "love your neighbor" and the "don't tread on me" ethos of the American Revolution. Loving your neighbor often means standing up for the freedoms that will provide for public virtue and opposing infringements on freedom that will limit public virtue.

People in tyrannical and authoritarian societies can possess the virtues, but they are not free to act upon the virtues, and therefore the virtues are possessed privately but practiced publically. For instance, acts of charity (i.e., love) may be highly regulated in an authoritarian state. People in North Korea, for instance, cannot speak up for those wrongly imprisoned in government-run detention camps. The lack of freedom limits public virtue. Tyranny limits the ability to love your neighbor; therefore, opposing tyranny is a loving thing to do.

Question 8.18

God told Jeremiah to "pursue the well-being of the city I have deported you to." What are some ways in which you can pursue the well-being of the state (whether federal or local)?

_____

_____

Question 8.19

Explain biblical conservatism.

_____

_____

Question 8.20

Christians seek to live in free societies because such societies allow individual practice of _____.

Classical Liberalism

In modern discourse, the word *liberal* is known almost entirely as a partisan label. People who identify as liberal tend to hold progressive views on gender and sexuality and to believe in a larger role for government in society. However, the phrase *classical liberalism* is different than this partisan description. Classical liberalism has its roots in many ancient, medieval, and modern philosophers, but came to prominence in the seventeenth century.[18]

The essence of classical liberalism is the belief in individual liberty, or individual freedom. Classical liberals believe that the role of government is to promote freedom in order to achieve public virtue. Freedom of religion enables a person to come to their own religious convictions and to act freely upon those convictions. This focus on freedom applies to persons, their labor, and their property: "the natural right of individuals to use their bodies, freedom, labor, and justly acquired property as they see fit, so long as they respect the equal freedom of others."[19]

Classical liberals were some of the first to speak out against slavery and in favor of women's rights.[20] The alternative to liberalism is state socialism. State socialism is the view that the government should control economic markets, industry, wages, and services.

Austrian economist Friedrich von Hayek argued that socialism restricts individual freedom, increases political power and the competition for political power, and negatively affects the poor. In his classic book *The Road to Serfdom*, he wrote, "As soon as the state takes upon itself the task of planning the whole economic life, the problem of the due station of the different individuals and groups must indeed inevitably become the central political problem. As the coercive power of the state will alone decide who is to have what, the only power worth having will be a share in the exercise of this directing power."[21]

Hayek was warning against the tendency of governments to increase control of private affairs. Eventually, when the government controls everything, the only way to effect change is to fight for political power. The result is that political power, and political control, becomes absolute. As Lord Acton warned, *absolute power tends to corrupt absolutely*. Hayek and Acton warned against

---

[18] See George Smith, *The System of Liberty: Themes in the History of Classical Liberalism* (Cambridge University Press, 2013).

[19] Smith, 2.

[20] Smith, 7.

[21] F. A. Hayek, *The Collected Works of F. A. Hayek*, vol. 2, *The Road to Serfdom: Texts and Documents*, ed. Bruce Caldwell (Chicago: University of Chicago Press, 2007), 138.

socialism because it limits individual freedom, threatens the rights of minority groups, and inevitably leads to corrupt societies rather than virtuous societies.

Classical liberalism sees the individual as the most vulnerable minority; after all, there is only one of *you*. If individual negative rights are protected and individual liberty is preserved, then everyone is protected. Alternatively, ideology that focuses on minority groups causes groups to compete or form coalitions to try and effect political change. Group politics tends to assume that all individuals of a group think and act alike or have similar experiences or perspectives. Much like a person who goes to prison might join a gang for personal protection amidst the violence of prison, so too, individuals are forced to identify with groups to endure the coercion of group politics and to effectively compete for political power.[22]

Classical liberalism offers an alternative to group or identity politics by seeing citizens, and treating citizens, as individuals. Individuals are expected to live according to the expectations of American citizenship (pay taxes, observe laws, register for the draft, serve on a jury when summoned, etc.). More importantly, the tacit expectation of citizenship is virtue. Do you think that the expectation of virtue is lost in modern society? If so, what do you think has contributed to the loss of public virtue as an expectation of citizenship?

Question 8.21

Classical liberalism promotes _____ _____ as opposed to _____ _____ of private affairs.

The Role of Government in a Free and Virtuous Society

If citizens are expected to live virtuously and contribute to human flourishing by supporting freedom and liberty, what are the expectations of government in the social contract? Let's reconsider the text of the Declaration of Independence from July 4, 1776:

> We hold these truths to be self-evident, that all men are created equal, that they are endowed by their Creator with certain unalienable Rights, that among these are Life, Liberty and the pursuit of Happiness.—That to secure these rights, Governments are instituted among Men, deriving their just powers from the consent of the governed,— That

---

[22] See Shelby Steele, *The Content of Our Character: A New Vision of Race In America* (New York: Harper Perennial, 1990).

whenever any Form of Government becomes destructive of these ends, it is the Right of the People to alter or to abolish it, and to institute new Government, laying its foundation on such principles and organizing its powers in such form, as to them shall seem most likely to effect their Safety and Happiness.[23]

Notice the phrase "to secure these rights, Governments are instituted among Men . . ." The job of citizens is virtue, and the job of government is protecting the rights of individual citizens.

Right now, you are probably enrolled at a college or university. You chose the college or university that you attend, probably for a number of reasons. Moreover, you chose (or will choose) your major degree or course of study.

College is a time of pursuing the very things that government is contracted to protect: life, liberty, and happiness. Presumably, you are in college to pursue a certain life. You are practicing certain liberties and freedoms (school of choice, degree of choice, etc.) because you think you will be happy in the chosen vocation for which you are studying.

Of course, there is a long-standing debate in the United States about how government should protect life, liberty, and happiness. In many ways, the contemporary disagreements between Republicans and Democrats go back to arguments about the role of government between the Founding Fathers. In particular, Thomas Jefferson and Alexander Hamilton took different positions on the role of government.

Jefferson preferred a more decentralized government, with power vested in the states. Hamilton advocated for a stronger federal government. Jefferson opposed a federal bank, fearing the involvement and regulation of the economy by the federal government. Hamilton, on the other hand, established the first national bank.

The arguments between Jefferson and Hamilton were not new. Thomas Hobbes and John Locke had similar debates in the seventeenth century. Hobbes believed in an absolute monarchy while Locke believed in individual rights and democracy.

Regardless of where you stand, it is important to think through what you consider to be the role of citizens and of government in a society. Oftentimes, people engage in arguments about politics without first discussing what they believe to be the roles and responsibilities of citizens and of rulers. Settling these questions will provide a foundation upon which to have more productive conversation about current political issues.

---

[23] Declaration of Independence, https://www.archives.gov/founding-docs/declaration-transcript.

Question 8.22

According to the Declaration of Independence, what is the primary job of the people, and what is the primary job of the state?

_____

_____

Question 8.23

A Federalist approach to the US Constitution is (select one)
   a) more decentralized
   b) less decentralized

A Time for War

If the job of government is protecting freedom in order to promote virtue, when (if ever) is it acceptable for a government to kill? This question applies to things like the role of police use of lethal force, and also to warfare. While the question of the legitimacy of government to perform capital punishment for its citizens who have committed a capital offense is an important one, we set it aside and focus our attention on this query: When is it just for a government to kill the members or citizens of another society?

The issue of war is complex. Philosophers like to start with definitions, so it is important to define war. Must war require a formal declaration, or is prolonged military conflict without formal declaration also war? For instance, World War II was a formally declared war by Congress, while Vietnam was only a prolonged military conflict. *Webster's* defines *warfare* as "military operations between enemies" and a "struggle between competing entities."[24] The latter use of war is metaphorical, such as in the war against drugs or the war on poverty.

Once we have defined war, we can define a good or just war versus a bad or unjust war. When is war noble and when should virtuous people support war? When should virtuous citizens take up arms and be willing to kill members of another country or society?

---

[24] "Warfare" in Merriam-Webster online, https://www.merriam-webster.com/dictionary/warfare.

Probably the most common and acceptable answer is self-defense. Most people recognize the right of a person or society to defend itself against lethal force or against forced rule. In 2022, Ukraine was invaded by Russian forces under the oppressive rule of Vladimir Putin. The doctrine of self-defense and consent suggests that Ukrainians were justified in responding with lethal force against such an unprovoked and illegal military invasion.

In his book *Summa Theologica*, medieval philosopher Thomas Aquinas laid out the requirements for just war. Just war theory, based on his teaching, is commonly divided into two branches: *jus ad bellum* and *jus in bello*. The principles of *jus ad bellum* and *jus in bello* were recognized by the United Nations Charter in 1945 and are still in effect today in international law.[25]

Jus ad bellum has to do with the conditions under which a government can justly enter into military conflict, and *jus in bello* has to do with the rules that govern militaries while engaged in military conflict.

In order to justify war, *jus ad bellum* says that a war must be necessary. The first question citizens should ask is if war is *necessary*. In order for war to be just, a government must have exhausted other means of settling the conflict, such as diplomacy. In other words, war must always be a last resort.

The second question citizens should ask has to do with the objectives of war: What does the war hope to accomplish? Just war has good intentions and reasonable outcomes. Just war cannot be fought over petty disputes or vengeance, for instance. The principle behind this rule is that human life is sacred and blood should never be shed without a noble and probable outcome. The outcomes of a just war must be reasonable. If the intentions are not defensible, and if the outcomes are not realistic, then the war cannot be just.

The third concern of *jus ad bellum* has to do with the legitimacy of government. Are the appropriate powers initiating the military action? For instance, the mayor of San Diego and the mayor of Tijuana cannot legitimately initiate military conflict across the US-Mexico border. Neither of these mayors has the constitutional power to command military forces, so no military conflict initiated by these individuals could qualify as *just war*.

The question of governing legitimacy is what often causes a conflict to be classified as terrorism, rebellion, or insurrection rather than war. War requires a legitimately recognized governing authority. Russia, for instance, has had ongoing conflict with Muslim separatists in the region of Chechnya, located near the Caspian Sea. Since Chechnya is a part of the Russian Republic,

---

[25] See Keiichiro Okimoto, *The Distinction and Relationship Between Jus Ad Bellum and Jus in Bello* (Portland, OR: Hart, 2011), 2.

conflict with Chechnya is considered an insurgency rather than a war. Calling the conflict "war" implies the legitimacy of the Chechen government and its forces. Calling the conflict "insurgency" denies the legitimacy of the Chechen government and its forces.

Jus in bello describes the rules for just war for governments engaged in military conflict. Many of the historical rules for *jus in bello* are obsolete given the nature of modern warfare. For instance, in an age of drone warfare, requiring combatants to be clearly visible and identifiable by their clothing does not apply. However, to this day, military aircraft bear military insignia and soldiers wear uniforms to distinguish themselves from civilians, both of which are principles of *jus in bello*.

The two main principles of *jus in bello* can be summarized by the words *discrimination* and *proportionality*. For a war to be just, combatants must be able to discriminate combatants from noncombatants (civilians) and must not intentionally target noncombatants. A military is unjust and breaks international law if it targets noncombatants for non-military purposes or in order to induce fear in the civilian population. The Russian invasion of Ukraine in 2022 is an example of an unjust war. Some ethicists have argued, for instance, that when dropping atomic bombs over Hiroshima and Nagasaki the United States violated this principle of *jus in bello*.[26]

However, here one must distinguish between an intent and an unintended, tolerated, consequence of an act. According to many philosophers, if the intent of an act is good, and one does not achieve that intent by an immoral means, then the act is morally permissible even if one forsees but does not intend bad consequences. So the dropping of the atomic bombs, some argue, were justified by this insight. Still, there is another condition for appropriate action to which we now turn.

The principle of proportionality in *jus in bello* says that a just war may include only that force which is proportionate to the good that is likely to be achieved.[27] For instance, most historians agree that the bombing of the German city of Dresden during World War II violates the principle of proportion because while there may have been a military objective, the use of high-explosive and incendiary bombs caused the deaths of up to 25,000 civilians.

---

[26] See F. M. Hamm, "Failures of Just War Theory: Terror, Harm, and Justice," *Ethics* 114, no. 4 (2004), 650–92.

[27] See Hamm, 650–92.

The bombing of Dresden on February 13, 1945, came three months before the surrender of the German High Command. The question is whether or not 25,000 civilians needed to die to achieve the military objective of unconditional surrender. The military argument for the bombing of Dresden is that it helped Russian allies to the east by cutting off escape routes for military retreat. The military argument against the bombing of Dresden is that the Russian forces had already overwhelmed diminished German forces and liberated Warsaw, Krakow, and Budapest.

The question of war helps to make clear the role of philosophy observed by Will Durant in his book *The Story of Philosophy*.[28] Durant argues that the job of philosophy is to provide a synthesis of human knowledge and experience. He uses war as an example. Scientists can tell us how to make a bomb, but philosophers can tell us when to drop a bomb. Philosophy takes questions related to human life, justice, and government and synthesizes them to reach conclusions about when war is just, and how a just war should be conducted.

Question 8.24

Distinguish between *jus ad bellum* and *jus in bello*. Include the two principles of *jus in bello*.

---

[28] See Will Durant, *The Story of Philosophy* (New York: Pocket Books, 1926), 19–28.

Chapter Review

Question 8.25

Match the author with the correlating idea/quote:

A. Jeremiah

B. Plato

C. George Berkeley

D. Friedrich Nietzsche

E. G. K. Chesterton

F. Lord Acton

G. Malcolm X

H. David Hume

I. Alexander Hamilton

J. Aristotle

K. Thomas Hobbes

L. Jean-Jacques Rousseau

_____ "Life of man is solitary, nasty, brutish and short."

_____ "If men were angels, no government would be needed."

_____ "Aristocrats were always anarchists."

_____ A "noble lie" may need to be told in order for society to function well.

_____ "Pursue the well-being of the city I have deported you to. Pray to the Lord on its behalf, for when it thrives, you will thrive."

_____ Any resistance to the state is resistance to God.

_____ Good politicians promote public virtue, and good citizens act virtuously.

_____ Governments are based upon a social contract between the governors and the governed.

_____ The few who are strong should rule the many who are weak.

_____ "It'll be ballots, or it'll be bullets."

_____ "Power tends to corrupt; absolute power corrupts absolutely."

_____ Governments are based on conquest, not contract.

Question 8.26

In the previous chapter we discussed virtue ethics. In this chapter, we discovered that Christians seek to live in free societies because such societies allow the practice of virtue. In what ways do free societies allow the practice of virtue? In what ways can the virtue of individual citizens contribute to the well-being of the state?

_____

_____

Question 8.27

Offer your own analysis of the American system of government, considering the following questions (you may need to do some research of your own as well):

a) Does the American government give way for the ultimate authority of God?

b) How does the American government incorporate elements of democracy, aristocracy, and monarchy? Where does it draw upon the strengths of these systems, and where does it suffer from the weaknesses of these systems?

c) Is the American government a biblical system of government?

d) Are there ways in which America today has departed from the ideas put forth in the Declaration of Independence?

What Is a *Good* Movie?

Plato said that philosophy is the "noblest and best of music."[1] Most people do not think of philosophy as something that (like music) brings enjoyment and pleasure. In reality, philosophy should help a person to know the truth and enjoy its beauty, as Robert Browning wrote:

> This world's no blot for us
> Nor blank; it means intensely, and means good.
> To find its meaning is my meat and drink.[2]

Philosophy is concerned with understanding in order to increase enjoyment. The point that Browning is making is that truth and meaning, like food and drink, are connected in human experience to pleasure and joy.

The subject matter of this chapter is aesthetics. Aesthetics is the branch of philosophy that deals with beauty and art. The goal of this chapter is to increase your understanding of beauty and art in order to increase your enjoyment of beauty and art and ultimately your joy in the Lord.

---

[1] Plato, *Phaedo*, translated by Benjamin Jowett, http://classics.mit.edu/Plato/phaedo.html.
[2] Robert Browning, *My Last Duchess and Other Poems*, Dover Thrift Editions (Mineola, NY: Dover, 1993), 44.

Art takes many forms. Plato mentions music and Browning food, things about which we all have opinions. Is Justin Bieber a better singer than The Weeknd? Are McDonald's hamburgers better than the hamburgers at Burger King? When deciding what movie to watch, many people check the reviews beforehand to try and pick a good movie.

This raises the question after which this chapter is titled: What is a good movie? For that matter, what is a good singer or a good hamburger? That we often rate and rank these things online seems to imply that not all movies, or singers, or hamburgers are equally good. Television shows like *America's Got Talent*, for instance, are predicated upon the idea that art can be judged. Beauty, it would seem, is not merely in the eyes of the beholder.

Of course we must make room for taste and preference, especially within similar categories and genres of art. Who is to say whether Mozart is a better composer than Beethoven? Yet we must not make the mistake of saying that beauty is merely subjective or that it is just a matter of opinion. Beauty is an objective quality about the world that we expect rational humans to recognize.

Beauty is not only objective, it is transcendent. Beauty goes beyond (i.e., transcends) opinion, time, or culture. While tastes about beauty may change, beauty has always existed and always will exist. For our part, humans recognized beauty and celebrated beauty because beauty is objective and transcendent.

Consider the concept of a scenic route. In where you live, there are probably roads that are considered scenic routes. The idea of a scenic route is that there is great beauty to be observed while driving.

California is blessed to have many scenic routes, including Highway One from Santa Cruz to San Francisco. The highway winds along the Pacific coast and features panoramic views of the ocean. A person who drives Highway One should immediately apprehend the beauty of the drive and understand why it is considered a scenic route.

Of course, not everything is beautiful. Most stretches of highway in California are not scenic routes at all, but are rather mundane, industrial, and congested. To call them scenic drives would be false and misleading. Some things are beautiful, and other things are ugly.

Part of the value of philosophy is that it helps to understand why some things are ugly and others are beautiful. We know that Vincent van Gogh's painting *The Starry Night* is beautiful, but philosophy helps us understand why. We know that prison cells, by contrast, are ugly, and philosophy helps us understand why.

In his essay "Of the Standard of Taste," David Hume shared a parable about two men drinking with others from a barrel of wine. Both men detect some foul taste; one believes the wine tastes metallic and the other leathery. Other people are enjoying the wine, but these two men find something distasteful and cannot explain why. Upon emptying the barrel, the men discover the presence of a metal key tied to a piece of leather. They always knew the wine tasted foul, but now they knew why.

Hume uses the essay to argue a few important points. First, not all wine is good. As we have said, beauty is not just in the eye of the beholder. There are standards of taste. If you do not think that Highway One is scenic and offers beautiful views, then something is wrong with you, not the Pacific Ocean. If you do not think *The Starry Night* is beautiful, then something is wrong with your tastes, not van Gogh's.

Second, Hume makes the point that we do not always know the reasons or arguments as to why something is beautiful, but that is not the same thing as there being no reasons or arguments for why some things are beautiful and other things are ugly. In Hume's story, the men eventually discover why the wine was bad, but even when they didn't know why, they still knew it was bad. Ancient people who were uneducated by modern standards knew the moon illuminated the night sky, even if they did not yet understand that it was because it reflected the light of the sun.

Third, Hume is challenging the reader to develop his or her tastes. A person who only eats fast food can develop a taste for nutritious and organic food, but it takes time and effort. A person who eats large amounts of refined sugar may not immediately enjoy or appreciate the natural sweetness of an apple. Yet, over time, tastes can be recalibrated to enjoy the natural sweetness of fruit.

So, too, Hume believed that people can develop their ability to identify, appreciate, and explain the presence of beauty in the world. He called this process of development the "discernment of beauty."[3] While Hume was right about the discernment of beauty and about our ability to cultivate tastes in regard to the enjoyment and appreciation of beauty, he was wrong about the nature of beauty because he ultimately rejected that beauty is an objective feature of the world: "Beauty is no quality in things themselves: It exists merely in the mind which contemplates them; and each mind perceives a different beauty. One person may even perceive deformity, where another is sensible of beauty; and every individual ought to acquiesce in his own sentiment, without pretending to regulate those of others."[4]

---

[3] David Hume, "Of the Standard of Taste," https://home.csulb.edu/~jvancamp/361r15.html.

[4] Hume, "Of the Standard of Taste."

The goal of this chapter is threefold. First, to explain the concept of beauty. Second, to give a context for modern discussion about beauty and art. Third, to outline the virtues of art so that you can not only appreciate but also contribute beauty to the world.

Question 9.1

Philosophy is concerned with _____ in order to increase _____.

Question 9.2

Which of the following is *not* a question of aesthetics?
   a) Is Bach or Beethoven a greater composer?
   b) Is it acceptable to steal your neighbor's painting?
   c) Does McDonald's or Burger King make a better hamburger?
   d) Is a house at the beach more beautiful than a house in the mountains?

Question 9.3

What does it mean that beauty is *transcendent*?

_____

_____

Question 9.4

Hume's parable of the two men drinking wine teaches us:
   a) Even if we do not know why something is beautiful, it still is beautiful.
   b) Our tastes may need to be trained or refined.
   c) There are standards of taste/beauty.
   d) All of the above.

Is Beauty Merely in the Eye of the Beholder?

First, "good art" means the art object possesses intrinsic beauty as a well-crafted work. Here, one seeks to discover the intrinsic beauty of the art object as an aesthetic end in itself. Does the object embody widely recognized attributes of beauty and, if so, what are they and to what degree does the object have them?

Second, "good art" means that the art object has the instrumental value of being a good means to fostering a non-aesthetic good of some sort. For example, a piece of "good art" may be such because it properly draws attention to the plight of the poor, to the preciousness of the unborn, and so forth. Here, the goodness of the art object is not its inherent beauty; rather, it is its degree of instrumental value in promoting some social, religious, political, or moral good. A work of art could be good in the first sense and not in the second sense, and conversely.

Aesthetic relativism is often—though not solely—expressed by "beauty is in the eye of the beholder." The main argument for aesthetic relativism is aesthetic disagreement: some people like one sort of music and others like a different sort of music. Who's to judge? What can an aesthetic objectivist (beauty and ugliness are objectively real) say in response to this problem? Here are four suggested responses:

1. We know the difference between an objectively real case of beauty or ugliness without having to know how we know that difference. In epistemology, there is a view called methodism (not the denomination) according to which before one can know something, one must first have a criterion for how one knows it. Logical positivism or empiricism (see below) are examples of methodism. It is rightly rejected because it leads to a viscous infinite regress: To know p (this art object is beautiful), I must first know q (an art object is beautiful if and only if it has symmetry) and r (this art object satisfies our criterion by having symmetry). If one is a methodist, now one must answer how one knows that q is a good criterion for beauty and how one can tell if the art object satisfies q. And so on to infinity. A better approach is called *particularism* according to which, while having criteria for how we know things is often important, we do not always need to know how we know something before we can know it. The particularist starts the project of knowing with specific cases and not with criteria. Sunset over Maui, Beethoven's Fifth Symphony, and the statue of David are beautiful; the city dump is ugly. Period.

2. People confuse taking pleasure in a work of art with having a proper aesthetic awareness of that work. These are not the same. One can like a poor work of art, and one can have an aesthetic awareness that properly justifies one's view that this is really good art even if one does not like it. Gaining pleasure from a work of art does not require training. Having proper aesthetic awareness of an art object does take

training (often apprenticing under a master) to have the wisdom to discern aesthetic beauty. People vary greatly in what does and does not please them. But there is much more agreement about what is beautiful and ugly among those with solid training in aesthetic awareness.

3. Objective aesthetic judgments should usually (though not always) be made within a specific type of art. Thus, it is hard to know what it would mean to claim a statue is more beautiful than a Beatles song. And within one general kind of art—e.g., music—it can be difficult to hold that a Beatles song is more beautiful than a specific piece of country music. That's because there are various specific types of music within this general kind of art. Though still difficult, it is usually easier to discern the difference in objective beauty within a more narrowly defined kind of art (e.g., within classic rock or country music). Aesthetic disagreement comes most often when we express different judgments in all but the last case. This leads us to the mistaken notion that the beauty of all art is a matter of personal preference.

4. A piece of art often has many aspects to it. Consider a painting. It may exhibit some degree of beauty in its color coordination, in its symmetry, in its geometrical layout, in its accuracy in representing its object in the world, and so on. A piece of art can be beautiful in one of these aspects and ugly, or at least less beautiful, in another. Aesthetic disagreement sometimes arises because some people are focusing on the ugly aspect of the art object while others are focusing on the more beautiful aspect. This sort of disagreement does not entail that the object does not possess objective beauty in at least some of its aspects.

Question 9.5

For something to be "good art," it must possess what two qualities?

    1.

    2.

Question 9.6

In epistemology, _____ claims that before we know something, we must have a definite criterion for *how* we know it. _____, on the other hand, suggests that we do not always need to know *how* we know something at first.

Question 9.7

The author gives four suggestions for avoiding aesthetic relativism. Summarize each in one or two sentences.

1.

2.

3.

4.

Current Theories about Art

In 2000, Chilean artist Marco Evaristti debuted his art piece called *Helena*. *Helena* consisted of ten blenders on a kitchen table. Each blender was filled with water and contained one living goldfish. The blenders were connected to an "on" button that, when pressed, would turn on the blenders and simultaneously liquefy the fish.[5]

Do you consider this to be art? Before we discuss what is good art or what makes art beautiful, we must first arrive at some understanding of art. In what follows, we will offer the most common theories about art and help to see their relative strengths and weaknesses.

The goal of defining art should reflect the value of art. Think of art like diamonds. Not every stone is a diamond, nor every object art. Diamonds are rated according to a grading system that takes into consideration things like color, cut, and clarity. This grading system reflects the value and rarity of diamonds and how diamonds possess qualities that other gemstones do not possess.

While there is not a grading system for art, the desire to define art reflects that art is special, meaningful, and rare. Defining art also helps to make sense of its value. While some works of art are expensive (even priceless), the value of art is sometimes personal or cultural.

The first theory of art is called institutionalism. According to this theory, something is art if the art community says that it is art. When French artist Marcel Duchamp displayed *Fountain* in 1917, few people believed that putting urinals on display made them pieces of art. Others argued that since the urinals were displayed at the Grand Central Palace (an art exhibit hall) in New York that *Fountains* was therefore art.

If simply being displayed as art makes something art, then the question "what is art?" seems to be settled. It appears to save one the time discerning beauty, as Hume instructed. The

---

[5] See Hugo Boogaerdt, "'Helena' by Marco Evaristti," Art & Electronic Media Online Companion, https://artelectronicmedia.com/en/artwork/helena-by-marco-evaristti/.

institutional theory also provides some criteria to distinguish that which is art from that which is not art. People want to know that art is not merely subjective.

There are many problems with this theory. A child's stick-figure drawing may be displayed as art on the refrigerator, while the *Mona Lisa* is displayed in the Louvre. Institutionalism would suggest that the child's drawing is not art because your refrigerator is not a part of the art world and your home is not a recognized art exhibit, like the Louvre. While there are many differences between a child's drawing and the *Mona Lisa*, most people probably believe that both are works of art.

Suggesting that only the art community can make something art is snobbish and authoritarian, characteristics that have long plagued the art community. Ideally, art is associated with creation, expression, and freedom. Putting the power to determine what is art into the hands of an elite group of people seems to be the antithesis of art. Further, exactly who counts as being a member of the art community, and why are they members and not others? These are difficult questions to answer.

In addition, the art community seems to be an inconsistent authority in regard to art. If all that is required for something to be considered art is to be recognized by the art community, then anything they say is art can be art. While it is true that beauty is all around us, not everything is art.

Art is a word we ascribe to any creation that possesses unique beauty in its form. A person who sits down and bangs away at the piano keys is not displaying art in the same way as Claude Debussy's masterpiece *Clair de lune*. There must be some standard for art that is above and beyond the art community.

The second theory of art is called *formalism*. Formalism is a view of art that says an object is artistic according to the perception (usually sight or sound) of its form. The lines of a painting, the strings of a symphony, shape of a sculpture—these are forms of objects recognized as art.

Of course, not every object with shape or that makes sound is considered art. A trash can, for instance, has shape but is not usually regarded as art. An electric drill makes sound, but is not art. How then do we distinguish artistic images and sounds from non-artistic images and sounds? According to formalism, Clive Bell has suggested that the form of art elicits what he calls aesthetic emotions. The value of certain forms consists in the impact made upon the senses. The meaning of art is therefore found in the forms presented to the senses.[6]

---

[6] See Clive Bell, "Art" (1914), https://home.csulb.edu/~jvancamp/361r13.html.

Formalism focuses on the form of the art. It draws attention to things like the brushstrokes on the canvas, the textures, the combinations of color, or the symmetry and proportion of lines and objects. The essence of art, according to formalism, is in the analysis of form.

The benefit of formalism is that it allows for new forms of art, such as abstract art. A Jackson Pollock painting, for instance, is abstract and does not present to the viewer a picture of anything in nature. Yet, there is a certain aesthetic appreciation many find in viewing abstract art, and formalism provides some explanation for this enjoyment.

In the same way that Aristotle differed from his teacher Plato by locating the ideal in the object and not in another realm of ideas, so too formalism emphasizes the art itself and opens up appreciation for new forms of artistic expression. A person who views Banksy's *Flower Thrower* painted on the streets of Jerusalem (rather than on a canvas hanging in a museum) is forced to contend with the work and consider and evaluate it seriously.

What is lost by formalism is an account of beauty as a universal property and not just a property of particular objects or works of art. The result is that art is reduced to individual taste and appreciation, contrary to what has already been observed about the self-evident ways in which beauty and art are not merely subjective matters of individual taste. If a person does not appreciate the aesthetic value of an opera by Giacomo Puccini, we would say that something is wrong with their sense of taste. It is either damaged (like a person whose taste buds cannot differentiate sweet from sour) or underdeveloped (like a person who has only ever eaten McDonald's chicken nuggets drenched in ketchup).

The third theory of art is called *emotivism*. While formalism focuses on the form of the art piece itself and not on the emotions elicited, emotivism is a theory of art that focuses primarily on the emotive impact of the art itself. In the words of the great Russian writer Leo Tolstoy: "Art is human activity consisting in this, that one man consciously, by means of certain external signs, hands on to others feelings he has lived through, and that other people are infected by these feelings and also experience them."[7]

Notice Tolstoy's emphasis on feeling. Emotivism says that art is not primarily about the art community (institutionalism) or analysis of form (formalism) but rather the emotions intentionally communicated by the artist to the audience. If an art exhibit (such as *Meow Wolf* in Las Vegas or Santa Fe) intends to instill a sense of disorientation and whimsy and succeeds, then it is successful art. In fact, the more the audience joins in emotion, the more successful the art.

---

[7] Leo Tolstoy, *What Is Art?* (Indianapolis: Bobbs-Merrill, 1960), 51.

Emotivism has a unique history, the story of which is worth telling in order to properly understand emotivism. American philosopher A. J. Ayer was a member of a school of thought called logical positivism. Before Ayers and logical positivism, though, there was a philosophical movement called, simply, positivism. French philosopher Auguste Comte was a leading figure in positivism who, along with others, said that human knowledge is limited to *scientific knowledge*, defined here as things that can be known by observation. Comte believed that societies evolve from early stages (metaphysics) to more advanced stages (science).

A problem faced by positivism, however, were the significant developments in modern science that were theoretical in nature (i.e., not based on empirical observation) such as magnetism, gravity, and electrons. Therefore, Ayers and others sought to recalibrate positivism to make room for scientific advancements in the twentieth century.

Logical positivism accepted the view of positivism that knowledge is tied to science (i.e., observation). However, in order to make room for modern scientific developments, logical positivism expanded knowledge to include theories that could be tied directly to observation but otherwise restricted knowledge to math, analytic logic, and sensory experience. By doing this, logical positivists attempted to avoid what they considered to be the speculations of metaphysics.

What does this have to do with art? The result of logical positivism was that ethical statements (i.e., right and wrong) or statements of judgment about things like aesthetics were excluded from the realm of knowledge. As a result, according to logical positivism, no one can say that something is right, wrong, beautiful, or ugly. Such statements, according to Ayers, were merely emotive expressions of taste.

So, when a person says that "murder is wrong," he means only an expression of emotion (i.e., "Yuck! Murder!" Similarly, when a person says, "The *Mona Lisa* is beautiful," what she means is something like, "Hurray for the the *Mona Lisa*!" For emotivists, ethical or aesthetic statements are non-cognitive expressions of the emotions. As such, they are neither true nor false.

Emotivism is helpful in that it seems correct to say that art has something to do with emotion. A sad song can make you cry, a comedic movie can make you laugh, and a horror novel can make you afraid. Cold and dispassionate reason about art can fail to appreciate the emotional impact that art has in our lives.

Despite this, emotivism abandons the idea that there is anything objective about art. Comte, Ayers, and other philosophers (referred to as "the Vienna Circle") rejected any knowledge apart from strict logical analysis or observation. Since the question "what is art?" is not answered by the standards of knowledge put forth by logical positivism, the conclusion is that there is no answer to the question and that art is solely a matter of the art observer expressing emotion, taste, and preference.

Logical positivism's claim that only things known by a small set of conditions (math, logic, and sensory experience) can be known is self-referentially incoherent: it does not meet its own standard of proof. The claim itself is not known by math, analytic logic, or scientific observation. If logical positivism is true, then it is false. In other words, it is self-defeating.

The fourth theory of art is called imitationalism. Imitationalism comes from the word *imitation*, and is the view that art is an imitation of reality. This view has led many artists to create paintings where the goal was to present an image as realistically as possible.

Bob Ross was a painter who appeared in a television show called *The Joy of Painting*. Bob was famous for his easygoing mannerism and his effortless painting. In particular, Bob tended to paint landscapes and seascapes: paintings of trees, mountains, rivers, and beaches. You never looked at a Bob Ross painting and asked, "What is that?" because Bob's paintings reflected, to some degree of accuracy, what nature looks like in reality.

In book 10 of the *Republic*, Plato argued that art is imitation (*mimesis*, from which comes the English word *mimic*). Remember that Plato believes in a world of ideas (forms) and the best thing a person can do is use reason to contemplate the ideal form of everything in the visible universe. For Plato, the idea of a tree is a higher truth than the object (tree) itself.[8]

However, even below the object is a picture of a tree. Plato might ask the following question to a person staring at a picture of a tree: "Why are you looking at a tree when you can be contemplating the idea of a tree? Why would you stare at a picture of a tree when you could at least be looking at the real thing?"

In some way, this makes sense. Most people appreciate "the real thing" as opposed to "a fake." Think for a moment about your favorite person in the world. Would you rather look at a picture of that person or be with them? Now think of a place in the world you have always wanted to visit, such as the Statue of Liberty in New York City. Would you rather look at a picture of the Statue of Liberty, or (if given the chance) go and see it for yourself?

Aristotle followed Plato in believing that imitation was true art, but he expounded Plato's view to connect with the beauty of virtue. In the *Nicomachean Ethics* he argued that virtuous living is a form of art:

---

[8] See also Aristotle's *Poetics*.

Further, men think that the happy man ought to live pleasantly. Now if he were a solitary, life would be hard for him; for by oneself it is not easy to be continuously active; but with others and towards others it is easier. With others therefore his activity will be more continuous, and it is in itself pleasant, as it ought to be for the man who is supremely happy; for a good man qua good delights in virtuous actions and is vexed at vicious ones, as a musical man enjoys beautiful tunes but is pained at bad ones.[9]

Art as imitation is rooted in the belief that art should be truthful. In both art and virtue there is beauty. Beauty, of course, is a great source of happiness. Art, in this sense, connects our happiness to reality.

Art as imitation and presentation of reality does not exclude things like fiction. The world of Harry Potter, for instance, is fictitious. However, the virtues and lessons learned by J. K. Rowling's readers are very real (e.g., friends should be loyal, courage is noble, etc.).

There are several benefits of the imitation view of art. First, it connects art to reality and to what some philosophers have called a "golden chain of being." Seeing a painting makes you think of the source of the beauty of that painting, which is nature. In turn, seeing nature makes you think of the source of the beauty of nature, which is God (or some transcendent source of goodness).

Second, the imitation view of art provides some standard by which to evaluate art and determine what is and is not art. Many people look at modern art and think, *That's just squiggly lines and blurry shapes; I could do that!* While those paintings require more talent and creativity than most people give credit, no one looks at Johannes Vermeer's painting *Girl with a Pearl Earring* and thinks, "I could do that!"

What are some weaknesses of the imitation position? Most obviously, most people do not share Plato's metaphysical commitment to Forms, to the idea that reason is superior to observation, or to a suspicion of the physical world. God made the world and declared that it was good, and God has equipped humans with both reason and sense to navigate reality. The Christian view of redemption includes a new heaven and a new earth, not an escape from these things.

Limiting art to that which is realistic limits creativity. Consider the Bible. It is filled with true stories, but some of them require a great deal of imagination, such as the snake speaking to Adam and Eve in the garden or the prophet Balaam's donkey speaking on behalf of God. What can we

---

[9] Aristotle, *Nicomachean Ethics*, chap. 9, Sacred Texts, https://www.sacred-texts.com/cla/ari/nico/nico104.htm.

learn from these stories? Humans, made in God's image, are likely to create art in ways that stretch the imagination and stretch the mind.

Impressionism, for instance, is a style of painting that was popular in the nineteenth century and practiced by such artists as Claude Monet and Henri Matisse. Monet painted a series of portraits of haystacks. Although the lines are blurry and the images dreamlike, it seems counterintuitive to conclude that it is therefore not art (or not good art). In fact, since all art fails to accurately capture reality, Plato ended up rejecting art. At the very least, the imitation view of art elevates certain art forms (like painting, because it is a visual media) over others (like music).

Having looked at the main theories of art, we can make a few conclusions. First, each of them has something to contribute to an informed perspective on art and beauty. Second, none of them seems to satisfactorily answer the question "What is art?" Third, they all try (but ultimately fail) to secure some foundation upon which to take art objectively.

The church should not, therefore, look to the secular art community to explain the reason for art or the definition of beauty. The secular art community can teach technical expertise (i.e., "how"). However, only philosophy and theology can explain the purpose of art (i.e., "why").

In what follows, we will consider an alternative approach to art. On this approach, art makes sense given a biblical view of God and humanity. We will argue that the best way to approach art is to start with God and the story of creation in order to establish a definition of beauty that can then be used to distinguish good art from bad art.

Question 9.8

The goal of defining art should reflect _____.

Question 9.9

For each theory of art, provide a definition, any problems that arise from the theory, and a representative artist.

Theory	Definition	Problem(s)	Representative Artist
Institutionalism			

Formalism			
Emotivism			
Imitationalism			

Question 9.10

In what way does formalism resemble the philosophy of Aristotle?

_____

_____

Question 9.11

True or false: Logical positivism relativizes ethical and aesthetic claims to mere preference.

Question 9.12

Give two benefits of the imitation view of art.

    1.

    2.

Why Humans Create

Art is creation. All of the above theories of art would agree. When a person makes art they are engaging in an act of creation.

Christianity provides the insight to explain why humans create. Humans create because they are made in God's image, and God is the Creator (Gen 1:27). Humans create because they are creations endowed with the special capacity to create, along with a natural desire to do so.

Of course, there are other examples of nonhuman animal creation in nature. For instance, you can look up the nests of the bowerbird or the sand art of the pufferfish. These (and other) examples of nonhuman animal art are always related to securing a mate and making babies; in other words, animal art in nature is always about sex.

Human art is unique and distinct in the animal kingdom. Humans create art for reasons other than sex, and often, for no reason other than the pure enjoyment of creation. Humans are also different because we are aware of art as art, work to preserve art as that which is beautiful, and praise the art of others.

Humans create, and we create in a way that is unique in the animal kingdom. Humans are not mere animals. The Bible starts with a statement about God as the Creator: "In the beginning God created the heavens and the earth" (Gen 1:1). God creates out of nothing (*ex nihilo*).

Every human creation is dependent on God in the sense that God is the ultimate source of the material and energy by which humans create (*ex materia*). As Paul said in Acts 17:28, "In him we live and move and have our being."

The Bible says that after creation God looked upon all that he had made and saw that it was very good (Gen 1:31). This verse is important because it tells us not only that God is good but also what he created was good. The word used for "good" (טוב) is translated elsewhere in Genesis as "beautiful." The same word can refer to both moral goodness and aesthetic beauty. God is good and beautiful, and what he created was good and beautiful.

Given this, it makes sense that humans, made in God's image, would be creative. It makes sense that humans would aspire not only to create but to create what is good and beautiful. It also makes sense that art and beauty have something to do with God, such that apart from God, these concepts simply do not make a lot of sense.

God is the source of beauty because he is beauty. He is the standard of moral perfection and also the highest possible experience of perceiving beauty. Theologians have called this the Beatific Vision. In the face of Jesus displayed in his glory, believers will see God: "Blessed are the pure in heart, for they will see God" (Matt 5:8).

As humans, we are living somewhere between the victory of Christ and the consummation of his kingdom. Our job is to walk by faith and not by sight (2 Cor 5:7). Art is a means by which we bring something that reflects the beauty of God into a fallen world; the light of God to the darkness and the order of God into the chaos. Our hope as Christians is that art would be like bread crumbs of beauty that would help lead a person to contemplate God who is goodness, beauty, and truth. Art—and natural beauty—opens us up and breaks down our resistance to receiving goodness and truth.

I have asked one thing from the LORD;
it is what I desire:
to dwell in the house of the LORD
all the days of my life,
gazing on the beauty of the LORD
and seeking him in his temple . . .
I am certain that I will see the LORD's goodness
in the land of the living. (Ps 27:4, 13)

If God is beauty, then when something of his character, will, creation, or order is observed we say it is beautiful because God is beautiful. In this way, the world becomes a window through which we observe the beauty of God. We delight in the window because it affords us the opportunity to delight in God. If it is true that worship is glorifying God by delighting in him, then the experience of delight in God and in the beauty of God's world is a form of worship: "And whatever you do, in word or in deed, do everything in the name of the Lord Jesus, giving thanks to God the Father through him" (Col 3:17).

When we delight in God's beauty, we are transformed to his beauty. As the church father Basil the Great wrote in his sermon on Psalm 29, "He who gazes steadfastly at the splendor and graces of [God's beauty] receives some share of it."[10] Elsewhere the Bible speaks of the beauty of holiness: "Don't let your beauty consist of outward things like elaborate hairstyles and wearing gold jewelry or fine clothes, but rather what is inside the heart—the imperishable quality of a gentle and quiet spirit, which is of great worth in God's sight" (1 Pet 3:3–4).

God's transformational beauty becomes an apologetic for the faith. In the context of Christianity, apologetics refers to defending the faith. The Bible speaks of defending the faith in places such as 1 Pet 3:15 and Phil 1:16. Examples of apologetics can be found in places such as Acts 17 and Acts 26:25 where Paul said to Festus, "I'm speaking words of truth and good judgment." As the church lives out the beauty of virtue in the name of Jesus, the virtue speaks in defense of the truthfulness of the faith. Augustine spoke of the "draw" of virtue in *Confessions*: "I was drawn to the peace I found in virtue, and repelled by the rancor I found in vice, attributing the former to unity, the latter to division."[11]

---

[10] Basil, Homily 14, in *The Fathers of the Church: A New Translation*, vol. 46, *Exegetic Homilies* (n.p.: Cima, 1947), 221.

[11] Augustine, *The Confessions of Saint Augustine*, trans. E. B. Pusey, https://www.gutenberg.org/files/3296/3296-h/3296-h.htm.

In summary, humans are creative because humans are created. Like a child imitating the mannerisms of its parents, the act of human creation is an act of imitation. God created humans in his image, and part of that image is the desire to reflect or display the beauty of God. When humans live in a way that reflects God's character, we call this virtue. When humans create something to be perceived, contemplated, and declared good, we call this art. When art is truthful and right according to who God is and what God has said, we say it is beautiful. When art lies or distorts some truth of God, we say it is ugly. Good art can also truthfully depict the ugliness of a fallen world.

Pornography, on the other hand, is ugly. It distorts God's purpose for sex. Sex is designed to strengthen joyful intimacy between a husband and a wife in the context of marriage. Sex in marriage is about loving, serving, and satisfying one another. Pornography lies about sex.

Pornography is the opposite of sex. Pornography serves the shameful act of self-service in which there is no ultimate, nonaddictive satisfaction. Sex in marriage honors and esteems those involved, while pornography exploits or degrades those involved. Sex in marriage builds up while pornography tears down. Sex in marriage builds healthy self-esteem, while pornography leads to self-loathing, which in turn leads to or perpetuates other destructive habits.

Given the source of beauty and the ability of art to bless or curse, in the next section we will consider Plato's warning about art. We will see the role of community in evaluating art and lay out some questions to help in the discernment of beauty.

Question 9.13

God looked upon all that he created and declared it "good." The Hebrew word for "good" can also mean _____.

Question 9.14

How does art become worship? What effect does this have on a believer?

_____

_____

Question 9.15

From a Christian perspective, what makes art beautiful?

_____

_____

The Role of Community

Plato warned against art. He knew that the poets had more of an influence on the minds of citizens than the philosophers. This warning seems to apply in modern times. For instance, do you think it is common for people to get their ideas about love and relationships from television or movies? Most people have watched more movies than they have read books.

Plato's warning about art stems from how he does not believe most people think about the truth of art but only whether they like it or not. By analogy, when you eat fast food you probably focus on the taste and not the nutritional value. If you thought seriously about the calories, fat, salt, and so forth, you might think twice about eating it or perhaps eat less.

Plato knew that popular art (poetry in his time or television and movies in modern time) had a message. Most people did not evaluate that message, but their thinking was nevertheless affected by the message. The danger, according to Plato's line of reasoning, was that art would lead people either to believe what is false or simply to be so entertained that they did not contemplate what is true. Eating fast food is bad for you but easy. Buying healthy ingredients and making a home-cooked meal is better for you but takes more time and likely costs more money.

Plato's solution was that the rulers of a city should control and regulate art. Plato did not trust the average person to make wise decisions about art. In the absence of self-control, Plato advocated for government control. To some extent, his advice is reflected in such modern practices of MPAA movie ratings, lyric warnings on music, and age restrictions on online entertainment. These regulations are hard to enforce with streaming entertainment; nevertheless, they reflect a Platonic fear about the power of art and the role of the community in regulating art.

From a Christian perspective, the Holy Spirit produces the fruit of self-control in believers. Yet, there is wisdom in seeing a significant role for one's faith community (i.e., the local church) in developing the discernment of beauty. Plato is right that individuals often lack wisdom and self-control. However, God has put individual believers into the church (the body of Christ) in order for them to both strengthen others and to be strengthened.

In terms of art, the church should be a place where the theology touched upon in this chapter is taught and reminded. These doctrines help Christians to remember God is the source and standard of beauty. Youth and college groups, for instance, can talk about popular movies and have guided discussion about the worldview of the movie. Churches should be places where questions are asked in order to train people to think about movies from a Christian perspective, rather than simply allowing online ratings to determine whether a movie is "good" or "bad." Ultimately, churches are equipped to provide thoughtful analysis about art in the world to help people make wise entertainment choices. In what follows, we offer four questions for Christians to encourage artistic discernment.

Question 9.16

The Greek philosopher Plato believed _____ about art:
   a)   It was pretty much useless.
   b)   Most people are aware of how art affects them.
   c)   Art has more influence on people's minds than philosophy.
   d)   Art is the greatest end of man.

Question 9.17

What two gifts has God given to help us discern between good and bad art?

_____

_____

Four Questions to Discern Beauty

In this section, we will use movies as examples of discerning beauty. These questions would apply to other art forms as well: music (especially lyrics), books, theater, and others. The goal is to avoid making simplistic judgments of art ("everyone else likes it," "it's made a lot of money," or "the critics love it") or trusting marketing categories ("but it's a *Christian* movie!") rather than applying what we have learned about the source and purpose of art.

   What is the point of the movie? Most movies have some ultimate point or message they are trying to get across. Spend some time ascertaining the point of the movie and then ask the all-important question: Is that true? Is the movie telling me the truth or is it lying?

For example, the movie *1917* tells the story of two young men in World War I who are called upon to risk their lives to deliver a message that will save many people. These characters (the protagonists) endure great hardships and danger on their way to accomplishing their mission. The point of the movie can be summarized in light of an early pessimist in the film who, upon giving the young men the message, says "hope is a dangerous thing." And yet, this hope sustains the young men through their perils and suffering and ultimately pays off.

The overall message of *1917* is true. Despite its "R" rating in the United States for violence and foul language, the message of the movie is truthful. The good guys are good for the right reasons, and good wins in the end. Those are Christian themes that, among other things, make it a good movie.

By contrast, the overall message of *No Country for Old Men* is false. The movie tells the story of a man named Llewelyn Moss whom, while hunting, comes across the remnant of a drug deal gone bad. Out of the carnage of the drug deal, Moss tracks one of the few survivors who manages to leave the scene with millions of dollars. Moss gets the money, but through a series of events, is discovered by the drug cartel. The cartel hires Anton Chigurh to track Moss and retrieve the money.

No Country is a movie with a fatalistic worldview. There is no place for confession, repentance, redemption, or forgiveness. One can only submit to fate.

In one scene, the mercenary Chigurh flips a coin to see if he will kill an innocent gas station attendant, asking the attendant to "call it." The audience knows that the outcome of the coin toss determines the man's fate. The gas station attendant expresses confusion, saying, "I didn't put nothin' up." Chigurh replies, "Yes you did. You've been puttin' it up your whole life. You just didn't know it."[12]

In the nihilistic worldview of *No Country*, there is no good or evil, no justice or mercy. The conscience of the movie (Sheriff Bell) is left to ponder his dreams. Bell represents the inability of rational and civil people to truly comprehend or accept that life is random and purposeless. It is implied that reason and morality are merely stories we tell ourselves to keep us from facing the meaninglessness of life. We should conclude that while movies such as *No Country* are to be commended for such things as the quality of acting, cinematography, and soundtrack, a discerning viewer will properly identify the worldview and conclude that it is false.

---

[12] *No Country for Old Men* (2007), directed by Joel and Ethan Coen, based on the book by Cormac McCarthy. Screenplay accessed online at https://gointothestory.blcklst.com/script-to-screen-no-country -for-old-men-163bc6656999.

What is the story of redemption? Every movie has a plot (i.e., story). In every good story, something goes wrong (i.e., tension). At some point, the protagonists (i.e., the main characters, usually seen as the "good guys" with whom the audience should sympathize) pursue a course of action that aids in resolution. Resolution means that whatever went wrong is made right. Another word for resolution, in this sense, is redemption. How is the wrong made right?

The biblical story of redemption is one of love, sacrifice, justice, and humility. In contrast, there are common ways that movies will get redemption wrong. For instance, some movies feature good characters who resort to becoming bad in order to bring about redemption. For instance, while the Batman movies are entertaining, the character of Batman is one who consistently resorts to evil in order to achieve good. The so-called Dark Knight is a vigilante who uses violence without legitimate authority (or accountability). This view that "might makes right" is the ethos of tyrants and bullies, not heroes.

On the other hand, consider *The Incredibles*, in which a family of undercover superheroes must come together to save the world. The movie features three primary sources of conflict. First, the superheroes have stopped being super because public opinion is against them. Second, the family at the center of the story has stopped working together. Rather than fighting crime they are fighting each other. Third, an old enemy of Mr. Incredible is seeking revenge, so he lies to his family in order to solve the problem by himself.

The resolution involves Mr. Incredible getting caught, confessing his lie, and realizing the strength of his family as a team and the importance of his marriage. The family comes to terms with their unique calling and figures out how to live in the world even though they are different and have a different purpose. By the end of the movie, the superheroes are back, because the world is filled with evil, and evil people must be confronted by good people of courage and strength.

According to genre, *The Incredibles* is not a "Christian movie," yet its message is consistent with Christianity. Knowing the story of redemption enables a greater appreciation of the movie. It also helps explain why its message resonates. Of course, Christians do not only watch movies that get things right theologically. However, Christians should know when the movie gets it wrong, and why.

What is the perspective on sin? Does the movie make clear the "folly of sin"? The Proverbs speak about the folly (or foolishness) of sin (Prov 24:9). Sin leads to bad consequences: Whatever a man sows, he reaps (Gal 6:7–8). The Bible warns that your sin will find you out (Num 32:23). Ultimately, of course, the wages of sin is death (Rom 6:23).

Movies can tell the truth by exposing the bad consequences of sin, or movies can lie by painting sin in a positive light and minimizing (or excluding altogether) those consequences. A movie that tells the truth is *Hamilton*. Based on the Broadway musical, the movie contains the song "Say No to This," which chronicles the affair between Alexander Hamilton and Mariah Reynolds. As Hamilton and Reynolds commit adultery, the backing chorus shouts, "No!" Later in the movie, songs such as "The Reynolds Pamphlet" reveal the public embarrassment of the affair, while "It's Quiet Uptown" explores the hurt Eliza Hamilton experienced because of her husband's infidelity. Toward the end of that song, the chorus sings "Forgiveness, can you imagine?" in recognition of Eliza's gracious forgiveness of her husband's unfaithfulness.

Most movies are less truthful. The James Bond movies, for instance, portray *as cool* a man who is a notorious womanizer. For all his daring, courage, and sophistication, Bond treats women like objects. Another example is 2019's *The Goldfinch*, based upon the Pulitzer Prize–winning "coming of age" novel of the same name by Donna Tartt.

The Goldfinch tells the story of Theo Decker. Orphaned when his mother dies, Theo pursues worldly sophistication as the benchmark of maturity. Absent virtue, Theo's sinful choices are background noise to his taste in clothing and furniture. The movie presents Theo as a self-taught sophisticate, when in reality, the character personifies moral pragmatism and selfishness.[13] Taste is never a substitute for virtue.

What are the virtues? Every movie has characters. The audience is meant to be sympathetic to certain characters—to like them, feel for them, and root for them. Despite their flaws, the protagonist(s) are characters we would commonly call "the good guys."

A good movie celebrates characters for the right reasons; characters who exhibit virtues such as hope, courage, and loyalty. The Lord of the Rings trilogy, for instance, is filled with virtuous characters like Bilbo, Frodo, and Samwise. While complex and flawed, we root for these characters because they exhibit goodness and have a noble purpose.

On the other end of the spectrum is *Deadpool*, featuring Ryan Reynolds as the anti-hero Wade Wilson (aka Deadpool). Early in the movie, Deadpool admits that he is no hero but rather a bad guy who commits murder in search of vengeance. Peter Parker's uncle Ben in *Spider-Man* said, "With great power comes great responsibility."[14] Deadpool, on the other hand, glories in his irresponsibility.

---

[13] *The Goldfinch*, directed by John Crowley (Warner Bros. Pictures, 2019).

[14] David Koepp, *Spider-Man*, directed by Sam Raimi (Columbia Pictures, Marvel, and Laurin Ziskin Productions), 2002, motion picture.

Deadpool invites you to root for a guy whose primary attributes are his penchant for murder, revenge, sarcasm, and nonchalance. These, of course, are not virtues. Deadpool is not a good guy who is rough around the edges; he is a bad guy who brags about being bad and uses his hardships as excuses for his behavior. Throughout the movie, he refuses to use his powers for good. It is hard to see anything in Deadpool that a person should aspire to emulate (i.e., imitate).

To conclude this section, consider the purpose of the above questions. The goal is to provide a framework for thought and conversation for the purpose of discerning beauty and its relation to truth. The goal is not to read Christian themes into art where such themes do not fit, or to impose a Christian worldview against the evidence within the movie. The principle of charity requires that Christians seek to understand the message of a film as it is presented and not as we will it to be understood.

Not every story is a Christian story. It is legitimate to see Christian themes where they exist. It is not legitimate, charitable, or honest to force such themes.

Question 9.18

True or false: The best criterion for judging whether a movie is good or bad is by finding out if a Christian produced the film.

Question 9.19

Which is *not* given as an example of a film that upholds a biblical approach to truth?

a) *Hamilton*
b) *The Dark Knight*
c) *The Incredibles*
d) *1917*

Question 9.20

Evaluate one of your own favorite films according to the criteria given above.

_____

_____

Cardinal Virtues for Christian Artists

In this section, we will explore virtues for Christians engaged in the creation of art. To this point, we have considered that God is the source of beauty. The purpose of art is to display the goodness, truth, and beauty of God to the senses. Beauty has intrinsic value, but art has instrumental value. The value of art is in its ability to give us glimpses of what is right or of the way things should be.

These ideas support a wide variety of artistic endeavors. Yet, they provide a groundwork for Christians to create. What follow are some ways in which Christians glorify God as they create, and these virtues inform both the process of creation as well as the product created.

First, be truthful. God is good, beauty, and truth. One cannot separate one from the others. Truth can be communicated in parables, myths, and other forms of nonfiction. In the words of English poet John Keats in his poem "Ode on a Grecian Urn":

When old age shall this generation waste,
Thou shalt remain, in midst of other woe
Than ours, a friend to man, to whom thou say's;
"Beauty is truth, truth beauty,—that is all
Ye know on earth, and all ye need to know."[15]

Pilate asked the question every society has asked: "What is truth?" Jesus is the answer. He is the way, the truth, and the life (John 14:6). Christian art does not need to explicitly invoke the name of Jesus, but it must conform to his truth and virtue.

Second, be creative. Banality (unoriginality) is the enemy of art. Christian truth does not always have to be serious. Danish Christian philosopher Søren Kierkegaard wrote: "By and large it is the most disastrous notion in the world that 'eloquence' has become the medium for the proclamation of Christianity. Sarcasm, irony, humor lie far closer to the existential in Christianity."[16]

Third, be technically excellent. The value of the art community is largely found in its ability to help artists develop technical excellence in their craft or medium. Doing all things to the glory of God means doing your best and striving for excellence.

---

[15] John Keats, "Ode on a Grecian Urn," https://www.poetryfoundation.org/poems/44477/ode-on-a-grecian-urn.

[16] Søren Kierkegaard, *Journals and Papers* (373), quoted in *Theological Aesthetics*, ed. Gesa Thiessen (Grand Rapids: Eerdmans, 2004), 196.

Question 9.21

Beauty has _____ value, but art has _____ value. What does this mean?

Question 9.22

Provide an example of an artwork that is truthful, creative, and technically excellent.

_____

_____

Humility and Art

In earlier chapters we discussed the biblical wisdom of knowing what you do not know. This chapter on aesthetics requires a closing reminder of that principle of intellectual humility. Some things should be quite clear. God is true beauty and the source of all beauty. Beauty is intrinsically good and is transcendental.

Humans create because they are made in God's image. God is the Creator. His creation is good. To display something created and declare its goodness is the origin of art. The ultimate purpose of art is to promote faith, hope, and love in the one true living God who is the source of all goodness, truth, and beauty.

These things we know.

Yet in the realm of art and aesthetics there is much we do not know about which we must be honest. Part of the reason for this is that human creativity is constantly pushing new forms of art, the creation of which exceeds our ability to analyze or even appreciate the ways in which beauty is on display. It takes time to develop the discernment of beauty.

When rock 'n' roll first came out, many Christians thought it was from the devil. Over time, it became accepted and even appreciated, and standards of taste were developed. Today, many churches have the kind of music that decades ago would have been forbidden. What can we learn from those "worship wars"?

When confronted with new forms of art, it is good to ask, "What am I supposed to appreciate about this form of art?" For instance, so-called jam bands like the Grateful Dead or Phish play songs live that are fifteen to twenty minutes long. Initially, it is hard to comprehend the purpose when you have grown up on a steady diet of three-minute pop songs. At some point, you realize the musical challenges and skills of improvisation that stem from jazz.

Asking the question about appreciation expresses humility and hope. As Christians, we have a standard by which to evaluate art reflected in the questions above. Yet, we should be excited and open to new ways of God's creative image being expressed. Given that the kingdom of God is ethnically diverse, we should be charitable and gracious toward sights, sounds, and tastes that come from other cultures. The church should learn to appreciate these artistic expressions as a way of loving others and honoring God.

Human knowledge is not exhaustive. Art is no different. We may never be able to explain the attraction of an M. C. Escher drawing of infinite stairs or many forms of music, for that matter. We can enjoy art without explaining it fully. There is enough we know to get our bearings and enough we do not know to keep us humble.

Question 9.23

How does humility help us engage with art?

_____

_____

Chapter Review

Question 9.24

How can art be used as an apologetic tool?

_____

_____

Question 9.25

Before reading this chapter, with which of the four theories of art (institutionalism, formalism, emotivism, imitationalism) did you most agree? Has this chapter changed your personal theory of art?

_____

_____

Question 9.26

The Greek philosopher Aristotle believed that art imitates life. Nineteenth-century writer Oscar Wilde believed the opposite: that life imitates art. Which position is most reflected in modern society? Should one of these outlooks be preferred to the other?

10

Conclusion

Philosophy is not boring. We said that at the beginning of this book. Hopefully, as we come to the conclusion of the book, you agree.

Neither is philosophy esoteric or impractical. Actually, philosophy applies to everything. It is probably the most practical field of study since philosophy relates to all of life.

Have all of your questions been answered? Probably not. In fact, you may have picked up some new questions along the way.

You are definitely not alone. The big questions about goodness, truth, and beauty are shared by other people all around the world. Since the dawn of time until the end of time people just like you have wondered, and will wonder, about where we come from, why we are here, and what it is all about.

Philosophy can bring people together in a common search for truth. Logic, the primary tool of philosophical investigation, is global. Even when we do not all agree on the answers, we can agree that the questions are important and worth asking. More than that, the questions discussed in this book remind us that we are human.

Mere animals have instinct, but humans have reason. Philosophy affirms what is unique about humanity. To reason is human. In the words of René Descartes, "I think therefore I am."

In the *Lord of the Rings* series, the character Aragorn was born to be a king but was living like a criminal, or what was called a "Ranger of the North." He is challenged by Elrond who says, "Put away the Ranger. Become the king you were born to be."[1] Reason by itself cannot save a person. Yet, faith seeking understanding is a means by which God changes us to become who he created us to be. By contrast, the Bible compares the wicked to unreasoning animals:

> But these people, like irrational animals—creatures of instinct born to be caught and destroyed—slander what they do not understand, and in their destruction they too will be destroyed. (2 Pet 2:12)

> But these people blaspheme anything they do not understand. And what they do understand by instinct—like irrational animals—by these things they are destroyed. (Jude v. 10)

Conversely, the Bible is both true and reasonable. Were it not, Jesus's instruction to "love God with all your mind" would make little sense. Loving God and taking the Christian faith seriously is both wise and rational.

Some people may find the idea of Christian philosophy to be a strange combination of words. After all, philosophy is about reason and Christianity about faith, right? As we have seen, Christian faith is reasonable. It not only makes sense, but it makes sense of everything else. Ultimately, if philosophy is the love of wisdom, and if Christ is the source of wisdom, then Christian philosophy is the truest form of philosophical expression. In a sense, all philosophy is bound to be "Christian" in the sense that God's revelation (nature, reason, virtue, etc.) is essential to philosophy.

> For from him and through him
> and to him are all things.
> To him be the glory forever. Amen. (Rom 11:36)

The Big Ideas

In this section, we offer summary statements about the previous chapters. These statements reflect what can be described as the "Big Idea" of each chapter. While few of us remember the details of

---

[1] Fran Walsh, Philippa Boyens, and Peter Jackson, *Return of the King*, directed by Peter Jackson (New Line Cinema and Wingnut Films, 2003), motion picture.

books that we read, hopefully you retain the big ideas in these chapter summaries along with key concepts of each chapter by section.

Chapter 1: Philosophy is a type of human exploration where the primary tools are logic and reason. It celebrates human freedom and the God-given ability to think. Humans are commanded to love God with all our mind, and Jesus embodies the unity of spirit and truth. Ideas have consequences and studying philosophy helps you avoid being taken captive by bad ideas (Col 2:8) and to advocate for truth (2 Cor 10:5).

God designed you and commands you to think. The rewards of truth (such as wisdom and happiness) are worth the pursuit. The four main branches of philosophy (metaphysics, epistemology, ethics, and aesthetics) constitute a worldview. The Christian worldview understands the triune God of Scripture to be the source of goodness, truth, and beauty.

Chapter 2: Loving God with all your mind and being wise is not just about you. These traits will bless others, help you succeed, and make a positive impact on your community. Philosophy as we know it starts around the sixth century BC and can be divided into four main eras: ancient, medieval, modern, and contemporary. Philosophers in each of these eras dealt with similar issues and questions, but each era is unique.

Ancient philosophers tended to focus on metaphysics and the nature of reality. Medieval philosophers were especially interested in the relationship between faith and reason in general and in regard to the reasonableness of Christianity in particular. Modern philosophy emphasized epistemology and tended to start from questioning what is real rather than reasoning about what is believed to be real. Contemporary philosophy has been marked by the professionalization and specialization of philosophy and an emphasis on language and detailed analysis.

Chapter 3: Philosophy is about asking questions that matter. The question of God's existence is the most important question dealt with in philosophy. The ontological, cosmological, and moral arguments are examples of arguments for God's existence. The primary argument against God's existence is the Problem of Evil.

The question of knowledge (epistemology) is another question that matters. God made humans to know the world and equipped them with reason and experience as means to obtain knowledge. Philosophers tend to debate epistemology and divide into two main camps: those who believe that reason is the surest foundation for knowledge are called rationalists, and those who believe that experience is the surest foundation for knowledge are called empiricists. These divisions go all the way back to Plato (a rationalist) and Aristotle (an empiricist) and persist today.

If God exists, then there are good answers to the Big Questions about human freedom and the meaning of life. If God does not exist, then it is difficult to avoid a loss of meaning (i.e., nihilism), knowledge (i.e., skepticism), morality (i.e., humanism), and just authority (i.e., anarchism or authoritarianism).

Chapter 4: Logic, reason, and argumentation are the primary tools of philosophy. These tools must be practiced with love and respect for others. Winning an argument requires more than reason. You must have emotional intelligence (empathy) and virtue (character). It is important to ask good questions, define terms, and take the time to understand other positions and the reasons why people hold those positions. This is one way that we love others in the context of dialogue and debate.

An argument is a set of premises that lead to a conclusion. Deduction and induction are two main forms of reasoning. A fallacy is a mistake in reasoning where the conclusion does not follow from the premises. Occam's Razor says that all things being equal, a simple explanation should be preferred. The Rules of Inference and Aristotle's Square of Opposition help to understand the logical relationship between propositions and the process of reasoning that leads to valid argumentation.

Chapter 5: Philosophy aims to help you live the good life. The good life is not about money, fame, or physical pleasure. These things are not bad in themselves, but they are neither necessary nor sufficient conditions for happiness. God is the good life.

Understanding the good life requires a proper understanding of the origin, nature, and purpose of humanity. The good life is both holistic and social. Love for God and others is the essence of the good life.

Chapter 6: Humans are noble and wretched. Made in God's image, yet fallen. Dostoevsky is right to say, "Man is a mystery." The Bible enables philosophers to unravel the mystery of man. The farther you go from biblical truth, the less you can expect to understand yourself (and others). Biblical anthropology refers to a biblical understanding of humanity.

The soul is the life of the body. When a person dies, the soul leaves the body. Humans have unique souls that are made in God's image, are self-aware, and maintain identity over time despite physical change. Different and distinct from the body and the brain, the soul is the thing to which a person ultimately refers when referring to themselves. Humans are indeed fearfully and wonderfully made.

Chapter 7: Ethics is the branch that explains morality and seeks to define goodness. God is the source of goodness, and efforts to explain morality apart from God fail. The reason why morality matters is because humans are created to reflect the character of God. A worshipful life reflects the goodness of God.

Christian morality looks to Jesus as the perfect and ultimate example. The Holy Spirit provides the power for moral transformation and character development. Virtue takes time to cultivate but leads to true and lasting soul-happiness. The goal is not to know about morality or to appear moral, but to actually be moral: "Morality isn't quite the same as being moral. It's more like parading one's morality. Moralizing is blaming others, while ethics is examining ourselves."[2]

Chapter 8: Political philosophy seeks to describe the ideal society. Morality has personal and societal benefits. Governments are instituted by God as servants for good (Rom 13:4) but their authority is not ultimate. The biblical role of government is not to provide for citizens (i.e., positive rights) but to protect citizens' right to flourish and prosper (i.e., negative rights).

America is an experiment in compromise between the rule of the one, the few, and the many. Since God is free and created humans in his image, and since virtue requires freedom, a basic duty of citizens is to protect and preserve freedom. Classical liberalism is the view that the role of government is to promote freedom in order to achieve public virtue. While there is a time for just war as a last resort, Christians should work to promote and preserve peace.

Chapter 9: Aesthetics is the branch of philosophy concerned with beauty and art. Taste is subjective but beauty is objective. Current theories of art fail to properly answer the question, "What is art?" Philosophy and theology are needed to explain that God is beauty. Art captures and conveys some truth of God's world to aid in human flourishing and in the cultivation of virtue.

Humans are made in God's image. We create because God is the Creator. We live in a fallen world, so human art can bless or curse. The Christian community should promote biblically informed discernment about art and beauty. Analyzing art's perspective on sin, redemption, and virtue is helpful to cultivating discernment. The virtues of art include truthfulness, originality, and excellence. Aesthetic discernment requires humility.

These are the big ideas of the book. These ideas matter because truth matters. Philosopher Will Durant summarizes the personal impact of the big ideas of philosophy in the introduction to his book *The Story of Philosophy: The Lives and Opinions of the World's Greatest Philosophers*: "We want to know that the little things are little, and the big things big, before it is too late; we want to see things now as they will seem forever—'in the light of eternity.' We want to learn to laugh in the face of the inevitable, to smile even at the looming of death. We want to be whole,

---

[2] C. John Sommerville, *The Decline of the Secular University* (Oxford, UK: Oxford University Press, 2006), 111.

to coordinate our energies by criticizing and harmonizing our desires. . . . We may be sure that if we can but find wisdom, all things else will be added unto us."[3]

Connecting the Dots

Philosophy is ultimately about synthesis. In college you learn a lot of different subjects. Philosophy invites you to connect the dots thereby creating a unified picture of reality; more specifically, a unified Christian worldview.

Thales, the earliest known philosopher in seventh-century BC Greece, wanted to know what things in the world (people, objects, etc.) had in common. What force binds reality together? Is there a unifying principle to the universe?

Durant has observed that the physical sciences isolate and analyze. The job of the sciences is to dig deep to explore and expand what is known. Philosophy is sometimes called the "queen of the sciences." She is bound to take new ground; to explore the butterflies of truth that cannot quite be pinned down and put under a microscope. She is the queen because she blazes the trail and all scientific research is done in the wake of her discoveries. All science was once philosophy.[4]

Today's world is in desperate need for thoughtful Christians who can connect the dots of human experience, both for their own sake and for the sake of others. This book has attempted to help in that endeavor. In his *Proslogion*, Anselm of Canterbury said, "I believe so that I might understand."

The Christian faith is like the line drawn between knowledge and experience that creates an intelligible picture of reality. Human knowledge (epistemology) makes sense if the Creator of the universe made the universe to be known and equipped humans with reason and physical senses that correspond to truth in the world.

Consider the alternative. Existentialist French philosopher Jean-Paul Sartre did not believe in God. He wrote his philosophical novel *Nausea* on the verge of World War II and his nonfiction *Being and Nothingness* during the Nazi occupation of France. In *Nausea*, Sartre explores the disconnectedness one feels from oneself and from the world in the absence of the meaning and purpose that come from God's existence. The main character of the novel (Antoine Roquentin)

---

[3] Will Durant, *The Story of Philosophy: The Lives and Opinions of the World's Greatest Philosophers* (New York: Simon & Schuster, 1961), xxv–xxvi.

[4] See Durant, chap. 1.

feels physically nauseous that the events of life, and his own existence to the world, are not "linked together."[5]

The vision for Christian philosophy presented in this book is one in which we hope you find a sense of orientation about yourself, the world, and your relationship to the world. Those who reject God and see no meaningful way to connect the dots of existence and human experience are left combatting the nausea of disorientation to which Nietzsche eluded in his famous section 125 of *The Gay Science* in which he declared the death of God:

> The madman jumped into their midst and pierced them with his eyes. "Whither is God?" he cried; "I will tell you. We have killed him—you and I. All of us are his murderers. But how did we do this? How could we drink up the sea? Who gave us the sponge to wipe away the entire horizon? What were we doing when we unchained this earth from its sun? Whither is it moving now? Whither are we moving? Away from all suns? Are we not plunging continually? Backward, sideward, forward, in all directions? Is there still any up or down? Are we not straying, as through an infinite nothing? Do we not feel the breath of empty space? Has it not become colder? Is not night continually closing in on us? Do we not need to light lanterns in the morning? Do we hear nothing as yet of the noise of the gravediggers who are burying God? Do we smell nothing as yet of the divine decomposition? Gods, too, decompose. God is dead. God remains dead. And we have killed him.[6]

The misguided notion of God's nonexistence is madness. The psalmist rightly said that it is foolishness (Ps 14:1). This is not to say that there are not reasons and arguments against God, but they are unconvincing. Even if you are not convinced by the arguments for God, in so far as faith is a matter of the will and of desires, hopefully you are convinced that you should *want* there to be a God. People seem to be more inclined to believe things they want to believe than those they do not.

More than anything, the message of this book is that God is goodness, beauty, and truth. If you reject God and the Christian understanding of reality, you do so against the weight of reason and evidence, against psychological well-being, history, science, and the arts. As C. S. Lewis portrays in his Chronicles of Narnia series, a world in which God exists is enchanted and magical.

---

[5] Jean-Paul Sartre, *Nausea* (1938), http://www.kkoworld.com/kitablar/jan_pol_satr_urekbulanma -eng.pdf, 32.

[6] Friedrich Nietzsche, *The Gay Science*, trans. Walter Kaufmann (New York: Penguin, 1974), n.p.

But a world without God is meaningless and bleak. In *The Lion, the Witch, and the Wardrobe*, Mr. Tumnus describes a godless world: "It is winter in Narnia . . . and has been for ever so long . . . always winter, but never Christmas."[7]

This book invites you to consider the world in which you want to live and, indeed, the world in which you are living. True happiness is knowing the God who gives life and makes life worth living.

The Value of Philosophy Outside the Academy

Few people pursue philosophy as a career in "The Academy" (i.e., in a professional educational setting such as a college or university or which involves professional research and writing). The normal path for such a career is to pursue a bachelor's degree, followed by a master's, and ultimately a doctoral degree in philosophy. While a career in philosophy is certainly possible and those interested should be encouraged to pursue graduate studies, a career in the academy takes a long time to achieve and jobs are competitive.

Despite these realities, philosophy has great value outside "The Academy." In addition to the personal benefits of philosophy for gaining wisdom and living the good life, there are practical benefits gained from philosophical study that apply to any range of occupations. Employers are looking for employees who have the kinds of skills that philosophy helps to cultivate.

A number of business leaders and tech innovators majored in philosophy. Peter Thiel is the cofounder of PayPal, an early Facebook investor, and author of *Zero to One: Notes on Startups, or How to Build the Future*. Thiel, a professing Christian, has talked about the impact of philosophy on his life, in particular, the French philosopher René Girard.

Other current leaders with degrees in philosophy include former Hewlett-Packer CEO and presidential candidate Carly Fiorina, hedge fund manager and philanthropist George Soros, Overstock.com founder and former CEO Patrick Byrne, and Flickr co-founder and Slack CEO Stewart Butterfield.[8]

Socrates is rumored to have been so enthralled by philosophy that he would forget to get dressed before leaving the house. That image, of the absent-minded philosopher with no earthly

---

[7] C. S. Lewis, *The Lion, the Witch, and the Wardrobe* (New York: Macmillan, undated), https://gutenberg.ca/ebooks/lewiscs-thelionthewitchandthewardrobe/lewiscs-thelionthewitchandthewardrobe-00-h.html.

[8] See Rachel Sugar, "11 Famous Executives Who Majored in Philosophy," Business Insider, August 8, 2015.

practical value, does not fit these business leader and tech entrepreneurs. Reid Hoffman, cofounder of the professional networking site LinkedIn, has been called the "philosopher-entrepreneur." He argues that philosophy teaches principles that have practical value for business leaders and entrepreneurs.[9] Hoffman and others are not successful despite their philosophical studies but because of their philosophical studies.

For example, as we discussed in chapter 6, philosophy seeks to explain and understand human nature. Insights about human nature influence practical business decisions related to social media. As Hoffman put it on the philosophy podcast *Greymatter*: "One of the things I've said about entrepreneurship is that it should include an embedded theory of human nature. If you develop a theory about how human beings identify themselves, connect with others, view themselves to be part of a group and pursue a theory of the good, the conclusions you reach can help you design a product or service that appeals to people on a fundamental level."[10]

Philosophy is not just about what you do but the kind of person you become. It is part of the so-called liberal arts or humanities that contain subjects, like philosophy, that are an integral part of freedom and humanity. These are subjects that help students to be free and productive citizens. As Henry David Thoreau said, "We seem to have forgotten that the expression 'a liberal education' originally meant among the Romans one worthy of free men; while the learning of trades and professions by which to get your livelihood merely was considered worthy of slaves only."[11]

Philosopher Scott Samuelson, author of *The Deepest Human Life: An Introduction to Philosophy for Everyone*, wrote an article in the *Atlantic* titled "Why I Teach Plato to Plumbers: Liberal Arts and the Humanities Aren't Just for the Elite," in which he observed, "Once, during a lecture I gave about the Stoics, who argue that with the proper spiritual discipline one can be truly free and happy even while being tortured, I looked up to see one of the students in tears. I recalled that her sister in Sudan had been recently imprisoned for challenging the local authorities. Through her tears my student was processing that her sister was likely seeking out a hard Stoic freedom as I was lecturing."[12]

---

[9] See Reid Hoffman, "The Philosopher Entrepreneur," *Greymatter* (podcast), July 20, 2021, https://greylock.com/greymatter/the-philosopher-entrepreneur/?utm_campaign=Newsletter&utm_medium=Email&utm_source=NewsletterMD.

[10] Reid Hoffman, "The Philosopher Entrepreneur," *Greymatter*, July 20, 2021, https://greylock.com/greymatter/the-philosopher-entrepreneur/.

[11] Henry D. Thoreau, "The Last Days of John Brown," Henry David Thoreau Online, accessed July 7, 2022, http://www.thoreau-online.org/the-last-days-of-john-brown-page4.html.

[12] Scott Samuelson, "Why I Teach Plato to Plumbers," *Atlantic*, April 29, 2014, https://www.theatlantic.com/education/archive/2014/04/plato-to-plumbers/361373/.

The value of philosophy extends beyond the classroom. Philosophical interests, once sparked, fan into flame character development, business insight, and perspective for life that can bring happiness in life's most challenging moments.

Go Forward

As you finish this book, and perhaps the class for which it is assigned, you may be asking yourself, "What next?" There are a number of possible next steps to ensure that the lessons learned in this book are not forgotten. Philosophy is like learning another language or a musical instrument; the key to proficiency is practice. How then do you practice philosophy?

Take another class. If you are reading this book as part of a college course and are intrigued by the subject and would like to go deeper, then we suggest taking another philosophy class. The subject matters discussed in this book sometimes have entire courses dedicated to them, such as ethics or aesthetics. If you take another class and continue to enjoy the subject, consider talking to your academic advisor about making philosophy your minor, your major, or perhaps one-half of a double major.

Choose one book. We have discussed key philosophical texts such as Plato's *Republic*, Aristotle's *Nicomachean Ethics*, Sartre's *Nausea*, or James's *The Will to Believe*. It is arguably better to truly know one important book than many lesser books superficially (i.e., without depth). If you see the value in philosophy but never plan to take another philosophy class again, you can choose one philosophy book and make it your goal to know that text well and to understand the author's ideas and arguments.

Listen to podcasts. If more classes or reading philosophers is not in your future, consider subscribing to a philosophy podcast. For general philosophy, check out *Philosophy Bites* or *History of Philosophy Without Any Gaps*. For Christian faith and philosophy or apologetics, look at *Reasonable Faith* or *The Reluctant Theologian*.

Practice the principles. This book has practical principles for philosophical thinking. For instance, in chapter 9 there are questions to ask when watching a movie to discern the movie's worldview. You can do this by yourself, but it is probably more fun to ask these questions with friends or with a Bible study or small group from church.

Explore your field. It is likely that philosophy is not your major nor will it be your professional career. However, inevitably there is some philosophical issue to be explored within your career field or field of study. For instance, philosophy of science raises questions about the nature of scientific exploration that those in the "hard sciences" (i.e., medicine, geology, astronomy, physics, engineering, etc.) are not quite as concerned with. For any career there are ethical issues that inevitably circle back to topics discussed in this book.

Philosophy requires what the Greeks called *scholé*. This word is the basis of the English word *scholasticism*, which pertains to education and schools. Originally, *scholé* meant leisure. It implied time to sit, think, ponder, and contemplate.

The modern world is largely defined by technology aimed toward expediency (fast) and efficiency (easy). Philosophy takes time and requires courage to ask hard questions. Think of philosophy as a lifelong pursuit or a long-term investment rather than a box you check or a class you pass.

Be Encouraged

The Spanish-American philosopher poet George Santayana wrote about the persistent pursuit of wisdom in "O World":

Our knowledge is a torch of smoky pine
That lights the pathway but one step ahead[13]

Santayana is making the point that it takes time and effort to experience the benefits of philosophy. If you have trouble grasping the concepts, you are not alone. It is common when reading philosophy to have to read a sentence, paragraph, or page more than once. Doing so does not mean you are not smart; it means you are smart enough to know that philosophy is difficult and requires careful attention.

Philosophy is for lifelong learners. David Hume made an important distinction between learning and education. Education produces beliefs, but learning produces impressions. Education is temporary and formal, but learning is ongoing and often informal.[14]

Ongoing philosophical education takes time and grace. Aquinas reminds us that sincere pursuit of truth must be accompanied by prayerful dependence on God's grace to illuminate our understanding.[15] Mere intelligence and intellect are not enough; you need God's grace.

As you continue to learn, put God first. In *Beware of Philosophy: A Warning to Biblical Scholars*, Norm Geisler says that when given a choice between lordship and scholarship, Christian philosophers should always choose lordship. Philosophy, in the end, is a form of spiritual warfare:

[13] George Santayana, *Poems* (n.p.: Bibliolife, 2009), 5.
[14] See Hume, *Treatise of Human Nature*, 1.3.10.1 and 1.3.9.19.
[15] See Aquinas, In *Super Boetium De Trinitate,* translated by Rose Brennan, Q.1., PR. 1, http://www.logicmuseum.com/authors/aquinas/superboethiumq1.htm.

In the final analysis, preserving orthodoxy is not a purely intellectual matter. It is spiritual warfare. "For our struggle is not against flesh and blood, but against the rulers, against the authorities, against the powers of this dark world and against the spiritual forces of evil in the heavenly realms" (Eph. 6:12). The enemy of our soul wants also to deceive our minds. He desires to destroy good teaching which leads to good living. By undermining our orthodoxy he can weaken our "orthopraxy." So we need to take on the whole armor of God in order to withstand the wiles of the Wicked One. It is noteworthy that this armor includes among other things the wide belt of truth which holds the rest of the armor together (Eph. 6:10–18). In brief, my conclusion is this: We cannot properly beware of philosophy unless we be aware of philosophy.[16]

Augustine made a similar point in *Confessions*: "Some there be that seduce through philosophy, under a great, and smooth, and honorable name coloring and disguising their own error."[17] While philosophy is a lifelong pursuit and requires God's grace to grant true understanding, it is worth it; not only because loving God with all your mind honors the Lord, or because the result is virtue and true happiness, but because philosophy will equip you with tools to guard yourself and others from what is false and therefore dangerous.

Standing for truth takes courage. The idea of encouragement means, quite literally, to impart courage. We hope this book imparts courage to your faith in Christ if you are a Christian. If you are not a Christian, our sincere hope is that God would use this book to bring you to personal faith in Jesus.

> *For from him and through him and to him are all things. To him be the glory forever.*
> *Amen.*

> —Romans 11:36

---

[16] Norm Geisler, "Beware of Philosophy: A Warning to Biblical Scholars," JETS 42/1 (March 1999) 3–19.

[17] Augustine, *Confessions*, translated by E.B. Pusey, Book III, https://www.gutenberg.org/files/3296/3296-h/3296-h.htm#link2H_4_0013.

ANSWER KEY

Chapter 1

Question 1.1:   acquired

Question 1.2:   False

Question 1.3:   reason

Question 1.4:   a) Martin Luther King Jr. and Socrates

Question 1.5:   Answers will vary.

Question 1.6:   False

Question 1.7:   a) believer and nonbeliever; b) human mind and God; c) the visible and the invisible

Question 1.8:   Philosophy invites us to take our thoughts and beliefs seriously, to define our terms, and to make sure our beliefs are consistent. When our beliefs are true and consistent, and when our actions reflect our beliefs, we exhibit integrity.

Question 1.9:   False

Question 1.10:   Socratic method; cooperative; truth

Question 1.11:   1. Socrates pretends to be impressed by his partner's knowledge of a concept.

2. Socrates asks a question to challenge his partner's definition of the concept.

3. Socrates and his partner unite in their pursuit of knowledge.

Question 1.12:

	Socrates	Jesus
Claimed to be the truth		X
Condemned to die by leaders who felt threatened	X	X
No interest in earthly riches	X	X
Gave answers		X
Only gave questions	X	
Resurrected after death		X
Astounded his opponents with his teaching		X
Used questions to provoke thought	X	X
Chose to die rather than escape	X	X

Question 1.13:   c) He knew his knowledge was limited.

Question 1.14:

__C__ Life is about happiness, understood as the absence of physical and mental pain.

__A__ This philosophical outlook argues that the truth will set you free.

__B__ Nature is divine.

__A__ Argues for a theoretical and practical approach to philosophy.

__D__ Philosophy is about defining terms, not about truth.

__B__ A wise person, according to this philosophy, focuses on the natural world.

C Followers of this philosophy resembled early Christians
    in their communal life.

Question 1.15:   *Philo* means love; *sophia* means wisdom.

Question 1.16:   truth; right living

Question 1.17:   Answers will vary.

Question 1.18:   b) Happiness is emotional stability.

Question 1.19:   *Eudaimonia* = deep and lasting happiness rooted in something that can-
                  not be taken away (i.e., a relationship with God). Philosophy is a pursuit of
                  truth to experience *eudaimonia*.

Question 1.20:

Branch of Philosophy	Deals with:	Explain:
Metaphysics	(Answer: Reality)	
(Answer: Epistemology)	Knowledge	
Ethics	(Answer: Morality)	
(Answer: Aesthetics)	Beauty	

Question 1.21:   goodness, truth, beauty

Question 1.22:   3, 2, 1, 4

Question 1.23:   Answers will vary.

Question 1.24:   In descending order: E, F, H, A, G, C, B, D

Question 1.25:   Answers will vary.

Chapter 2

Question 2.1:   Answers will vary.

Question 2.2:   False

Question 2.3:   Answers will vary.

Question 2.4:   Answers will vary.

Question 2.5:   In descending order: E, F, G, B, C, A, D

Question 2.6:   c) They contributed greatly to Greek social and military prowess.

Question 2.7:   change; permanence

Question 2.8:   Plato; Aristotle

Question 2.9:   material = wood; efficient = carpenter; formal = idea of table in carpenter's mind; final cause = eating/sitting

Question 2.10:   False

Question 2.11:   cosmological; Aquinas

Question 2.12:   faith; reason

Question 2.13:   In descending order: E, D, E, C, A, B, C, C

Question 2.14:   Epistemology is the study of knowing.

Question 2.15:   Answers will vary.

Question 2.16:   Answers will vary.

Question 2.17:   In descending order: C, E, D, B, A, B

Question 2.18:   Answers will vary.

Question 2.19:   In descending order: C, A, B, C, A, B, A, C, B

Question 2.20:   Answers will vary.

Question 2.21:   Answers will vary.

Chapter 3

Question 3.1:   intelligence; courage

Question 3.2:   Answers will vary.

Question 3.3:   False

Question 3.4:   humanizing; life affirming

Question 3.5:   Answers will vary.

Question 3.6:   Answers will vary.

Question 3.7:   In descending order: C, B, A

Question 3.8:   Answers will vary.

Question 3.9:   evil

Question 3.10:   b) Plato

Question 3.11:   F

Question 3.12:   Aristotle

Question 3.13:   incontinence; impulse; desire

Question 3.14:   Answers will vary.

Question 3.15:   Answers will vary.

Question 3.16:   Answers will vary.

Question 3.17:   ethics; metaethics; normative ethics; applied ethics

Question 3.18:   Answers will vary.

Question 3.19:   Answers will vary.

Question 3.20:   Answers will vary.

Question 3.21:   In descending order: G, L, O, A, B, R, E, P, Q, N, J, H, C, F, K, I, D, M

Question 3.22:   Answers will vary.

Chapter 4

Question 4.1:   logic; reason; argumentation

Question 4.2:   ideas

Question 4.3:   grace; love

Question 4.4:   Persuasion is a change of mind that results in a change of action. Pressure is indoctrination, manipulation, and coercion.

Question 4.5:   b) pathos, ethos, logos

Question 4.6:   Answers will vary.

Question 4.7:   Answers will vary.

Question 4.8:

Premise	General	Particular
All red dogs are named Clifford.	X	
My new car is a sedan.		X
All apples come from trees	X	
No snakes have legs.	X	
Sarah's dog doesn't feel well.		X

Question 4.9: inductive; deductive; deductive

Question 4.10: Answers will vary.

Question 4.11: c) Judge whether the source of the argument has a good reputation.

Question 4.12:

Argument	Fallacy	Explanation
I got sick last time I ate rice, so I must be allergic to rice.	(Causation/correlation)	Answers will vary in each explanation.

Sure, I don't like your cat. Cats are all just selfish, obnoxious creatures.	(Hasty generalization)	
You can't trust that article. That came from a journal from Berkeley, which is a wildly liberal school.	(Genetic fallacy)	
Look, there's nothing wrong with getting drunk every so often. Everyone has gotten drunk at some point in their life.	(Appeal to the masses)	
If we allow students to have service dogs, then they will want all kinds of service animals. Pretty soon, this campus will be a zoo of all kinds of exotic creatures.	(Slippery slope)	
Stephen told me the test was on Thursday. But he is a bad student, so I'm not going to trust his opinion.	(Ad hominem)	
Sure, I may have cheated on my exam. But I saw you cheat on your quiz, so what's the difference?	(Tu quoque)	
Churchill led England to resist the Nazi regime, which led to the end of the war. He is undoubtedly the most influential man in history.	(Ambiguity fallacy)	
You should not discipline your children. Think of how sad it makes them when they think you are angry with them.	(Emotional appeal)	

I don't agree with Catholics. They all wear robes in church and chant strange music.	(Straw man)	
Jerry claims that he is libertarian, but he voted for a candidate who supports gun control. Obviously, he is not a libertarian.	(No true Scotsman fallacy)	

Question 4.13:   ambiguity

Question 4.14:   Answers will vary.

Question 4.15:   a) top left; b) bottom right; c) top right; d) bottom left

Question 4.16:   Particulars are limited to contextual, specific objects whereas universals are abstract, conceptual objects.

Question 4.17:   False

Question 4.18:   Ockham's Razor is a helpful tool to process possible explanations that prevents unnecessary speculation and conspiracies. It attempts to get right to the argument at hand.

Question 4.19:   a. 2
b. 1
c. 2

Question 4.20:   Answers will vary.

Question 4.21:   A. Slippery slope
B. No true Scotsman
C. Hasty generalization
D. Tu quoque

Question 4.22:   Answers will vary.

Chapter 5

Question 5.1:   aim

Question 5.2:   Answers will vary.

Question 5.3:   b) An affirmative answer to life's deeper questions

Question 5.4:

Approach to Life	Explanation	Possible Errors
Answers will vary for each category		

Question 5.5:   Answers will vary.

Question 5.6:   Answers will vary.

Question 5.7:   d) Humans no longer need the idea of God to find meaning.

Question 5.8:   love of one's fate

Question 5.9:   False

Question 5.10:   Answers will vary.

Question 5.11:   life with God

Question 5.12:   Aseity is the simplicity of God's being.

Question 5.13:   Answers will vary.

Question 5.14:   "At the same time justified and sinner"

Question 5.15:   Answers will vary.

Question 5.16:   a. Modern View
                 b. Modern View
                 c. Modern View
                 d. Ancient View

Question 5.17:   Answers will vary.

Question 5.18:   False

Question 5.19:   Answers will vary.

Question 5.20:

A. Bertrand Russell

I "My formula for greatness in man is! [*sic*] *amor fati*: the fact that a man wishes nothing to be different . . . for all eternity."

B. A. W. Tozer

E "Life moves pretty fast."

C. Isaiah

D "How happy is mankind, if the love that orders the stars above rules, too, in your hearts."

D. Boethius

G "A meaningful life is, first of all, one that within it has the basis of an affirmative answer to the needs or longings that are characteristically described as needs for meaning."

E. Ferris Bueller

H Is addicted to "retail therapy."

F. Flannery O'Connor

J "Life is for the living."

G. Susan Wolf

K "There is nothing on this earth more to be prized than true friendship."

H. Ariana Grande

F "I do not know you[,] God[,] because I am in the way. Please help me push myself aside."

I. Friedrich Nietzsche

C "Seek the Lord while he may be found; call to him while he is near."

J. Langston Hughes

A "The good life is one inspired by love and guided by knowledge."

K. St. Thomas Aquinas

B "Salvation apart from obedience is unknown in the sacred scriptures."

Question 5.21:   Answers will vary.

Question 5.22:   Answers will vary.

Question 5.23:   Answers will vary.

Chapter 6

Question 6.1: Material, efficient, formal, and final

Question 6.2:

a. *Ruach*	Answer: Spirit
b. *Palah*	Answer: Soul
c. *Nephesh*	Answer: Wonderfully

Question 6.3: anthropology; ethics

Question 6.4: False

Question 6.5: Answers will vary.

Question 6.6: e) All of the above

Question 6.7: Answers will vary.

Question 6.8:

Viewpoint	Description	Proponent
Dualism	Answers will vary in each section.	
Idealism		
Occasionalism		
Physicalism		

Question 6.9: Answers will vary.

Question 6.10: False

Question 6.11: Answers will vary.

Question 6.12: c) There is no proof of human essence beyond what we perceive.

Question 6.13:   dehumanization

Question 6.14:   False

Question 6.15:   universalism, annihilationism

Question 6.16:   anthropology

Question 6.17:   Answers will vary.

Question 6.18:

A. David Hume — **M** God communicates ideas directly to the human mind.

B. John Calvin — **E** "What is a human being that you are mindful of him?"

C. Aristotle — **D** "The first fruit of love is the musing of the mind upon God.

D. Thomas Watson — **K** If two things are identical, everything true of one is true of the other.

E. King David — **A** "And were all my perceptions removed by death . . . I should be entirely annihilated."

F. René Descartes — **J** It is preferable to be absent in the body and present with God.

G. Jesus — **L** There is a time to be born and a time to die.

H. Nicolas Malebranche — **F** "It is certain that I am really distinct from the body, and can exist without it."

I. Thomas Nagel — **C** "To attain any assured knowledge of the soul is one of the most difficult things in the world."

J. St. Paul — **B** "Something was taken from Adam, in order that he might embrace, with greater benevolence, a part of himself."

K. Wilhelm Leibniz — **I** "What is it like to be a bat?"

L. Solomon — **H** Only God has causal powers.

M. George Berkeley   **G** "Fear him who is able to destroy both soul and body in hell."

Question 6.19:   Answers will vary.

Question 6.20:   Answers will vary.

Chapter 7

Question 7.1:   d) Intelligence and character

Question 7.2:   Answers will vary.

Question 7.3:   right living

Question 7.4:

Statement	Moral Naturalism	Moral Realism
Morality is objective.		X
Moral claims have the same truth value as biological facts.		X
Moral principles arise from observations about the world.	X	X
Christian ethics most resembles this view.		X
Allows morality to adapt to social and personal norms and convictions.	X	

Question 7.5:   Answers will vary.

Question 7.6:   virtue; deontology; consequentialism

Question 7.7:   a) virtue

Question 7.8:   Answers will vary.

Question 7.9:   Answers will vary.

Question 7.10:   Answers will vary.

Question 7.11:   Answers will vary.

Question 7.12:   eudaimonia; blessed

Question 7.13:   Answers will vary.

Question 7.14:   personal; social

Question 7.15:   Answers will vary.

Question 7.16:   false

Question 7.17:   conscience

Question 7.18:   Answers will vary.

Question 7.19:   freedom

Question 7.20:   False

Question 7.21:   c) hope

Question 7.22:   making a decision

Question 7.23:   Answers will vary.

Question 7.24:   Answers will vary.

Chapter 8

Question 8.1:   d) A person who adheres to a specific political party

Question 8.2:   Answers will vary.

Question 8.3:   False

Question 8.4:   Answers will vary.

Question 8.5:

A. Friedrich Nietzsche

C There exists a social contract between those governed and the governor(s).

B. David Hume

A The few who are strong should rule the weak.

C. Jean-Jacques Rousseau

B Governments are based not on contract but on conquest.

D. George Berkeley

D Christians should never rebel against governing authorities.

Question 8.6:   Answers will vary.

Question 8.7:   Authority is a normative notion according to which something with (genuine) authority has the right to command compliance. Power is a descriptive notion according to which something with power has the ability to force compliance.

Question 8.8:   social contract

Question 8.9:   Answers will vary.

Question 8.10:

	Authoritarian	Totalitarian	Tyrannical
Absolute power invested in the government	X	X	X
Tyrannical in nature		X	X
Absolute power invested in one person		X	X
Lacks any checks and balances in government	X	X	X
Allow some, albeit little, freedom for individuals		X	X

Question 8.11:   Original sin

Question 8.12:   Answers will vary.

Question 8.13:   On the basis that power would be fully given to the people

Question 8.14:   Answers will vary.

Question 8.15:   a) the church

Question 8.16:

	Positive Right	Negative Right
Each citizen has the duty to go to school until of age eighteen.	X	
No citizen may trespass upon another's land.		X
Each citizen has the right to an attorney if taken to court.		X
No citizen may murder another citizen.		X
The state will not interfere in any private religious practice.		X

Question 8.17:   b) Negative rights

Question 8.18:   Answers will vary.

Question 8.19:   Answers will vary.

Question 8.20:   virtue

Question 8.21:   individual freedom, government control

Question 8.22:   virtue; protecting individual's rights

Question 8.23:   a) more decentralized

Question 8.24:   Answers will vary

Question 8.25:

A. Jeremiah   __K__ "Life of man is solitary, nasty, brutish and short."

B. Plato   __I__ "If men were angels, no government would be needed."

C. George Berkeley   __E__ "Aristocrats were always anarchists."

D. Friedrich Nietzsche

B A "noble lie" may need to be told in order for society to function well.

E. G. K. Chesterton

A "Pursue the well-being of the city I have deported you to. Pray to the Lord on its behalf, for when it thrives, you will thrive."

F. Lord Acton

C Any resistance to the state is resistance to God.

G. Malcolm X

J Good politicians promote public virtue, and good citizens act virtuously.

H. David Hume

L Governments are based upon a social contract between the governors and the governed.

I. Alexander Hamilton

D The few who are strong should rule the many who are weak.

J. Aristotle

G "It'll be ballots, or it'll be bullets."

K. Thomas Hobbes

F "Power tends to corrupt; absolute power corrupts absolutely."

L. Jean-Jacques Rousseau

H Governments are based on conquest, not contract.

Question 8.26:   Answers will vary.

Question 8.27:   Answers will vary.

Chapter 9

Question 9.1:   understanding; enjoyment

Question 9.2:   b) Is it acceptable to steal your neighbor's painting?

Question 9.3:   Answers will vary.

Question 9.4:   d) All of the above.

Question 9.5:   1. intrinsic beauty
                  2. instrumental value of being

Question 9.6:   methodism; particularism

Question 9.7:   Answers will vary.

Question 9.8:   the value of art

Question 9.9.   Answers will vary.

Question 9.10:   Answers will vary.

Question 9.11:   True

Question 9.12:   1. Reflects on the source of beauty
                  2. Discerns a standard of what beauty is

Question 9.13:   beautiful

Question 9.14:   Answers will vary.

Question 9.15:   Answers will vary.

Question 9.16:   c) Art has more influence on people's minds than philosophy.

Question 9.17:   community; Holy Spirit

Question 9.18:   False

Question 9.19:   b) *The Dark Knight*

Question 9.20:   Answers will vary.

Question 9.21:   intrinsic; instrumental

Question 9.22:   Answers will vary.

Question 9.23:   Answers will vary.

Question 9.24:   Answers will vary.

Question 9.25:   Answers will vary.

Question 9.26:   Answers will vary.

AUTHOR INDEX

SUBJECT INDEX

O

obedience, 15, 125, 133, 164, 168, 171, 182, 194–95, 200
Occam's Razor, 108–10, 252
O'Connor, Flannery, 127–28
ontological argument, 63–64
ontological parsimony, 110

P

parable, 179, 222, 244
Parmenides, 37, 39
particular, 42, 93, 107–10, 151
particularism, 225
partisan, 191–92, 199, 212
Pascal, Blaise, 19, 23, 34, 54–57
    Pascal's wager, 55
    Pensées, 19, 23, 55
pathos, 90, 102
patriotism, 209–10
Paul, 4–5, 8, 146, 156, 167, 181, 194, 236
Pensées (Pascal), 19, 23, 55
person, 143–46, 150–51, 154–56, 163–64, 208
personhood, 145–46, 153
persuasion, 89–90, 92
phenomenology, 50
philosophical theology, 43
philosophy
    ancient era, 39–41
    contemporary era, 49–50
    definition, 2, 13, 15, 251
    medieval era, 42–43
    modern era, 45–47
    nature of, 30–31
    value of, 18, 256–58
physicalism, 149, 152, 154
Plantinga, Alvin, 64
Plato, 3, 9, 25, 30, 39–40, 63, 65, 73, 82, 146, 158, 174–75, 183, 192, 196, 203–4, 221, 231, 238, 251
    "Allegory of the Cave", 40
    The Republic, 9, 20, 25, 40, 82, 117, 158, 192, 196, 203, 231, 258
political philosophy, 24, 191–92, 194, 196, 199–201, 253
politics, 2, 14, 18, 39, 70, 191–92, 199, 205, 213–14
pornography, 177, 182, 237
positive right, 208, 253

positivism, 225, 230–31
power, 65, 89, 120, 122, 128–29, 142, 145, 151, 167, 178, 181, 194, 196–98, 200–203, 205, 212, 214, 216, 228, 238, 242–43, 253, 260
pragmatism, 49, 204, 242
prejudice, 187
premise, 63, 93–96, 99, 112, 252
pressure, 89
presupposition, 11
probability, 64, 94
probability theory, 55–56
problem of evil, 42, 67–68, 251
problem of universals, 42
purpose, 40, 81, 122, 141, 243–44, 252
Pyrrho, 69
Pythagoras, 37

Q

questions, 3, 35, 60–62, 103, 118, 218, 251

R

racism, 177, 179, 187
Rae, Scott B., 187
rationalism, 25, 37, 40, 50, 70, 251
reality, 24, 37, 50, 110, 251, 255–56
reason, 2, 7, 9, 11, 25, 36, 40, 42–43, 89, 210–11, 249–52
redemption, 28, 123, 125, 146, 159, 180, 232, 240–41, 253
reductionism, 37–38
Reid, Thomas, 71–72
relationship, 2, 18, 21, 27, 87, 157, 159, 182–84, 238
relationship with God, 23, 56, 83–84, 125–28, 132–35, 140, 167, 172
responsibility, 73, 75, 192, 242
resurrection, 8, 28, 67, 71, 84, 146, 167, 180, 210
revelation, 5, 115, 122, 125, 166–67, 250
rhetorical triangle, 90
Ross, Bob, 231
Rousseau, Jean-Jacques, 195–97
Rummel, R. J., 197
Russell, Bertrand, 20, 49, 84, 126

S

sacrament, 156
salvation, 5, 84, 132–34, 167, 181
Samuelson, Scott, 257